MURDER IN GRAND CAYMAN

An Inspector Thompson Mystery

C. Davis Fogg

Copywrite©2016 by C. Davis Fogg
All rights reserved.

ISBN: 1533466653
ISBN 13: 9781533466655

This is a work of fiction. Names, characters, places and incidents are the product of the author's imagination or are used fictionally.

Cover design: Terry Greene Cover photo: C. Davis Fogg Author photo: Kate Driesen

Other books by C. Davis Fogg:
Diagnostic Marketing (Addison Wesley)
Team Based Strategic Planning (AMACOM)
Implementing Your Strategic Plan (AMACOM)

CHAPTER ONE

One of the oddest calls in my life, Charlie Braun thought, hanging up the phone. Even Gil Baxter, the eccentric former Chairman of Baxter Investments, isn't immune from murder. And now I've been summoned. He rehashed the conversation with Anne, Baxter's sister.

"Charlie, you heard the news about my brother Gil, right?"

"No, what's happened?"

" He's been murdered. You have to go to his condo in Cayman tomorrow to inventory his possessions, bank accounts, securities holdings, and safe deposit boxes. Then report back to me. I want to know how much money he has, where."

"That's pretty short notice. What about his wife?"

"Brenda's out of town – on an Antarctic cruise, won't return for at least a week. As you know, I'm the executrix of Gil's estate. I'll handle all of his legal and financial matters from now on. It's imperative that you're there tomorrow, Charlie."

"What's the rush?" Charlie asked, absent-mindedly patting his paunch, the result of many rich dinners.

Anne had ignored his question. "I'll fly you to the island on Gil's executive jet. Find out every detail you can about the murder. Inspector Thompson is investigating. Meet with him first, and give him all the help you can. Get back to me in two days." Click.

"Hello…a? *Hell is right. You'd think a big-league hedge fund owner would have extra security for one of those fancy Grand Cayman condos. But with the drugs that guy ingests, he may not know what the hell he's doing half the time.*

Help. I'm not a criminal lawyer, just their estate, and finance guy. Get involved in a murder investigation? That's a job for the local pros.

Charlie crunched on loose gravel leading up to the tarmac and let out a slow whistle. The aircraft was a Gulfstream 650, the fastest and highest-flying civil plane in the sky. It could cruise at 510 miles per hour at 51,000 feet. Clanking up the steps, he entered and took it all in. The 60-year-old Ivy Leaguer wasn't easily impressed. But this sure warranted a whistle. The interior made the luxurious cabin of a Bentley look like a

Ford. The seats were crafted from buttery ivory leather. The cabin trim was a rare brown-black-veined African mahogany. It could seat, with space to spare, ten people on two sofas and four high-backed swivel armchairs on either side of large, foldable worktables. The handsome tables, trimmed in brass, featured a chessboard made of exotic woods. Galley, bathroom, and shower were in the rear.

Charlie removed his windowpane tweed vest and jacket, and settled into a swivel seat toward the front of the aircraft where he could stretch his legs out. He noticed that, if needed, the chair could be made up into a comfortable bed in its own private capsule for cross-country or international flights.

The flaming redheaded flight attendant was dressed in a tailored, short-skirted blue suit, red scarf, and high heels that showed her luscious legs to great advantage. When she bent over to serve a pre-flight glass of Crystal champagne, her blouse peeked open, revealing most of her ample, enticing, white breasts that had been shielded from the ravaging sun by a scant bikini top.

"Would you like anything else before we takeoff?" she asked.

Charlie got goose bumps when he felt her fingers linger on his arm through the fabric of his white button-down shirt. He thought, *yes, immediately seeing himself as a Bondian character, stripping off his Saville Row attire, and ravaging her on a couch. He would join the ten-mile-high club experienced by few.* Charlie always had a penchant for sexy young women, but this one had "do not touch" written all over her. Besides, he was on a client trip in a client's plane, and had to behave himself.

"No, thanks," he said.

When in the air, Charlie was served a "snack": Blinis with beluga caviar, and sour cream followed by wild Icelandic salmon with capers, onion and egg, and toast points. Dessert was a small rectangle of dark chocolate mousse. The champagne flowed freely and Charlie didn't turn down a glass. He would arrive a very happy man, quickly, and in style.

Though slightly woozy, Charlie pondered the marital-financial arrangements of the Baxter family which were, to say the least, unusual. Gil and his reputedly toxic wife, Brenda, lived semi-independent lives, cohabiting about half the year and doing their own thing the other half. Brenda lived off a pile of money given to her by Gil. Lucky lady, she'll inherit plenty more to keep her beyond luxury for the rest of her life.

Looking out the window, the island had yet to come into view. *Hmm,* Charlie thought, *Grand Cayman seems to be the nexus of their time together and their financial affairs. Why anyone would want to spend so much time on a small, hot, isolated, overcrowded island is beyond me. But I'll just keep to my policy of not getting involved in clients' personal lives and bizarre habits. How the heck am I going to relate to British-bred police on Grand Cayman? Except for a couple trips to London as a tourist, I know nothing about England and the English. Hardly spent enough time to get even a whiff of the culture.*

Charlie was a bit of an odd duck. Some might say an eccentric man who liked a challenge, and was charmingly avuncular. Married decades ago, his wife had died in an auto accident, and they had no children. He was now a confirmed bachelor. Charlie enjoyed and cared about people and easily struck up conversations with anyone that caught his interest: somebody sitting next to him on the subway or a billionaire client. They were all people with stories as far as he was concerned. Maybe his friendly smile and the fact that he was not an imposing, striking person (hair fleeing, he was sort of deceptively average), induced people to trust him. His wry sense of humor and penetrating, inquisitive legal mind resulted in a lucrative practice. Between his legal fees and inherited money, he was financially comfortable enough to pick and choose the cases he worked on.

Settling into his cushy seat, Charlie relaxed and thought,

Maybe I'll have time to do some scuba diving and photograph the Lion Fish on the western side of the Island. Can't believe the weather kept me from there the last three times I was here. Nothing like the serenity of being underwater with coral and fish, away from the two-legged animals. Ahh, it's a good life, you got, ol' Charlie.

Champagne prompted heavy lids, and he napped for the remainder of the flight

The plane landed on time at Grand Cayman's Owen Roberts Field and parked in front of the ramshackle executive terminal, sharing the apron with a dozen and a half other executive jets. Probably weekenders with houses on the "McMansion" East End of the island. The executive terminal used to be the main terminal when there were only a handful of commercial flights a day. Charlie recalled that it formerly had an ill-repaired thatched roof that, during the rainy season, drizzled water on the concrete floor and often sopped unlucky passengers and their baggage. The old terminal used to be staffed by one lackadaisical customs official anxious to get back to his nap or to gabbing with a policewoman. There might be one or two dented, dirty cabs around and one person to carry luggage. Today, the renovated executive terminal was spruced up with a new thatched roof to maintain the character of an exotic island, and a spiffy waiting room for its privileged guests. The thirty-year-old "new" commercial terminal was an unattractive mix of architectural forms and decorative treatments. It was a hubbub of activity with over sixty commercial flights a day, a lot of them wide-body jets, discharging thousands of passengers. It was a sign of the island's explosive growth.

Charlie dodged traffic, walking across the airport entrance road to the small, cramped and crowded Avis Rent-a-Car office. He greeted Samuel, the brown, slender, balding, middle-aged manager of the agency whom he had known for some thirty odd years. They reminisced about the past when there were no stoplights on the mosquito-plagued island, and only a couple of cops who had little to do. There was one hotel, four or five dive operations, and no fast food joints. Builders were putting up the first three condo complexes. A small number of savvy divers came each year, and Avis had a five-car agency operating out of a downtown gas station with seasons old cars. Their larger office, across the street from the terminal, was built about thirty years ago and handled a substantial portion of the car rental business on the island. Samuel, the manager, was a born-again Christian and let you know it. He gave each renter a business card with the saying: "Come to God and Come to Avis, Grand Cayman." Handing over the car keys, he said: "May the good Lord be with you on your journey through our little paradise. And don't whack up my car."

Almost in a vacation mood, and wanting a bit of fun during his grim duty, Charlie rented a brilliant yellow Jeep Ranger convertible. He would never put the top down, of course, in the blistering heat, but the car made him feel young. He imagined himself riding on the sand, skirting the surf, gin and tonic in hand, a scorching, red-haired movie star like Christina Hendricks in the passenger seat, drinking in the sea and air, heading for a secluded spot where they couldn't be observed. It wouldn't happen even if there were time, but worth a fantasy.

Charlie immediately made a right out of the parking lot, head-on into oncoming traffic. Still a bit foggy from imbibing on the jet, he'd forgotten that the British drive on the left and almost had a front-end collision with a Leyland lorry that wheeled around him; horn blasting, at the last moment.

Christ! Guess Samuel's prayers are necessary after all. Charlie fought his way through the mammoth midday, LA-like, traffic jam on West Bay Road to the Four Seasons Hotel on the northern end of Grand Cayman's spectacular Seven Mile Beach. He tucked himself into a luxurious beachfront suite and poured two-fingers of Balvenie 21–year-old single malt scotch from the bottle he'd picked up at duty-free.

After all, if I'm going to work, why not work in comfort with a bit of a buzz? My dead client never had problems with my lush spending habits, so I might as well make this dull assignment enjoyable. Who is he going to complain to anyway?

Charlie picked up the phone and called Inspector Thompson. An operator answered in a lazy island voce,

"Police Department. How may I help you?"

"Could I speak to Chief Inspector Thompson please?"

" Of course, he just came in." Thompson picked up on the first ring and tersely said,

"Thompson here, make it quick, I'm in a hurry."

"Inspector Thompson, I'm Charlie Braun. I believe you know that I'm here to deal with the Baxter's personal affairs."

"Yes, I know. I'll fill you in on the murder when I see you. I also need you to identify the body. We'll go to the morgue after the condo visit. I'll meet you at Blue Diamond Condominiums at 8 AM tomorrow. Don't be late. I don't have much time.

Charlie thought, *asshole.*

According to Baxter's sister, Gil and Brenda lived in an "over-the-top" 8,000 square-foot penthouse suite in the Blue Diamond Condominium Tower, the most expensive and grandiose condo on Grand Cayman. And that was saying something. There was a young couple that lived with them, and seemed to do little but lounge around, eat out, look beautiful, and run minor errands. Some said that they were personal trainers, but Baxter and his wife were not into exercise and health, so having trainers was puzzling. No one knew what they really did, but he'd likely find that out from Thompson.

The police seemed to know all that's about in Grand Cayman with the rich, financial heavies, and the criminal element. Not a good place to get arrested because, while English law is the law of the land, its application can sometimes be a bit rough on hard-core criminals or anyone else unfortunate enough to threaten the peace of the island.

Briefcase in hand, he ambled over to the formal, lavishly furnished dining room for lunch, and to mull over the job ahead.

Charlie took out a yellow legal pad and listed what he needed to do. He had to run over to Cayman National Bank and Barclays to look at Gil's "honest" account balances, account histories, and freeze the accounts as the law required. His bills, debts and ultimately estate, had to be settled from those assets. There were two secret accounts that Gil, a bit smashed and mellow, had told him about some years ago. They contained "insurance money" that Gil had laundered and buried, in case the IRS or his wife came nosing around.

I don't know the source of the money or where it is hidden, and don't want to. If any of the funds were ill-gotten, there's a distinct possibility that I could be dragged into some nasty IRS tax fraud case or hotly contested will situation. Having no knowledge is the best defense. And, God forbid, I should get crossways with Brenda. The IRS would be a cakewalk by comparison.

Charlie ate a meal of grouper in a light butter and caper sauce. Good, but not up the standards of his usual five star-famous-chef, New York restaurants. He tossed down the rest of his second, generous Balvenie, and left a $40 tip for superlative service before heading to the banks.

CHAPTER TWO

Two Days Previously, Detective Inspector Harry Thompson was drowning in immense piles of routine paperwork that had accumulated over a couple of weeks. He was thinking: How much of this useless shit can I get away with trashing, when Chief Inspector Gibbs had rushed into his office.

"Harry, there's been a murder. Gil Baxter, and I don't need to tell you how important the guy is. The uniforms have secured the scene, and the forensics crew is on its way. Get out there, and find out what happened. And solve the Goddamned thing fast. We need this like a hole in the head after the rash of house break-ins that hit the front page last week."

"Address?"

"Diamond Condos on upper West Bay Road."

"Whadda we know."

"Nothing except that his throat's been cut. Messy. Looks a slaughterhouse. Blood all over the place."

"Where are last two week's reports, by the way?"

Harry went silent.

"Nice try. Cut out the paperwork and half of us would lose our jobs. Civil Service bureaucracy. But right now, get your ass out of here and report back to me as soon as you have a handle on the Baxter case. I'll notify the next of kin."

Harry mumbled to himself: *Americans. Too much money, arrogant, difficult to deal with. Too much trouble. Baxter is a complete asshole and druggie. And with a lawyer involved, there'll be trips to the American Counsel General, ponderous inquiries by customs and immigration, and annoying pestering by relatives of the deceased. The Finance and Fraud Ministry will pour over financial records, and lawyers will be swarming all over the place. And I'll be in the middle of this crap until I catch the culprit.*

Thompson was a widower. He had yet to find a companion that would even partially fill the dark void left by his wife's death. A decade ago, a recently paroled and vengeful murderer that Harry had arrested, stalked and murdered his wife one night as she walked home from an exercise class. He was caught shortly thereafter and sent up for life. Harry understood that the Bobbies had "trouble" bringing the guy down. He was arrested and returned to the station house with multiple broken bones innumerable cuts, bruises and contusions. He was 5'11" and weighed 175 pounds. The residue of the travesty was Harry's barely contained anger and fury when chasing big-time criminals. Particularly murderers. It was his way of getting even.

Eventually, Thompson got bored. After golf, diving, shooting sporting clays, and a bit of socializing, he ran out of things to do. Too much time on his able and restless hands, he applied for a Detective Inspector's job in Cayman's CID. Shy of experienced personnel, they hired him.

Thompson seemed like the perfect man for a Rolex Submariner tall, taut, athletic, fit and tanned with a thin craggy wind-worn face and pronounced dimpled chin. He looked a bit like Daniel Craig. He was developing slight crows feet in the corners of his eyes and a little bit of sag of the chin and waistline. Other wise, he looked ten years younger than his fifty-three years. He had a military bearing gained during his post-university Army service and combat experience during the Falklands war. He exuded cool confidence and fierce intelligence. When Thompson looked at someone with his blue, yellow-flecked, Paul Newman eyes, they felt as if they were the only person in the world that counted.

His standard mode of dress on and off the job was traditional British Colonial flared khaki military shorts with matching short-sleeved bush shirt and brown hiking boots. He cut quite a figure.

CHAPTER THREE

Harry left headquarters and walked smartly across the parking lot through humidity so thick, you could practically bite chunks off and chew them like a sausage. The fluorescent lime-yellow stripes on his blue and white BMW 535i police car reflected the noonday sun, and he hopped in. Siren screaming and red and blue lights flashing, he sped through traffic, weaving from one side of the road to the other, leaving a trail of angry motorists. Thompson recklessly snaked his way through the tangled assemblage of police, police cars, and the medical examiner's van to the front door of the condo complex. A uniformed, snooty-looking doorman that dressed more like a Beefeater than an employee of a rich man's tropical haven, opened the door. He was directed to the private elevator, which whizzed him to the penthouse.

"What do we have here?" Thompson asked the officer guarding the door.

"Sir, we have one Gil Baxter. Been here for a while, and getting as ripe as week-old fish, if I do say so myself. Forensics and Detective Odigbo are waiting for you."

"Thanks, I'll find my way in."

Thompson walked into a sculpture-filled foyer flooded with light and decorated with clouds of exotic, white Caribbean Star Valley orchids. The overwhelming stench made him gag. Definitely not the orchids, he thought. It smelled like dead meat overlaid with the distinct metallic smell of blood. Thompson put on a gauze mask, stretched on white nitrile gloves, and tugged cloth boots over his shoes to prevent evidence contamination.

He entered the living room, a sumptuous space decorated in white. Highly impractical near a beach, but it was clean. Almost pristine. The expansive room accommodated two large seating areas with couches, chairs upholstered in Missoni patterned white-on-white cloth, an assortment of tables, lamps, plants, and colorful abstract art on the walls completed the scene. *Money, money, money*, he thought.

The corpse was on its back, one arm flung over its head, the other tucked in next to the chest. A huge pool of dry, crusted, brown blood that had poured from Baxter's cut throat, made a dark, stark pattern, shaped like the state of California, on the white rug. The temperature was over 100 degrees and the humidity in the high nineties. The construction crew working next door had likely turned the electricity off and forgotten to turn it back on. That had accelerated the decomposition of the body which did not help Thompson's mood.

Brady, chief of forensics, kneeling by the body, pointed at Baxter's head, "This is all you need to see. All of the action was on the neck."

Maggots, as well as birds that had flown in through the open patio doors, had done their work. The body looked like a cadaver being dissected by a med student. Flesh was plucked from everywhere on the body. Bone visible. Residual skin on the face was wrinkled and stretched over the skull. Eye sockets and nose cavity were dark, vacant voids. His mouth was a gaping hole and looked like a grinning jack-o-lantern. The flesh that remained was a putrid shade of green-gray. Thompson went over to the body. The morgue guys were understandably anxious to get the carcass out of the apartment.

"How long's he been dead?" Thompson asked.

"Given the advanced state of decomposition, I'd say about a week or a bit longer."

"What do you think happened?" he asked Brady

"It's a textbook case. Assaulted from behind, throat slit, and the blood rush from his carotid artery splattered the patio window. That artery will spurt four pints of blood until the heart has nothing to pump and the brain shuts down without oxygen. That's a lot of liquid—like spilling a half-gallon of milk on the floor. Look at the finger trails on the glass. He tried to stop his fall, which, of course, he couldn't. He probably lived for five or six seconds once he hit the floor."

"Murder weapon?"

"Throat was cut with a large knife with a razor-sharp, serrated edge. Might be a dive knife--an item as common as dirty, stray dogs on the island, except that it was specially sharpened. We didn't find a weapon. We'll send trace evidence to the lab and see what that turns up."

Thompson turned to Odigbo.

"How did the murderer get in? Any signs of forced entry?"

"The housekeeper who found the body hadn't been here for over a week. On vacation. She said that the Baxter's always kept the entry door locked even when they were at home. But the door was slightly ajar when she came to work. There's no other way to get into the place unless you rappel from the roof or were Spiderman and could climb or fly up twenty stories. No sign of a struggle or fight. So it was likely someone he knew and let in. Maybe a workman or business acquaintance. Or the murderer had a key.

"Another thing. The neighbor across the hall rushed out when she heard our ruckus and told me that a couple in their mid-twenties lived with the Baxter's. She believed their names were Pat Sweeny and Savannah Lord. About two weeks ago she overheard something about their taking a trip to Cuba. She hadn't seen them since. She pinched her nose as if the very thought of the pair reeked. She'd said the man was spacey and his muscular body usually oiled and covered with tattoos—arms, legs, back, back and chest. Quite an eye for detail, this lady had. She remembered death's head inked on one foot, USMC, and the Marine shield on the other. His girlfriend, the housekeeper reported, looked like a Penthouse centerfold. Always 'struttin' it. She'd wander around the complex and beach topless, wearing a bright yellow, string bikini bottom that left absolutely nothing to the imagination. Got men's tongues hanging out behind her wherever she went."

Thompson said, "We already know about them. Strange situation. Where's the housekeeper now?"

"On her way downtown to make a statement," Odigbo replied,

"Lady seemed interested in all of the 'police stuff,' as she called it. An avid fan of CSI and Dexter."

"More than one murderer?"

"We don't know. No signs of Baxter being held down or anything else that would indicate two."

"How about prints?"

"Piles. Covering the killing room, which is no surprise given the number of people who lived here. But the door handles were wiped clean. We'll do a search of our database and IAFIS' records. When you bring suspects in for questioning, we'll print them and run the prints through the databases as well. The electronic fingerprint scanning system takes only minutes. If we get a hit, we'll at least have someone who was recently in the apartment that I can question them any way that I want. And I mean any way"

"Anything else?"

"Yes. We found a cache of drugs hidden in the toilet tank. Stupid place to hide them. Everyone who watches TV knows that that's where the cops look first. I don't think Baxter would give a dam if caught. He'd buy his way out. The booty will go to the lab for analysis, but it looks like crystal meth, coke, maybe heroin, and ecstasy. These guys liked to party."

Thompson, along with Odigbo, took a quick tour through the rest of the condo's rooms. At first look, nothing seemed disturbed. There were untouched jewels in the woman's underwear drawer. They were immediately removed for safekeeping. Odigbo said, "A burglar wouldn't have overlooked those treasures. Robbery or vandalism did not seem to be the motive. According to the cops canvasing the condominiums, no one in the residences, condo office, or parking garage, noticed anyone or anything out of sorts in the past week or two. Sweeney and Lord seemed to be the only suspects at this point, unless their Cuban alibi checks out."

"Find the live-in couple fast," Thompson said to Odigbo. "And bring in Brenda Baxter as soon as she returns from her cruise."

The lawyer, Charlie Braun, was on his way. He had lists and photos of valuable items as well as pictures of the entire apartment and will take a complete inventory. When Braun's job was finished, Thompson would know for sure whether anything was missing. Thompson hated the idea of having a foreigner, particularly a lawyer, messing around in his backyard, taking his time and asking stupid questions. He despised lawyers, and particularly the brash, hyper-aggressive, and uncouth New York type.

Hardly have anything to go on right now. Thompson thought. *Brutal murder, no weapon, no motive, and three suspects. I'll see Braun at the morgue tomorrow so he can view the body. I'll blow him off as soon as possible. Otherwise, he'll be a royal pain in the ass.*

CHAPTER FOUR

The next morning, Inspector Thompson drove to the Four Seasons to pick up Braun and take him to the morgue. Braun was to view Baxter's body to assure the executrix that the dead man was, indeed, Gil Baxter.

Braun got into Thompson's car with a pleasant, "Hello, I'm Charlie Braun."

"I know."

"And how are you?"

Thompson did not answer.

"Had a good flight down. Private—on one of Baxter's planes. Hope to get my business done in a hurry and get out of here in a couple of days if I can."

"Good," Thompson snapped, and then went silent.

Braun tried a few more pleasantries, but Thompson answered with blunt, growly, hmmps," and drove the rest of the way to the morgue in studied silence.

Charlie looked at Thompson and thought, *Looks like a tough-ass British Colonial, man of few words, used to controlling everything, and hell to get along with. Pulling information out of him will be like pulling teeth without an anesthetic.*

The one-story morgue façade boasted happy colors, pink masonry-covered, cinder block walls and aqua blue shutters, meant to blend in with the "colonial island look" of the surrounding buildings. It was located on a narrow street behind the former British colony's stately, old, palm-fronted library, the geographic center of town. The library's street was narrow and once laid out for horses, carriages and merchant carts. It was lined with shops selling diamonds and jewelry, T-shirts, knickknacks, and other "touristy" items, and the inevitable here-today-gone-tomorrow bars and restaurants. Such was the detritus that a once-sleepy and beautiful island collects once cruise ships start to disgorge 10,000 intrusive but profitable visitors a day on a postage stamp-sized island with a population of 58,000.

The inside of the morgue was a simple affair. Three stainless steel tables were hooked up to blood drains with what looked like hospital operating room lights hanging over them. Neatly laid out on small tables next to the larger autopsy tables, were the usual tools of the trade: a Stryker vibrating saw for opening the skull, scissors, scalpels, forceps, rib-cutters, bone saws, sewing needles, chisels and hammers, and a scale for weighing organs. The scale reminded Braun of his neighborhood meat market without the butcher paper. This was small arsenal that would assault our bodies, once dead. Fewer instruments than in most home fix-it-up tool kits.

The Medical Examiner slid Baxter's body out of one of the two-dozen refrigerator trays and uncovered him from top to bottom. Charlie gasped and turned pale. "It's him." He'd never seen a "raw" blood-drained white corpse before...much less one that had been moldering and attacked by maggots, bugs, and birds. The cold, long-dead skin made the body look like a stiff, waxy, ravaged alabaster statue--a figure from another world. There was the usual "y" shaped, stitched-up incision from the shoulders to the belly where the severed organs had been removed for examination. The brain was removed by cutting the skull over the crown from one ear to another. The intact scalp was re-stitched, holding on the crown and covering the cavity where the brain once was. His gums had deteriorated, probably due to the use of meth. Track marks on his arms showed where he injected drugs. His name was sloppily written with a magic marker on a toe tag.

"He died about a week or so ago," the examiner said. "See the slashed throat?" Obviously the cause of death."

The c roughly turned the body on its side. "Look at the bruises on the small of his back. The murderer probably put his knee there for leverage when he slit the throat. We found no other indications of foul play, no other trauma, no illnesses. It will be a couple of weeks until we get the tox screen back from Miami. On the face of it, he looks like a pretty heavy drug user. Local tests showed alcohol levels high enough to get him arrested twice over for drunk driving."

In an attempt at humor, Charlie said, "Can I tell Annie that Gil is truly dead?"

"Ummh," grunted Thompson. "What about the slit throat?" he asked the examiner.

"That tells us a lot. First, it was a very strong person who cut his throat. Notice that the gash is deep, and cut through tough ligaments and tissue through the larynx. We think that the assailant was a man, about 5'10" to 6 feet tall, who cut Baxter from behind with his right hand, given the angle of the slash. It appears that Baxter was leading the murderer to the balcony when the man kneed him in the back, yanked up his head by the hair, and slit his throat. No signs of defensive wounds.

"Take a look at the torn edge of the gash. See the rippled edge of the cut? Look at my Dacor dive knife over there on top of my scuba gear. A knife like that might have been the weapon. If so, the blade had to be specially sharpened to cut through all of the muscle and tissue in the throat to the spine. It had to be. The serrations are too deep for a kitchen knife."

"So, what we have," Thompson said, "is the body of a very rich and mysterious man, killed by someone known to him or that he let into his condo voluntarily. His throat was cut a week or so ago, and the murder weapon may have been a dive knife, the criminal a relatively tall man. Other than that we haven't a clue to the murder. We don't know the motive. When Braun finishes his detailed inventory of the condo, we'll know if anything has been stolen or is out of place, though I doubt it. I found nothing out of sorts when I inspected the place."

Braun added, "To add to the turmoil, Brenda, his Goddamn wife, left conveniently on a pseudo-scientific cruise to the Antarctic about a week ago and is unable to return to land for at least a week. I'm the family's representative for the time being, and I have power of attorney for all of Baxter's affairs. I suggest that we solve this fast."

Thompson grimaced." We?"

"Yes we. You will have information that I'll need, and I'll have information about the Baxter's that will help you."

Thompson flicked Braun a contemptuous, sardonic look, and said, "Thanks for the summary."

Charlie thought, *if this continues this way, I'll be sucking hind tit in this investigation. Guy's snarky attitude sucks. Won't be able to do my job. No way in hell is that going to happen. I'll have to make it clear to Thompson that he can't cut me out.*

I can see a blowup coming soon.

Thompson was thinking, *I've got to get wannabe detective off my back. Give him the absolute minimum of the information that the wants and cut him loose.*

Charlie hoped that toddy or two might loosen things up a bit. *I'd like to get him to help me. Or he might just try to screw me up and make matters worse…or boil over.* " Would you join me for lunch at Sunset House? We can discuss the case, and besides, I haven't seen the Slavins who own the place in quite a while and would like to say hello."

Thompson agreed. *Maybe I can give this man a little innocuous information fast, and send him packing.*

CHAPTER FIVE

Thompson and Braun drove the short distance up Church Street to Sunset House, a collection of twenty cottages and hotel rooms frequented by hardcore divers. Situated not on a beach but on striated red-brown hard rock and ancient dead coral called the Iron Shore. It overlooked West Bay and was a mile or so away from the near-white, brilliant sands of Seven Mile Beach. Serious divers went there for three or four dives a day; lots of camaraderie with fellow divers; a first-rate dive operation to cater to their needs; fast boats; a cheap, mediocre restaurant with humongous burgers and fries; and one hell-of-a bar. Locals as well as divers congregated in the bar's small, intimate, thatched-roof, open-air watering hole. It was a place to drink without swarms of tourists, who were curiosities to be watched with amusement. Once the "bar buzz" got going, the local and dive community rumors flew like mosquitoes at dusk—usually unencumbered by fact.

Charlie and Thompson entered the seaside drinking spa, and Charlie said to the bartender, "Hi Johnny, long time no see."

Johnny, the slender Caymanian bartender, was on the black-black side of the island's gradated color spectrum. He was dressed in his usual flamboyant Hawaiian shirt, faded cargo shorts, flip-flops, and slightly disreputable straw fedora. He threw a wide, white-toothed smile. "Hi, Mon. You come see Johnny. Want to toss the local politics and dirt?"

"Of course, but later. I have a bit of business to transact."

Braun turned to Thompson. "Heinekens good for you?"

Charlie signaled Johnny to bring the beer to a nearby table and they sat down.

Thompson said nothing and looked out toward the sun-sparked ocean.

Trying to break the ice, Charlie said, "Harry, I caught the scuba diving bug when the industry was in its infancy and began frequenting Sunset House in 1965."

"Then, the only tourists were a few thousand divers seeking some of the most beautiful and un-trafficked dive sites in the Caribbean. There were no traffic lights, maybe two cops, and the Holiday Inn was basically a hotbed joint for divers and the locals. Maybe there were two or three condominiums, a few stores, and that was it. It was nice. Now the place is overrun with tourists, condos, traffic, and high prices. I understand that crime in this once 'leave your door open' society is rising, due to the massive influx of laborers from other islands and the growing drug culture imported by Jamaicans. Of course, you know that. Sad."

Thompson raised his eyebrows at Charlie and fielded a desultory shrug and uttered a dismissive "humph."

"Do you dive?"

"Yes, when I have time, not often."

The beer arrived and Thompson and Charlie clinked their glasses, and uttered the obligatory "cheers." They ordered burgers and fries, which couldn't be screwed up too much.

Thompson, tensing, abruptly said, "Let's get on with it. What are you here for?"

Charlie, annoyed, replied in measured words. "I've got a hellofa job in front of me collecting the financial information for the executrix of the estate. I have to talk to banks, lawyers, and investment companies. I need to get out of Cayman fast. I have other business to attend to and have to deal with Brenda Baxter as soon as she gets back. She's an arrogant piece of work. Money and power are her motivators and constant quest--also a prime motivation for murder.

Thompson noted Charlie's irritation. *Righteous prig. Wants to play detective, huh? We have to dog the financial angle down; why not let Charlie do it for us. He has expertise that we don't.*

Charlie thumped his glass down and signaled for another round. He hoped that a little booze-buzz would warm things up a bit.

"You can help me in the investigation by answering a few questions," Thompson said. "Do we know if Baxter's recently had a fight or conflict with anyone? Enemies? Anyone who would want him dead?"

Charlie hesitated, quelling his annoyance at Thompson's unfriendly demeanor. "Given all the people he screwed during the last sub-prime mortgage scandal, I wouldn't be surprised if a lot of people wanted his head. I'll find out what I can, but Brenda's the best source when she gets back from her trip."

"What do you know about Gil and Brenda?"

"A lot. They've been clients for decades, ever since Gil started getting rich. I handle their legal work and estate affairs. He was from Des Moines of all places. An area you don't expect a big time moneyman to come from. Upper middle-class family, parents involved in the city—Board of Education and all that. Good, solid, boring Midwestern citizens. Father owned about a half dozen McDonalds. Went east to school—University of Vermont and got an MBA at Wharton."

Thompson looked Charlie in the eyes, and said "Work?"

"Got a job with JP Morgan. Had a knack for trading. Worked 80-hour weeks and got promoted to Senior Vice President quick. Rich as hell. Left the firm to found Baxter Investments, a hedge fund. It was very successful. His clients were New York wealthy and society types."

"What about his personal life?"

"Gil was a hell raiser. Ran with fast crowds. Fast cars—Maserati's were his favorites. Always in New York's places-to-be-seen: clubs, fancy restaurants, gallery openings, society balls. Did coke and booze. Out all night all the time. Liked to be seen with celebrities. You hear of the designers, Michael Kors, Calvin Klein and Tommy Hilfiger? All friends. Loved women—the more powerful, sexy and 'willing,' the better. Lots of affairs. Particularly loved wives of the rich and famous. I guess he liked the intrigue and deception involved in nailing a married woman. Temper. Arrogant. Thinks, well thought, he knew it all; could get away with anything. One night he got boozed and coked up and threw a punch at a guy at the 'The Standard,' a hot disco-driven, red-rope club where the 35 to 50s crowd goes. The guy was hitting on a model that Gil was after. There was a small brawl before the bouncers broke it up. The guy brought charges. I negotiated the best settlement I could, but it still cost him tens of thousands."

"And Brenda?"

"Brenda's got flaming red hair and a temperament to match. Handsome, not beautiful. Regal. Attracts men like a Venus flytrap. Blue blood. Tough. As arrogant and condescending as Gil unless you're important. Has money; loves money and attention. Artsy. Into big-time designer fashion. In short, a brazen bitch. Once, after a very well lubricated society ball, a freaked out wife caught her in bed with her husband—Chairman of the Hudson Art Museum. She unexpectedly came home from a trip and found them in the master bedroom. Apparently, Brenda, naked, mounted on and piston-humping the husband yelled 'get the fuck out. I'm coming.' After she did, she got on her clothes and asked the frantic wife for an umbrella because it was raining. Classic Brenda."

"How do you know all this stuff?"

"From the resulting divorce. The injured wife took on her unzipped hubby. Brenda relayed the graphic testimony. She enjoyed giving the lascivious details. She had a ball, so to speak. Gil was off in Asia doing something or somebody or both and didn't give a shit about Brenda's transgressions. The divorce was granted. Zillions of bucks changed hands. In sex and everything else, she gets what she wants,"

"How did they get together?"

"They met at a sweaty end-of-the-summer, let-it-all-hang-out party in East Hampton. Hot music, hot anything-goes crowd. Filled with celebrities and younger debauched pillars of society. Both in lust that night, they fell into one of their host's beds. They surprised themselves, found out that they liked each other, or at least could become companions and playmates. They married a few months later. I think Brenda had a few affairs after their marriage, but nothing like Gil's prodigious action. The relationship was rocky. Fought a lot, over money; trivial things. Took separate vacations; lived apart some of the time. A marriage of sex, convenience and lifestyle. That's about all I know."

"That's a ton," Thompson said, impressed in spite of himself. "They sound like el primo pieces of work. Where do they live?"

"The 77 million dollar penthouse at the Plaza on Central Park South."

"Swish. What were they worth?"

"That's no secret. Billions."

Relaxing some after a third beer, Charlie asked, "What's your game plan?" Thompson looked at Braun. He wasn't about to divulge his strategy, but he'd offer a few morsels.

"The Department will continue with routine police work. We'll canvas the neighbors again to see if they saw or heard anything. Go through the files of our usual suspects who have violent records, see if any merchants have seen suspicious activities or men around the time of his murder. And who knows what 'suspicious' is, given the potpourri of people who wash in and out of this island daily."

"And how are going to find the perp?"

Did he really say "perp"? I really don't need a wanna-be detective. And "we"? When the dinosaurs return.

"You heard the examiner's findings. We'll ask questions and look for a six-foot, well-muscled male who might be a diver, probably knew Baxter, and may have bought a dive knife lately. Besides the island's dive shops and operations, we'll question the major restaurants and bars. That's about all we can do except hope that he doesn't kill again. Seems like a personal crime. An out-of-towner or very sophisticated person. Too pat, too smooth, too clean for one of the locals."

After three mellowing beers, Braun thought, *maybe if I tell Thompson about some of my background, he'll loosen up some and tell me about his.*

Squelching his annoyance and putting on his best face, Charlie changed the subject in hopes of warming up Thompson and asked, "Why are you here?" You're a Brit and I would think you'd stay in the home country."

"Like it here. Relaxed culture. Didn't want to be in cold and rainy England for the rest of my life."

"Tell me about your toughest case?"

Seizing an opportunity to brag a bit and establish his credentials, Thompson said,

" I spent 25 years in London's Criminal Investigation Department (CID). I was responsible for handling everything from robbery and assault, to some of the most gruesome murders and the bloody results of violent drug wars in central London. I solved the most the most grotesque serial killing in half a century—the rape and murder of eleven young prostitutes."

Charlie leaned forward and put his elbows on the table to hear better over the din of the bar's growing population.

Twelve girls had been raped, dismembered, and their parts stuffed and preserved in 55-gallon drums filled with formaldehyde. The "caskets" were left in a remote little-visited swamp well outside of the city. The victims fit a profile. The twelve were well-built, prostitutes. Good-looking blonds in their late teens or early twenties, who hadn't been working the streets very long. When we opened the drums, upturned faces in a tangle of arms and other body parts greeted us. I retched. My heart thumped; my pulse soared. I was infuriated. I wanted this killer in the worst way,

"We called the psycho-nut 'Bible John' because he pasted a bastardization of a Bible verse on each victim's 'coffin.' Two of John's favorites were: "For the wages of sin is death" and "Everyone who would not seek the God of Israel was to be put to death." I caught John after a three-year hunt. I installed CCTV monitors at most of the hooker hangouts, and finally saw a man forcing a young blond into a car with a visible license plate. I identified him and his address from the plates. Would you believe that a murderer would be stupid or arrogant enough use his own plates on a car? A SWAT team ambushed him, and killed him in a blaze of gunfire, but regrettably, not before 'Bible John' had killed his last victim."

"Love the heat of a hunt, and the adrenaline rush of bringing a criminal to ground. I got a lot of commendations and promotions out of my handling of tough-to-solve crimes.

Thompson paused. "I don't know why I'm telling you all of this. You seem to be the type that makes people want to talk to you"

"I'm a lawyer. It comes with the territory."

"What about you?"

"Not a particularly exciting life," Charlie understated. I'm a widower too. Lost Lorraine in a horrible auto accident. I'm semi-retired. Service a handful of long-standing clients, play a lot of golf and go to a lot of charity functions and dinner parties. Come down here to relax, see old friends and scuba dive. Not much interested in women. When it's dark and I've had a couple of drinks, I often sense Loraine's ghost wisping in the curtains or sitting in her favorite chair watching me. Really. I'm not kidding. Sometimes it's a very lonely life. I guess we're two bachelors in the same sad barrel of grief. "

"Yes, we're certainly in the same sad boat, Thompson added."

Seeking a way to get closer, Braun said, "By the way, Inspector, I'm going to do a couple of dives in the morning. It's Saturday. Would you like to join me?"

"Maybe some other time. My boss is breathing down my neck to get this thing solved. Fast. Who do you dive with?"

"George Savage. Been diving with him for 35 years. "

"He's the best. Will probably be a good source of information"

"There's another guy, Zane. Only goes by that name. Few know his last name. He might be good for information. Always seems to know what's going on in the island. I'll ask both about the tattooed Bobbsey Twins that live at the Baxter's. I'll look Zane up. He's been hanging around the diving scene and dive boats for decades. He takes pictures of tourists coming off the cruise boats, and underwater and onboard pictures of divers. Sells to them at a ridiculous price.

Well, Thomson thought: *maybe not such a bad guy after all. The financial and legal angle may play big in the murder's motive. Besides, he knows the personalities and quirks of the Baxters. I can use him.*

"Keep me informed about your progress." Thompson said to Charlie.

"Of course, if you'll keep me in the loop on your progress on the investigation."

"We'll see what I can officially let you know," said Thompson, getting up to leave.

After Thompson left, Charlie sidled up to the mahogany bar for a final beer and chat with Johnny. He said to himself, *I hope that I'll find people and documents that will help solve the mystery. But what, where, and when? Better damn well get moving.*

CHAPTER SIX

The demons returned on the evenings when Charlie was home alone. It slipped into his psyche like gas seeping slowly from a stove and swirling around him. After his meeting with Thompson was no exception.

Charlie sat in his Ritz Carlton room without a companion to talk to. He'd only bothered to throw his suit jacket and briefcase on a chair. He turned on one dim light. The black visage returned. He usually avoided night at home in New York by going out with friends for dinner, to society functions, the opera or symphony, jazz joints, and many of the cultural advantages of the city. Anything to escape being alone at night and to satisfy his burning need to be around people. But in Cayman, there was no companionship, no close friend that he could share his thoughts with. Dining alone was an anathema, and there were no events that piqued his interest. Nothing to distract him so he didn't have to face the beast. His thoughts always returned to his wife, Lilly, and the feeling that he was responsible for her death.

Charlie and Lilly were hit in Cayman by a lorry speeding on the wrong side of the road. Every time he thought of the tragedy, slow-motion images of the accident flashed through his head. Lilly's airbag had not deployed. The car careened off the road. Her head hit the dashboard and she was killed instantly. Her seat belt held her waist tight against the seat. Her torso was bent over at the waist like a rag doll held tight by a kid. Blood streamed down her face. She wasn't breathing. Charlie had yelled her name. He shook her, slapped her. No response. The last thing that he remembered, in his shocked state, were the taillights of the ambulance carrying her body to the morgue. The red dots faded symbolizing to Charlie the last of her blood streaming into the ether. He always blamed himself for not swerving out of the lorry's way. When alone, he drank more than he should. The substantial settlement from Jaguar for the faulty airbag did nothing to assuage his guilt. He donated the money to the Metropolitan Museum and the Museum of Modern Art.

I've got to get myself out of this morose morass. I have to find someone to go to dinner with me, to events, to the movies, to a bar just to talk. The only person I know is Thompson. I'll call him to go on a dive with me tomorrow.

CHAPTER SEVEN

It was dusk and daylight was rapidly fading with a slight pink line just over the horizon. Inspector Thompson trudged up the steps to his small house and opened the front door. He was greeted by a dark room with no signs of life. Vacuum-like silence. No hello by anyone. No flowers. Not even a cat or dog. He switched on a lamp and saw the crummy furniture that looked like it was on its third life, heading toward the grave. He didn't give a damn. This was a bachelor's pad for sleeping and eating only.

The house was sparsely decorated. His past was ever present. On a bookshelf, there were many pictures of his murdered wife, and the two of them on the many vacations that they took all over the world. There were images of their friends at parties, and their dog, Sherlock. It looked like a shrine—a place to bring the past present. His many commendations peppered the wall. There was a picture of him with London's Police Commissioner giving him a citation and promotion for closing the serial killer case. A yellowing, framed London Times headline and first page heralded the end of the case. The accompanying photograph was a picture of Harry bringing the hand-and-foot-chained culprit in for booking. There was group picture of Thompson and his department.

Harry poured himself a neat scotch and plumped down in his lumpy armchair. *Christ, the Commissioner and pols are all over my ass to get this case closed. It's snake pit. I'm without clues and this is going to be a long, hard pull. Too bad I can't convince the boss and the press of that. And this Charlie guy. I don't know if he will help or distract from the investigation. Best wait a while and see what he can produce. An extra hand on the legal-financial side would be helpful.*

Though nostalgia was not a frequent occurrence with Thompson, his mind turned to his glory days in London.

I miss London. My assistant Henrietta was a peach. Waiting for me in the morning, was tea—cream and two sugars —two current scones with clotted cream and boysenberry jam. Paperwork to be signed, urgent memos and notes sorted in order of priority and everything in its place, and easily found.

My schedule would be laid out. Thank God she organized me. I hate office detail. Without her I would get nothing done. I miss the low buzz of voices from ten detectives in the bullpen spiked by the occasional laughter at a joke. Or the yelling from a criminal being dragged in for booking. Loved the work. But herding a bunch of detectives, and being lead on key cases was too much. What sane middle-aged man would put up with that insanity? Burned out. Miss London, but this is a great deal for me. A boutique detective operation, great people, and a friendly climate. All in all, I have an excellent situation.

Thompson fixed himself a frozen microwave dinner, tuna alfredo with broccoli. He watched the tele news, had another double scotch. At nine, exhausted, he fell into deep and dreamless sleep. At eleven, the phone jangled its jarring, insistent and raspy bell. "Jesus, who the hell is this? I was sound asleep.

A slightly slurred American voice came on the line. "It's me, Charlie. Sorry to wake you up, but I have an idea. Lets go diving with George Savage tomorrow. It's Saturday, and you should take some time off

"Can't. Too much work. Have to get a lot of shit out of the way so I can get on with the Baxter case. No way in hell."

Charlie said, "help me out here. Maybe we can kill two birds with one stone. Focus on some beautiful sights and relax as only one can with nothing to intrude—no phones, no case to worry about, no invading people.

And we can ask Savage what he knows about the Baxters and the case. He knows a lot of what's happening on the island. And he may know a lot about Pat and Savannah. Harry, it's only three hours out of the day. You can be back in the office by eleven-thirty."

Thompson thought for a minute. *Maybe this is a chance to get to know this guy better and find out what he's all about. The dive will wake me up and destress me. Usually does.*

"You're on. When and where?"

"Usual place—dock by the Lobster Pot restaurant at quarter of eight."

"See you then."

Thompson hung up and went back to a restless sleep. His "monkey brain" kept turning over problems with the Baxter case. He woke at seven, bleary-eyed and tired..

He got up heated up a cup of coffee, threw his dive gear in a bag, and lumbered out the front door.

CHAPTER EIGHT

Charlie woke up at 5:45 AM to a sunny, crystal clear morning. *Perfect day for a couple of dives with George Savage. They'll clear my head before digging into the Baxter mess. Savage, an old friend and dive boat operator, knows a lot about island happenings via its feverish grapevine, and might be helpful in the investigation.* He called George who said in his typical gruff, clipped, no-nonsense, and standoffish voice: Who is it? Who is it? It's too damn early. Meet me at the boat ramp next to the Lobster Pot Restaurant at 8." Click.

Harry rang a grumpy Thompson.

"Time for diving. I'll pick you up at 7:30

"Yes, 'hummph'."

Braun had been diving with Savage for at least 40 years. Savage is a rugby-playing Scot with a heart of gold and a spine as tough as rebar. He stood about five feet ten. And, as opposed to his slim, younger days, his middle-age spread stretched the limits of his scarred, long-out-of-fashion, black wet suit. He definitely wasn't into the current lycra-clad, sleek, color-splashed, upscale diving world that he catered to. Discriminating divers funneled through his dive service, and his following was large and loyal. He also headed up the Association for the Preservation of Cayman Reefs for the past three decades, and knew almost everyone in town.

George had replaced his old, sloth-slow pontoon boat with a new, very fast 30-foot rigid inflatable boat—the kind that the Coast Guard uses on harbor patrol. The boat carried twin 140-hp Yamahas, and he could get to any of the dive sites in short order, including the challenging diving on the distant North Wall. He only took twelve people, so the diving was comfortable and the groups usually friendly.

Charlie and Harry unloaded their gear from the yellow jeep, and carried it down the dock beside George's boat. Charlie slid his old mesh dive bag, along with his wetsuit (absent one knee pad and patched in various placed) onto the deck. The old, well-worn suit was bleached by the sun and saltwater, from blue to gray. Most divers would have replaced their wetsuit before it got into this disreputable shape.

George gave him a firm hand climbing over the side of the boat.

"Well, Mr. Braun, where the hell have you been?" George asked with a good deal of faux-aloof formality. "I've been looking for you for the past year, and you've not graced my doorstep or bank account."

"I've been working, George, so I can pay your damn exorbitant fees and the cost of living on this over-rated money pit." They both knowingly laughed.

"And who are you dragging onto my yacht?"

"I'd like you meet detective Harry Thompson from CID. We're working together to solve the Baxter murder case. The killing was a tragedy."

Thompson blanched. *Christ, 'we' again.* He strained to keep quiet.

Savage said, " I'm not sure it was a tragedy. He was a real prick. What are you doing with the case?

"Just some estate affairs."

Savage shrugged his shoulders and addressed Charlie. "Say, remember when we had to pull out those fools that damn near killed themselves on a night dive?"

"Yes," Charlie said, "I remember the rescue as if it were yesterday. The arrogant idiots didn't know squat about diving. Dived at night in a heavy current downstream from the boat. A real no-no no matter how experienced you are. Couldn't possibly swim against the current back to the anchor line and were swept away. We got them just before heavy breakers threw them into the reef, half a mile away. If we hadn't heard them yelling and seen their flashing lights, they would have died or ended up like a mess of dog food."

George turned away from the rest of his guests and continued talking while he quickly and deftly hooked up Charlie's and Harry's scuba gear. He secured the air tanks to the back of their buoyancy compensators (A jacket that a diver wears to put air into or flow out of allowing him to hover neutrally in the water at any depth). He paid particular attention to attaching the regulators—the breathing mechanism—to the tanks. He checked the tank's pressure gauge to insure that they were full of air, and returned the rig to a rack holding a row of a full tanks for the then oncoming divers. George tossed Charlie's face mask to him. The mask had prescription lenses allowing Charlie to see clearly underwater. Then came the long, flexible, highly visible, yellow-lime fins. Charlie and Harry started the acrobatic struggle of putting on their skintight wetsuits that had shrunk during storage, and fit like a pair of very tight skinny jeans. Even with the water temperature a bathtub 85 degrees, a diver can chill quickly without a warming wet suit.

"Who's onboard, by the way?" Charlie asked.

"Usual lot. Six of them are old hands, been diving with me for decades, and just want to get into the water. Maybe you know one or two. The others," George said, with a note of disdain, "are your am-there, almost-there, and hope-to-get-there-soon rich business and financial types."

"Not a charming group, huh?"

" Mixed bag. Some really nice people. But see the hoity-toity preening dudes in the sun on the starboard side? They'll be showing off the latest glitzy gear, getting in sexy poses, telling everybody how rich and great they are, and extolling the exotic dive spots that they've been to all over the world. I don't complain. They can pay the $170 toll for the trip.

"Where would you like to go today? The rest of the boatload won't care," George said,

"How about Tarpon Alley? It's a deep, cool, beautiful, relaxing dive. There's none better."

"You got it." And off they went.

Tarpon Alley was a site off the North Wall of Grand Cayman where the reef plummets from the sunlit surface into the pitch black of the Cayman Trench. At 25,000 feet deep, it's the second deepest in the world, next to the Pacific's Mariana Trench, which is deeper than the tallest mountain on earth. The water is crystal clear with over 100-foot visibility. At 70 feet down, there is a wide sand-bottomed cut with coral heads rising over 50 feet on either side creating a natural underwater valley. The cut was likely formed over the centuries by water surge and vicious storms that had worn and torn away that part of the reef. The current constantly pulsed through the protected lagoon from the open ocean, bringing nutrients into the area. At least 20 tarpon usually hung out in the cut, waiting for schools of baitfish, or other small fish to foolishly swim by. A six-foot, 125-pound tarpon looks like an elegant, sleek, silvery, miniature WWII submarine with a snout and a mouthful of tiny sharp teeth suitable for their prey. They're considered a prize game fish. The grand animals are not good eating, but will give a fisherman a long and tough fight before becoming exhausted and pulled into a boat. They usually move slowly and majestically through the water until they see food. Then they become an eating machine: a silver flash moving through the water at warp speed. It's mesmerizing to see them suspended in the water, finning to hold themselves in place with the sun streaming through the water, dappling their lustrous bodies and the sand bottom. Always magical to Charlie and Thompson.

George dropped the pair at Tarpon Alley to give them a solitary, easy, calm, relaxing dive. He took the remaining divers to another location further up the reef to explore the fish and coral. After 35 minutes, Charlie's dive computer signaled that his bottom time was almost up, and his air was getting low. On his way up to the boat, which had returned to pick him up, he made the obligatory "safety stop" at fifteen feet to blow off bend-causing nitrogen, surfaced to a blazing noontime sun, and returned to the boat.

On the ride back to the harbor, wet and chilled on the outside, but wonderfully warm and de-stressed inside, Thompson asked George about the Lord couple.

"Oh yeah. They go out with me occasionally. They're strange live-ins with the Baxters at Diamond Condos. Said to be trainers. There's something weird about them. Muscles and outrageous tattoos all over their bodies. And I mean all over. Always look like bulked up and sun-basted Barbie and Ken dolls in scant show-all bathing suits. A bit spacey. Watery bloodshot eyes. Look hung-over every time they come on board. Probably do drugs and booze. They keep to themselves, which is fine by me. Don't trust them. Stay away from them. They come, they pay, they dive passably, they go away. I don't know much about the Baxters, but the whole kit and caboodle looks odd to me. If you want to find out more, go find Zane. He's pretty piped into the tourist trade and also has a foot in the darker world of the island."

"Many thanks. " Thompson said. " We have a couple of urgent things to deal with now, and then we'll get to Zane."

Charlie went off to chase down the money; Thompson to find Pat and Savannah.

++++++++++++2/24/16 6:55 AM

CHAPTER NINE

The policeman guarding the residence let Charlie into the condo. Thompson had promised to leave the condo "as was," awaiting my more detailed inventory.

Charlie did a quick sweep of the apartment, using an old photo inventory and lists of important items. All of the paintings and prints on the wall were untouched. He was particularly concerned about the Giacometti sculpture and the Warhol and Thomas Eakins paintings. These three pieces alone were worth $200 million. Seemed a bit much to put museum-quality art in what is essentially a glorified 20th floor beach house. But, he guessed., if you've got the bucks and you want it, and you can get it, you can put it anywhere you please. They were fortunately untouched. The effete party animals and coke-sniffers that the Baxters seemed to attract will likely be the only people to see these gems if they notice them at all. A pity.

Of course the trainers, probably consider Norman Rockwell or the Penthouse Centerfold, pinnacles of art, can't miss them. Doubt that they had a clue about their history and beauty.

Charlie made a mental note to get the art and valuables out of there and into safe storage as soon as the police released the place to him. The furniture, silverware, and electronics were untouched. The maid had cleaned the rotten meat out of the refrigerator. The police cleanup, air conditioning, and very strong, sickeningly sweet-smelling lavender disinfectant failed to mask the awful odor of death. The police had found and removed $200,000 in cash, not an unusual amount of money for a man that has a $1,000,000 limit on his credit cards. But the Baxter's inventory noted dozens of uncut and cut gems. They were not in the house. Subsequently they didn't find them in the Baxter's lockboxes. They were gone with no idea where they might be.

A brown stain remained on the sullied white carpet. Charlie could visualize the body hitting the floor, twitching in its last moment of life and blood slowly spreading over and being sopped up by the carpet. He wondered if Gil had felt the blow, seen the floor coming up at him, realized that he was going to die.

Stain aside, the place was spotless. It looked as if Gil had just entered the immaculately groomed apartment after a long absence and was immediately murdered. Had the murderer been waiting in the apartment or did Gil know him and let him in? Could the man have been disguised as a deliveryman or maintenance worker? There were a lot of questions to be answered. The crime scene yielded nothing according to Thompson and forensics—no murder weapon, no prints, no trace elements. Not a clue, save the suspicion that the murder was committed with a sharp dive knife by a tall man.

Charlie then took to rummaging through drawers. Gil's desk contained unimportant business papers, personal correspondence, the usual bank statements, purchase receipts, and Cartier engraved stationary. The only correspondence of interest was a letter from a friend named Herb saying that he was looking forward to seeing Gil on the island sometime this month, to discuss "their problem." He would inform him of his travel plans. The envelope was postmarked Montauk New York, but there was no name or return address on the letter or envelope. Brenda's well-organized desk yielded nothing of value, though it was fun to read letters from Brenda's female friends about the foibles of this person or that; the whiney, troublesome kids; affairs or soon-to-be affairs, and problem husbands. It was superficial stuff. The wall safe contained ordinary items such as Gil's passport, residency certificate, and routine financial documents. There was nothing else of interest.

Charlie rifled the bedrooms and came up with little, save a drawer full of appliances—not the kitchen type but the other kind—handcuffs, studded black-vinyl body suits, dildos, whips, and gags. Seems that the family that plays rough together stays together, at least for six months of the year. He wondered what kind of relationship Gil and Brenda had with the dynamic duo. They apparently lived with the Baxters for a good part of the year and traveled all over the world with them as court to their royalty. Charlie also wondered where he'd find them. He was tired. First there was the murder, then executor Anne's call to his office and a hurried trip to Grand Cayman. Then followed Thompson, the smell, the murder scene, the morgue, and the puzzling players—Brenda, Gil, the dynamic duo. It was befuddling. He felt that he deserved a treat.

He decided to pack it in for the day and have a fine European-style dinner at Eduardo's in the Coconut Plaza strip mall on Seven Mile Beach. The restaurant is tucked away in an ignored corner of the old and faceless strip mall, where you would expect a convenience store with blazing fluorescent beer signs. Eduardo's is a "find" for those lucky enough to stumble upon it, and it has fine continental food.

Charlie said hello to William, the Caymanian who owns the place, before dinner, he dawdled and relaxed over a nice 2002 Louis Jadot Cordon Champaign. He preferred the much more expensive Crystal, but the restaurant didn't carry it. Charlie had garlic-studded lamb roast garnished with potatoes, artichoke hearts and garlic, served with a Domaine Dujac 2009 Pinot Noir. He ended the evening with a Cognac Prunier XO. He felt that he deserved the feast after the morning and morgue. He'd figure out how to approach Jonathan Brooke, the Baxter's lawyer and financial adviser in the morning. Maybe he could get a handle on the Baxter's financial status through Brooke. Anne Baxter said that he had the key to the king's treasury.

CHAPTER TEN

Two weeks before Gil Baxter's murder, Brenda Baxter was in New York on one of her periodic "breaks" from the toxic world of Gil. She was in a fury. She needed to calm down and think long and hard about her future. As far as she was concerned, he was a philandering, drug using drunk; a son-of-a-bitch who was rich as Midas. Brenda retreated to the Cloisters on the north end of Manhattan Island. There was no better place to mull over a difficult problem than that quiet and contemplative oasis in the middle of New York's madness.

The Cloisters were built in the 1930s from a grant from John D. Rockefeller Jr. They were reassembled, limestone block by limestone block, pillar-by-pillar, stained glass window by stained glass window from three medieval French cloistered abbeys. The buildings dominate the wooded hill and have a stunning, uninterrupted view of the wide, smooth-flowing Hudson River and the New Jersey Palisades. One thousand medieval paintings adorn the walls of a museum, and the site is dotted with sculpture and other artwork from the period. Medieval flower and herb gardens rest outside the cloister walls, among the paths and benches that make up a small walking park.

Brenda sat on a stone bench in an herb garden. The sweet and pungent aroma of roses, lilies, violets, fennel, sage, iris, and rosemary, calmed her nerves for some reason she did not know or care about. Perhaps in medieval times, these herbs, flowers and scents had medicinal value, maybe an ancient tranquilizer. Maybe they exuded some mystical or magical force. Brenda didn't care. She was steely-calm, she was collected, and she was ready to figure out what the next step in her life would be.

For a few minutes she thought about how good life with Gil once was. They married just out of college, young graduates living in the then-cheap East Village on his starting salary at J.P. Morgan. A leading financial institution, Morgan started Gil in the acquisitions and mergers department, where he quickly rose from junior associate to a key member of acquisition teams. His salary and bonuses soared. He went to the investment side of the company where they invested in stocks, bonds, mortgage securities, and companies. He was a star, making a good $20,000,000 a year and still far from the top. They were tough years--six or seven days a week on the job, no kids by design, and little time together. Sure, they lived in a huge apartment at Fifth Avenue and 86th street, but that was small compensation for the mini-marriage they had.

It didn't get any better when Gil left Morgan a very wealthy man, and started his own hedge fund. As Forbes Magazine said: "Gil Baxter, in a remarkably short five years, has built one of the largest and highest-performing hedge funds in the country. A gold mine for investors who can cough up $10,000,000 for an initial investment." Gil's personal fortune was a billion dollars at that point.

Then came the drugs. Gil got hooked on cocaine. It started at a celebrity charity party for the World Hunger Fund hosted by Beyoncé. An agent arranged a night in bed with a hopeful starlet, Claudia Greene--and why didn't Gil try a snort just to prime himself? He did. Nothing was ever the same after Gil found and drifted into his new, intoxicating, star-studded, drug-propelled, woman-littered life.

The live-in dynamic duo, our supposed personal trainers, were about the last straw. For a while, Gil's little concubine, Savannah, and her boyfriend, Pat, provided a lot of entertainment, dope, and sex. There were the four ways, one on ones, and two on one, and God knows what's. Initially it was fun. After a while, it became disgusting. Gill couldn't keep his hands out of Savannah's pants, not that she wore them very often. Then the two became invasive, underfoot, and self-entitled. They were more than I could take. Disgusting. Put me over the edge.

What was I doing while Gil went off on his charging stallion? Anything I wanted-- spending money on second, third, and fourth homes -- Grand Cayman, Palm Beach, New York, and Monaco -- jewelry, clothes, flying wherever I wanted in a company Gulfstream, and having affairs with a number of very discrete and wealthy men who had time, money, and the urge for me. They appreciated my youth and vigor, and I was happy to provide it while I was young and before my time under the plastic surgeon's knife. The best of the bunch was Norman, divorced former head of a Fortune 50 company. He had a beautiful home in Bermuda, only an hour and a quarter away. I could leave for a "shopping expedition" after Gil went to work early in the morning and be back in time to welcome him home at seven or eight at night—very happy, relaxed, and very, very satisfied. Norman was a gracious host and an insatiable swordsman. When Gil was out of town or the country, the sky, literally was the limit. It was coast-to-coast fun. And the pilots, discrete anyway by profession, were bribed to keep their mouths shut.

Brenda sighed and put her head in her hands in sad resignation. She stared into the nothingness of the cobblestone path in front of her until the stones blurred and tumbled like a kaleidoscope in her mind. There was no other answer. Gil would have to go. Soon. There were a couple of ways she could think of getting rid of him. Some more permanent than others. She would go on a planned trip to Antarctica and make up her mind how and when.

CHAPTER ELEVEN

Dawn crept over the East River and a dazzling orange sliver of sun poked over the horizon. The black Mercedes 650 SL slipped around the corner of 86th and Fifth Avenue with Brenda's regular driver, Guido Pizzarelli, at the wheel. He had been chauffeuring Brenda for years, and they had become friends.

Brenda got in and said, "Guido, we're going to Teterboro to pick up the Gulfstream G650, Gil's new toy and the hottest, most expensive business jet on the market. We'll make our flight from New York to Buenos Aires in ten hours, forty minutes shorter than commercial airlines. I'll pick up a charter the rest of the way to

Ushuaia on the tip of Patagonia. I'll overnight there and join Abercrombie and Kent's cruise ship in the morning. So you won't see me for a few weeks.

"By the way Guido, Gil tells me that your family has been of great help to him over the years. Aren't they in the garbage hauling, construction, and cement businesses?"

"Yes Mam. Been in business one way or another since the family came from Sicily in 1820. Early on, they worked farms and provided labor for the construction industry. They graduated to supervising construction jobs and then to owning their own business developing small commercial buildings. The other businesses came later as the family grew and a few died off, leaving a lot of money to invest. Some of the deaths were unexpected, if you know what I mean. Usually followed arguments with other families. They deal with other matters I'd rather not speak of. Let's just say if you needed something, no matter how rough or tough, you'd be dealing with my extended family. We'd be honored to do business with you. Anywhere. My uncles and cousins are very wealthy and very reclusive, so I don't see them much. But they are extremely good at what they do."

"Where do they live?"

"Mostly in estates or very nice houses on Long Island. A few have homes back in the old country."

"So, what is this mob killing that goes on from time to time. Does it really happen? What about the killing of Gino Ferragio in The Castile restaurant last week?"

"Quick hit—in the door and out again, two shots. Spaghetti and blood all over the place. The cops are blaming the Lucchese mob for a revenge hit on the Gambino gang. Apparently the Gambino's were edging in on the Lucchese's New Jersey drug interests. That kind of territorial grab is a serious 'no-no' and always invites a bloody retaliation. But the cops really haven't a clue, according to the papers."

"So, if your family is so rich, what are you doing running a car service?"

"They started me out in the simplest, safest business that they own—if you consider driving in New York and New Jersey safe. But I love it. Meet all kinds of interesting people and make good money. I supervise fifty cars and drive a few exclusive clients, like you, myself. Eventually I'll work my way into the mainstream businesses. And those businesses are really tough, now that the Russians, Ukrainians and Chinese are chewing up the turf. In other words, we're in a brutal and bloody fight just to keep a piece of the pie as big and as profitable as it's been in the last few decades."

As they pulled up to the plane, Brenda said, "Guido, I may soon have some very sensitive, tough and lucrative work for you and your family. I'll be in touch."

"Bye," Brenda said to Guido, then greeted the pilot, copilot, and flight attendant on the stairs to the plane. Wheels were up at 7:30 AM and they would be in Buenos Aires in time for dinner. She would be on the boat two days later to decide Gil's fate.

CHAPTER TWELVE

There were thousands of people in colorful island dress ringing Georgetown Harbor to witness the invasion of Grand Cayman by two pirate ships and their swashbuckling, sword-wielding buccaneers. The event was part of Pirate's Week, Cayman's annual, weeklong celebration of the island's history and culture. It offered local color, music, drink, dancing, and a generally good time.

The "marauder's" purpose was to land, capture, and carry off the Governor of the island to an unknown fate—usually the poolside bar at the Westin Hotel on the north end of Seven Mile Beach. The governor, Sir George Kirkpatrick, was Queen Elizabeth's representative to the country. Sir George, a cordial, engaging, outgoing man, had largely ceremonial duties. He participated in negotiations with other countries, opened Parliament, attended important events and ceremonies, and was responsible for defense of the island--not that Grand Cayman required any. The real power rested with the locally elected Premier, Ministers, and Legislative Assembly. But the Governor looked very impressive in his formal, white, British Naval uniform dripping with medals; or in the long-tailed black morning coat and striped pants used to greet important foreign visitors. For today, dressed in white Bermuda shorts, knee-length socks and polo shirt, he was just out for a bit of fun.

Harry was jostled by the excited, Caribbean-music-driven, wiggling Pirate's Week crowd, and found himself bumping butt-to-butt with a tall, animated, sexy Caymanian woman. He turned to apologize and was then packed-in, front-to-front, chest-to-breast. Quite a nice feeling, he thought. They laughed.

"I'm Harry Thompson," he said.

She raised her eyebrows and with a mock disapproving look, said, "It seems we got to know each other intimately without knowing each others' names, or for that matter, anything about each other. You owe me an apology."

"For what?"

"For sexually assaulting me," she said, with an amused look on her face.

"You're not serious."

"Of course not, it felt good."

They laughed and bumped butts again.

"I'm Amanda Carter," she said, extending a hand. "I know you. Big hero. Saw your picture in *The Compass* last week. Seems you broke up a nasty robbery ring. In the job of arresting headline-catching criminals are you?"

"All in a day's work."

Harry quickly sized up Amanda. She had a throaty, sexy laugh, not unlike Lauren Bacall's. Looked like 25, but more likely thirty-something. Her mischievous, large, brown eyes glowed at him. Her glistening black hair was pulled up to emphasize an elegant long neck adorned with a fine West African cowrie shell necklace. Dangling from her hears were long, gold filigree earrings. Coffee-with-cream colored skin, she wore a stylish low-necked, spaghetti-strapped sundress made from a deep orange, yellow and brown contemporary Nigerian print. She was obviously proud of her African heritage.

Harry was smitten. Searching for something to talk about and in a rare, slightly discombobulated state, he said, "How about the spectacular weather—not too hot and not a raincloud in the sky."

Amanda looked at him and said, "Why are you talking about this weather bullshit?"

Harry babbled on. "And what do you think of the tree-hugger environmentalists trying to block the new golf course on the east side of the island?"

Amanda said, "Let's cut to the chase, Harry. Do you want to go out with me tonight or not?"

Harry recovered nicely and wasted no time in saying, "Can't wait. Hear that the band at Royal Palms' is mind-blowing, the dancing's always great, and the scene is high voltage. Why don't I pick you up at eight? What's your address?"

Amanda gave Harry her address in a posh part of town and turned to leave. She walked a few steps, looked back and snuck a peek at Harry. He was staring at her. She waved and they both smiled.

Harry and Amanda drove in his British racing green Range Rover down a graveled road through two long lines of old, stately palms and into the Royal Palms' jammed parking lot. Even at nine o'clock the place was jumping. The club was Cayman's premier place for drinking, dancing, and those seeking a dance partner, a new connection, or a steamier night—maybe stealing out on the dark beach and making love in the warm surf. It attracted the 20-50s crowd, with most in their thirties. Some were married, most not. A single woman at the circular mahogany bar would wait but a moment before she was asked to dance. Raucous laughs radiated in waves from the bar. Patrons sang the lyrics to tunes being played by "The Beach Rebels," a Jamaican mainstream rock and reggae band. Six bartenders, blurred in motion, were quickly serving their customers and moving on to the next. After all, the faster they moved, the more customers they could serve, the faster the reorders, and the more the tips. Kitchen staff shuttled back and forth, from kitchen to bar to kitchen, with typical island food such as jerked pork, fried conch, and curried chicken, all with sautéed plantain. And, of course, the universal foods—hamburgers, fries, and wings--were on the menu.

To get away from the crowd and take in the scene, Amanda and Harry sat on the low stone wall separating the large wooden dance floor from the beach. The area was lit with dozens of multi-colored lanterns hanging overhead, and gently swinging in the breeze. A flock of dancers exuberantly bounced, twirled and gyrated like spinning tops. Their happy faces were beaded with sweat in the hot, humid night. Harry slipped his arm around Amanda. She didn't resist and leaned into him.

"You're a beautiful woman, Amanda. An Egyptian princess. Your skin is a remarkable shade of tan that I don't see much on the island. "

Harry traced a finger slowly down the back of Amanda's neck.

She scrunched her shoulders at the tingling sensation, smiled, laughed, and said, "I'm a light one, which makes little difference on the island. But it does in the States and Europe where "light blacks" are more accepted than "black blacks." That distinction is breaking down, fortunately. To understand me, you need to understand where we Caymanians came from."

"And where was that?" Harry said.

"We were settled over the centuries by slaves from much of the rest of the Caribbean, merchant seamen from France, England, and Portugal, and brigands fleeing from justice. That's why the range of people's colors range from pure black to light like me. Rumor has it that there were at least half a dozen pirates operating from the island, but that has never been substantiated. This agglomeration produced people of every color from black to almost white."

"So what about your family?" Harry asked.

"I'm a Carter, and our history starts back in the 1600s when a Portuguese seaman and a woman, once a slave from Jamaica, started a family. The family began to import cloth and dry goods from Jamaica. Our supermarket, real estate, food franchises, and food import businesses grew from that small start."

"Impressive. I'm aware of the power of the Carters, Browns, Kirkwoods and Powells. Do you have a day job?"

"Of course. Doesn't every modern woman? I flip burgers 8-5 every day but Sunday, when I attend church three times a day."

"Seriously?"

"No. I manage the family's retail businesses--six supermarkets, a handful of gas stations and convenience stores, and the Burger King franchises. The food import, gasoline, and real estate businesses are run by other family members."

"Quite a job. That's a rough business. Doesn't leave you with much time to party does it?"

"More than you would think. I have two brothers reporting to me that are trained to run the operation and do the 24/7 heavy lifting."

"Ever married?"

"No, and I never intend to be. I like my independence. I've had a few short-term partners but no life commitment."

"With your beauty and talent, I suppose that you have lots of suitors."

Amanda chuckled. "Yes, but they don't last very long."

Harry kissed her lightly on the lips and led her to the dance floor. Amanda was happy, and didn't care where this was going. It was going to be good…at least for one night.

The Beach Rebels launched into Busy Signal's hot Reggae tune, "Jail Juice." Harry and Amanda danced energetically and aggressively, as if they had been dancing together all of their lives. Every turn, wiggle, bump and grind, was executed to perfection. At the end of the piece, they collapsed into each other's arms. It was love, or at least lust, at first sight.

They left early. Amanda and Harry rushed back to Thompson's place and made love, made love again, and again. And then they collapsed, exhausted, on the bed. Harry thought, *I hope that this turns into a hot affair.*

CHAPTER THIRTEEN

Jonathan Brooke, Attorney at Law and Financial Adviser, danced around the fringes of the law. That is to say that he specialized in investments and offshore banking officially, and hiding and laundering money unofficially. He was a shark disguised as an English gentleman—soft spoken, tall, slender, and polite. He always wore a light tweed suit and vest in the office with a watch on a chain hanging from vest to a watch pocket—hardly the garb that you'd expect in torrid Cayman. He got a "first" in law from Trinity College Dublin, and cut his teeth with Lloyd's International Bank in Bermuda. His boss at Lloyds, Jeremy Stuart, was on the payroll of the Mexican Sinola drug cartel. Walsh found Brooke a willing student with few principles other then making money. He taught him the art of wiring funds though multiple banks in many countries so that the money was untraceable. Brooke struck out on his own and established his financial advisory company in Grand Cayman. When Miguel Gonzales, the formidable, feared and brutal head of the cartel, asked Stuart who he might hire to handle Caribbean money laundering, he recommended Brooke.

Grand Cayman was the hub of the cartel's Caribbean drug operations, including Jamaica and Barbados. There were the offices of hundreds of offshore banks, making cash laundering easy. There was air and sea transport, including commercial and private aircraft, fishing vessels, private yachts and sailboats that could move cash and drugs in and out of the country. There were easily bribable key custom banking and government officials. This made for smooth shipping and communication for its agents throughout the Caribbean islands. Brooke's legitimate financial advisory service, including the Baxter's two accounts, was the perfect front for Gonzales' purposes.

Brooke was not looking forward to a visit from the Baxter's lawyer. Braun had called him to arrange a courtesy visit to talk about Baxter's financial affairs. He would have to be very cagy and give the man nothing while appearing to give him something. Charlie was ushered through the door by Brooke's prim and proper middle-aged English secretary, and greeted Brooke:

"I'm Charlie Braun, and really appreciate your taking the time to see me."

" My pleasure. Please make yourself at home."

Braun noticed a model of a sailboat on Brooke's bookshelf and, to get the conversation going said:

"I see you like to sail. Looks like a wonderful boat."

"Yes," Brooke said, "it's a 46' Leopard catamaran, the fastest yacht on the island. Makes 12 knots in a brisk wind. Great for entertaining—three staterooms below, galley and table that seats ten above. It's my stress reliever. Nothing like a quick trip to Cuba, Jamaica or Maiquitta in northern Venezuela to relax. We'll have to go out for a spin sometime. I'd enjoy your company. We'll sail around the north end of the Island where I keep the boat."

"That would be great, I'd enjoy it. May I call you Jonathan?"

"Of course, and I assume that Charlie's alright for you?"

"Yes"

"Gil's murder was a horrible thing. The grapevine said that it was pretty brutal. His few friends were shocked. Any suspects, any obvious motive?

"Nothing yet."

"Will you let me know about funeral arrangements? Will he be buried in the States?"

"Yes to both questions. There will be a memorial service here soon. Getting the body home quickly is one of my duties."

"Well, what can I do for you?"

"I'd like as much information as you can give me about Baxter's accounts. Aside from balances and holdings, it would be good to get a twelve-month history of transactions. If there are any irregularities in the accounts, we'll follow up to see if they relate to the murder. The police have already subpoenaed their cell phone, landline, GPS and credit card records for the last three months. I have a power of attorney from the executrix of the estate to handle all of Baxter's affairs."

"Well, let me ask a question. Why isn't Brenda handling all of this? Too upset?"

"She's on an Antarctic cruise and won't be able to get here for at least a week. Maybe longer"

"Unfortunately," Brooke lied," I don't think that an American power of attorney is valid on the Island. Until I get a Caymanian court order validating the power of attorney, I can't give you any information. I'm sure that you understand client confidentially. I can verify that both Gil and Brenda have personal investment accounts here, but no more. "

"How about a contact in the Finance Ministry? I'd like to familiarize myself with Island financial rules and regulations."

"Of course. Go see Gerhard Birmingham. He's assistant to the Finance Minister and will have all of the information that you need. I'll call him to give him a heads up that you'll be contacting him"

"Many thanks for the connection and your time. You've been very helpful."

"Enjoyed meeting you."

After Braun left, Brooke called Birmingham who was on his payroll and said: "I'm sending over a Charlie Braun to ask questions about financial regulations here. Give him as much misinformation that you can get away with. Send him on a bureaucratic wild goose chase. And tell him, true or not, that he needs Cayman court approval for a US power of attorney to be valid here. I want to confuse him and make his investigation convoluted, time consuming and as difficult as possible. Maybe he'll get frustrated and go back to the States and stay out of Gil Baxter's financial affairs."

"I'm happy to cooperate."

On his way to the car Braun thought: I checked. A US power of attorney is valid here. Brooke's a bad liar.

CHAPTER FOURTEEN

Savannah Lord was drop-dead gorgeous and sexy to an extreme. Rumored to be a centerfold model for Penthouse, she certainly fit the stereotype—flaming redhead with sharp green eyes, legs as tall as the Empire State Building, tanned skin like bronze butter and one wicked tongue.

After a desultory education at a two-year girls college, and lounging around the house for a year, her Connecticut parents kicked her out, insisting that she support herself. She tried modeling, but, according to the trade, had looks, but didn't have "the look". She wasn't too red hot happy about leering agents and groping photographers anyway. Not qualified for much of anything, she aimlessly drifted between waitressing, hostessing and receptionist jobs but hated them—didn't make enough money and they were just plain boring. Beneath her. Slave labor in her view. But she took to aerobics and became good enough to lead a few classes. Much to the surprise of her parents and herself, she worked very hard to become a junior instructor. Gwynn, one of her aerobics instructors who had become a good friend, persuaded Savannah to take scuba diving lessons with her. Savannah, game for almost anything, agreed. She was enticed by the talk and pictures of beautiful tropical fish swimming through clear, warm waters, brightly colored corals, and "creepy crawly" things that called the ocean bottom home. Experienced divers showed her pictures of laughing, sun-drenched, beer-drinking people relaxng and laughing on the deck of a dive boat. She heard that the dating scene was torrid, and some really neat guys and gals went on trips all around the world to dive. She was hooked.

Savannah didn't know what she was getting into. It was waterborne boot camp. In the beginning, her training was more of an endurance test, a water stress test, than an introduction to a pleasurable pastime. Their instructor was a former Marine Corps Drill Sargent that taught accordingly. It was not a democracy. First, there were the dire warnings that you could kill yourself diving if you did something stupid. Then, learning to put on and take off a mask underwater and clear it when flooded. They swam exhausting laps in the pool, treaded water for ten minutes, and learned CPR. Those who weren't scared to death, continued through the course. They learned how to assemble and use their gear—air tanks, air regulator, weights and buoyancy compensators. Then the last test of all—the terrorizing "doff and don." They individually threw their unassembled scuba gear, with air from their tank turned off, into the deep end of the pool, and descended without a mask, effectively leaving them blind. The gear was reassembled by touch and air turned on before a safe ascent to the pool's surface. They were warned to make an ascent by rising slowly, breathing normally, and not holding their breath. The latter can cause a deadly embolism when air enters the lungs and blood stream. Cheers went up for everyone who succeeded. It was like a coming of age ceremony. The written exam was duck soup by comparison.

The class had to make four "test" dives before getting certified. The first two were in an abandoned granite quarry near Branford, Connecticut. The quarry dives were easy and meant to teach them how to use their skills in open water. But they were ghostly, dark as twilight, and smelled like cesspools. Visibility was poor, maybe twenty feet, slimy rocks, and stringy algae, made the dive very unpleasant, like swimming through a green haze. The bottom was strewn with old refrigerators, tons of beer bottles, and tires. There was even the carcass of a burned car. Savannah expected to find a body from a mafia hit any minute. At least there was something to look at besides the muddy, icky, and rock strewn bottom. She climbed out of her second quarry dive, wet suit covered with gunk. She was very comfortable in the water, but wondering exactly what she'd signed up for.

The second two dives were off the coast of Beavertail Park in Jamestown, Rhode Island, a popular and safe Northeastern dive site. There was a world of difference. She loved the feeling of weightlessness in the open water and the grace with which she could move through the water. She could go deeper and see amazing sights—fish, cold-water anemones, lobsters, crabs, and various types of snails. The fluid motion of sunlit sea grasses swaying like ballerinas in the gentle ocean swells mesmerized her. Both the ocean and quarries were cold as hell. Wet suits were a necessity, and you were always miserably damp and chilled when you took it off.

Savannah heard other divers talk about the warm water and beautiful underwater sites in the Caribbean. Gwynne persuaded her to take a trip to Grand Cayman for a few days of diving. She loved the diving there so much that she decided that she would suffer the pain of getting her Professional Association of Dive Instructor's Divemaster rating. This classification would allow her to lead groups and guide divers underwater. She looked forward to getting a job in the industry. She vowed she would never dive in cold water again and decided to ply her trade in Grand Cayman, which was considered one of the el-primo locations for diving and partying by the serious diving crowd. Easy to get to, British Protectorate, Safe, and beautiful diving. Why not, she thought. Cayman attracted a hoard of young people that loved the island atmosphere, good diving, water sports, and parties.

The non-stop party scene was not bad either. If there was not a party being thrown by someone from the diving community, there were plenty of hot bars and nightclubs to entertain. Divemasters usually decided to stay a couple of years, as did Savannah. Then, they became island bums, hopping from island to island looking for fun or work, or went back home and got serious about making a living. Savannah landed a job to crew on Jimmie Hester's popular dive boat that catered to Gen-Xers. She found a nice little house to share with two diving instructors in a small, quaint, residential section of West Bay. She took a second job as a part-time personal trainer and aerobics instructor at Gold's gym. She was tan, employed, and had her choice of young men. Her parents were out of her hair. So, life was good.

CHAPTER FIFTEEN

Pat Sweeny, a long time instructor at Gold's, came from a tough neighborhood in the South Bronx. Not a murderous, turned–to-rubble neighborhood like those featured in the media and movies about deprivation and crime, but close enough. He barely graduated from high school, and could have cared less about his education. He was frequently in trouble for sassing teachers, truancy, smoking pot, and poor grades. His blue-collar parents didn't give a damn. He ran with a gang of boys who occasionally got into fights, did drugs, (meth a favorite), and generally flaunted society. Pat and his friends weren't headed for a pleasant, productive life.

Pat was a tall, dark "Mediterranean handsome," well-muscled man. He always had a day's growth of photogenic stubble—the type that was currently popular on male models. He worked out almost daily at the local "Y," and had a set of abs that looked like a washboard. He could press 250 pounds. It was the only thing that Pat ever pursued with vigor and commitment.

Pat and his buddies, yearning for drugs and cash, robbed a closed-for-the-night drugstore, forgetting that narcotics and cash were locked in a safe. It didn't even occur to them that the store had a police-linked alarm system, and a closed circuit TV surveillance system. Caught, they were charged with breaking and entering and, as juveniles, were put on a year's probation and community service. Being minors, their felony would not be part of their public record. They were warned that they would be adults soon and would face prison if they got caught in a felony again.

Pat decided that he'd better fly right for a while. He managed to get a menial job cleaning equipment at the "Y." Over the course of four years, he worked his way up to a fitness instructor's job. He was technically very good, and the ladies loved his hard body and his exciting, slightly illicit, "wink-wink," tough-guy manner. A buddy had taken an instructor's job at Gold's gym in Grand Cayman in answer to an ad in *Muscle and Fitness Magazine.* After a few successful months on the job, he recommended Pat as a starting instructor. Pat managed to scrape together enough money to go to Grand Cayman, and was hired on the spot. Gold's arranged for his work permit

At the age of twenty-three, he was on his way.

Pat hustled Savannah as soon as she showed up at Gold's. She appeared in a sleek electric-blue Lycra body suit with shoulder straps and a low-low cut top that showed her cleavage to a distinct advantage. Their affair started out as a few after-work drinks with the gang from the gym. Then they went alone on a real date—supposedly to watch the spectacular Cayman sunset at the famous, carved- mahogany bar at the Holiday Inn--a loosey-goosey go-to place for the young, young at heart, and those trolling for a date--same or opposite sex.

On their first date, Savannah rebuffed his advances beyond a few kisses and a little fondling that left Pat hyper-aroused. Frustrated. He vowed to conquer this woman. Savannah liked playing games and spacing out the fun. So she teased him on the second date—kissing, fondling, but backing out of sex at the very last minute. She sent a very frustrated, "blue-balled" Pat home to contemplate his next move. Pat desperately wanted this woman—the only woman that he had not been able to quickly conquer. A challenge. On their next encounter, she didn't mess around.

To be more precise, she did more than mess around. After dark, with the colored lights from the Holiday Inn bar reflecting on their faces, and the band playing a gentle Caribbean calypso tune, they stripped naked in the dark shadows of a grove of thick, drooping casuarina trees. They waded waist deep into the provocative, dark shallows of the gentle surf. The light from the stars illuminated them so they could dimly see each other's bodies. When the heat of the ocean warmed their wanting groins, Pat kissed her hard, and ran his tongue around her nipples, which were tingling and standing at attention like palace guards waiting to march. Savannah was wet. Very wet, and not just from the mellow swells. Buoyed by the water, floating on her back, she locked her legs around Pat's waist, quickly inserting his ready penis into her. They rocked gently in rhythm with light waves, and then accelerated, pumping forcefully and rapidly and with abandon until the water frothed and splashed around them. They erupted at the same time. Savannah's piercing cries were drowned out by the surf, wind, and music. They were one for a moment, and, as it turned out, would be for some time.

Flushed and spent, Pat and Savannah crept out of the water, bare-naked, fully lit by the bar lights, and slightly embarrassed. They ran to the protection of the casuarina grove. "Ahhhh. That was out of sight," Savannah said. "I haven't been fucked hard and furious like that since my coming out party. Massive orgasm. Twice." A few patrons glanced knowingly and with amusement at the nude ghosts lurking in the shadows. They put on their clothes and, after they settled at a table by the ocean, Pat made a brash proposition.

"I live with a couple named Gil and Brenda Baxter. They're loaded. I'm their personal trainer. Why don't you move in with me at their condo? I'm sure that I can persuade them that they need a female trainer as well as me. After all, it's luxurious room and board, and ready cash on the side. All we have to do is one training session a day, maybe two with each, and run errands now and then. We can eat any meals that we want there. We would travel with them on their private jet on various domestic and foreign soirées." We'll quit our jobs at the gym, and you can quit your divemaster's job at Conner's operation. We can get paid, laid, and live the life of luxury. It won't be hard to take. What do you think?"

"I like you a whole lot, Pat. But this is pretty sudden. I'd like to wait a while and see how we get along."

"Fine. I'll approach them when you're ready. Please decide soon."

It only took Savannah a couple more dates to make up her mind to move in and for Pat to make arrangements with the very willing Baxters. *What the hell, Easy living, more money, less work, and a compatible companion. How bad is that? If it doesn't work out, I'll just leave.* She uncomfortably sensed that there was more to this gig, but couldn't put her finger on it.

CHAPTER SIXTEEN

"Christ," Gil said, wringing wet with sweat, as he crawled off the rowing machine. "Half an hour's enough. I'm exhausted."

Savannah said, "You haven't finished the Nautilus circuit, so get your ass in gear. Fifteen more minutes."

Gil sighed and reluctantly went back to work.

Savannah had been living with Pat and the Baxters for a week. They had one training session in the morning to sweat out the inevitable drug-booze hangovers and often one "for real" in the afternoon. The morning session ended with a sauna followed by a massage. Savannah massaged Gil, and Pat, Brenda. Gil almost always ogled Savannah when he got off the massage table with a sporting erection tenting the towel around his waist. He raised his eyebrows, tilted his head and gave her a lascivious smile. She knew exactly what he wanted, and she was quick to pack up the exercise table and get away from him. Moans, rapid breathing, and earsplitting cries came from the room where Pat and Brenda were. It didn't take a lot of thought to figure out what was going on—aerobic sex.

That night, Gil insisted that they take an evening cruise on his yacht and sail to a secluded cove on the east end of the island. They would have a light dinner prepared by the crew and go for an evening swim.

The yacht was the luxurious 100-foot, sleek, two masted four-sailed, ocean-going Julie Mother. It was bought from an Italian media tycoon for 20 million dollars. There was a large master bedroom, four guest cabins, and space for the three crew needed to sail and maintain the boat. The lounge had African mahogany walls, with sparkling bright brass portholes that beautifully contrasted with the wood. There was a couch and three chairs covered with creamy-soft tan leather and a glass and mahogany table in the middle. The usual instruments, for the pleasure of guests--barometer, speed indicator, chronograph, compass, and depth finder--were fastened to one wall. Another wall held an entertainment center with a large screen television set, HiFi, WiFi router, and loads of CDs and DVDs. The yacht could do 16 knots in a strong wind and once held the speed record for its class from Italy to Miami. All in all, a memorable and ridiculously expensive yacht.

The 22-year-old Swedish, blond, luscious, and bra-less cook, adorned with short shorts and revealing T-shirt, served dinner. Their dinner consisted of fresh lobster salad, with island mango and paw-paw drenched with raspberry coulis for dessert. There was copious champagne, of course. After dinner, they hung over a side rail of the boat marveling at the carnival of vibrant coral colors illuminated by underwater lights. The occasional spider crab moved slowly over the bottom, claws opening and closing in front as if engaging an enemy in battle. Tiny lobster eyes beamed red in the light, as they peered out of their reef crevices. Two mating octopuses sped across the reef, the male trying to capture the smaller female. The male was an angry red, his quarry changed her colors in a useless attempt to blend in with the background and hide. The foursome refilled their champagne and passed around a joint. Gil surreptitiously dropped a pinch of ecstasy in each champagne glass.

Twenty minutes later, Gil stood up and said, "Christ, I feel like I'm floating in the clouds, can do anything. Anyone want to climb the mast? Mine," he laughed. "I'm horny Brenda, come on to me, you luscious babe."

Not likely, Brenda thought, looking at Pat with let's-go-do-it eyes. Gil suddenly stood up and grabbed Savannah by the waist and tossed her in the water. She surfaced, laughing hilariously, and said, "Gil, get your goddamn ass in here, you sleazy bastard. You aren't going to get away with this."

Gil stripped off his skimpy bathing suit and followed his ecstasy-fueled erection into the water. He caught up with Savannah, and they splashed water at each other like courting teenagers. Gil playfully pushed her under, and when she surfaced, she, him. Submerged, Gil stripped off her bikini bottom and shot to the surface behind her, laughing. He put her in a cross-chest rescue carry and pulled her over to the diving platform at the stern of the boat. High as hell, she was a willing target. She no sooner had started to climb up on the platform when Gil grabbed her legs and entered her from behind.

Shit, Savannah thought. *Is this what this job is all about?*

She found out later that she was right. Sex was to be a mainstay and paid the room and board.

CHAPTER SEVENTEEN

Pat took the joint from Savannah's ample lips and took a hit. Instant mellow. It was Maui Wowee, the best and most potent mind-altering weed that could be had. They had personally imported it from Hawaii on last winter's debouch with the Baxters. Pat, spaced as hell, leaned back and said, "You know, a couple more years of muscle training and non-stop fucking the Baxters and maybe we'll have enough bucks to live anywhere we want, any way we want…and not have to jump and ask how high or how prone every time they belch. I love the four-ways, don't you?"

"Not really. It's like being tangled in sweaty seaweed. I'm fucking tired of the whole deal, particularly the bitch ordering me around like chattel. Treats me like shit. I bought into becoming their live-in trainer, not a sex object at their beck and call. Parading around in a string bikini with my tits hanging out all day long for Gil's pleasure isn't remotely sexy anymore--particularly when he's sporting his ball-hugging Speedos with his overlapping hairy gut and saggy erection. When he has a few snorts, he's ravenous, and I'm sore for days. And she came on to me last week. I'm just plain tired and want to get out of the whole damn mess. And yeah, the free drugs and money are great. So how do we get out of this thing with a lot of money?"

"I don't know."

"OK, asshole. You got us into this; you figure how to get us out. Rich."

CHAPTER EIGHTEEN

Visions of gold glittered in Pat's eyes. He figured that he and Savannah wouldn't be allowed back into the Baxter's apartment except to gather their things under police supervision. Pat wanted to rifle the place to see if anything valuable, portable, and salable, could be had. Worst case, if they got caught, they would claim that they just came back to get some clothes. After all, they were trusted with a key. And if someone found what they stole was missing, they'd claim that they weren't there. There should be no witnesses to their presence.

Pat and Savannah went out for a simple dinner at 8:00 PM, and made sure that they had a chat with the desk manager at the Holiday Inn before they went to their room. He would remember that they had been in for the night. Then they left their room at 3 AM, the darkest part of an already dark night. They were careful to exit by an isolated emergency door so they wouldn't be observed by anyone and identified as going out on the night of the robbery. They drove past the Diamond Condominium Towers, put their lights out, and parked at the back of the adjacent condominium's secluded parking lot. They quietly moved to the glass entrance door. Pat carefully peered into the lobby. The night doorman was known for slacking on the job. And sure enough, he was snoozing and snoring restively in a cushy armchair reserved for guests.

Pat and Savannah decided to avoid the noisy elevators, lest the noise and bells wake the doorman or they run into residents. They entered the dimly lit, gray-painted emergency stairwell, and began the climb up 20 steep flights of stairs to the Baxter's penthouse condo. In their condition, it was an easy hike. They arrived at the door that opened into the hall, in front of the Baxter's apartment. Pat opened it a crack to see if the police had left a guard. No one was there. Blue and white police tape used to mark off the crime scene was strung across the outside door. There was a large sign proclaiming that this was a crime scene, and anyone entering the property without permission would be prosecuted. They put on latex gloves and carefully removed the tape so it could be put back in the same way that they found it. Pat turned the key to the door. It clicked, and the door swung open. Once inside the entrance hall, they turned on their shielded flashlights, which illuminated bouquets of dead flowers—a far cry from the usual lavish display of fresh blossoms. They moved into the living room.

"Holy Christ," Savannah said, "The place is a fucking mess, furniture dragged helter-skelter, books and papers all over the floor. Fingerprint dust on every frigging surface. It smells like a gym locker room."

Pat pointed to the dark purple-brown, crusted stain on the white rug. "This must have been where it happened. Creepy. Gives me the shivers. Feel like the bastard is staring at us. I want to scour the place for anything valuable that the police might have missed. Might as well get last dregs of money out of the place before Brenda comes back, and we sure as hell don't know when that will be."

"So where do we start?" Savannah interjected.

"Let's do the obvious first. You go through Brenda's desk. Call me if you find anything that looks important. Then go through the closets. Be on the lookout for boxes, envelopes, clothes, anything that might have something hidden in them. Look under chairs and behind pictures. Tear the backing off pictures to see if there is anything of interest. Put any booty on the bed in the master bedroom. Then we'll do the rest of the house. I'm going to start with Baxter's office.

"You OK?"

"Pat, I'm scared. If we get caught, we're going to end up in jail."

"Don't worry about it. We're not going to get caught—now get on with it."

Savannah started with the small compartments in Brenda's elegant antique cherry drop-front desk. *It's odd that a beach condo would contain such formal furniture, but there's no accounting for taste or what the Baxters would do.* The desk contained nothing but routine business correspondence and letters from friends, check books, bills, and detritus that most peopled collect and never throw out. The checkbook showed a balance of $45,567. *Maybe we can find a way to get our hands on this. Pat has forged a signature or two in his life.*

In the bottom drawer, there was a sturdy unlocked metal box. Pat said, "I'm amazed that the cops didn't take all of this evidence with them right away. Sloppy work." Pat fumbled the box, while attempting to put it on the desk. It crashed against the desk and careened to the floor with a loud "thunk." A yipping dog started a high-pitched, harsh chorus of barks from the apartment beneath them. Feet padded out from one end of the apartment and stopped directly below them. They froze. Didn't breathe. Their eyes were wide open in fright. Then the elevator stopped at the entrance to the Baxter's condo. There was hard pounding on the door. Someone yelled "Gil, Brenda, are you in there?" The doorknob rattled back and forth. There was a moment of silence. Maybe the person was listening for more sounds from inside. They were as still as a marble statue. A minute that seemed like an hour passed. Footfalls moved back to the elevator. Its doors shut and it whirred down to the next floor. They held their breath for a moment and then exhaled, relieved but tense and on alert. They opened the lock box.

They found letters, photographs, a camcorder, and uninteresting memorabilia. The still pictures were time-stamped four years ago. They then cranked up the video in the camera. It obviously taken by Brenda, lying prone on the bed and pointing the camera down her body toward the foot of the bed. The series showed a humongous, erect, purple penis entering the fame. Then a muscled man filled the whole frame, and there was a sequence of him mounting her. There was a small camcorder with a video of two men doing a repertoire of sexual acts with Brenda. Savannah wondered if Brenda got off on the pictures or if they were kept as "insurance" to blackmail her consorts if they ever leaked word about their indiscretions. "Well, she sure gets around to get off," Savannah said. "I wonder if Gil has a collection like this? I see enough of his appendages in the raw. Wouldn't be surprised if he has a few secret cameras installed abound here. Pervert."

There were letters and some financial papers in the box. A few dealt with Brenda's investments held by Jonathan Brooke and a list of jewelry and other valuables held in a safe deposit box at the Butterfield Bank. "My god," Savannah said, a queen's ransom is in there." The two safe deposit keys were taped to the inside of the box, which Pat immediately pocketed. There were sets of directions to two private planes sometimes parked on the periphery of Owen Roberts Field. The tail numbers were included so that the aircraft could be identified. Savannah rifled the closets and bathroom, coming up with little except pornographic costumes for their "dress up" nights, and a box full of adult toys.

Baxter's desk was from the Cayman Colonial Era and was made of oak with grooved joints and dowels holding the panels together—one of those stern and monumental pieces of oak furniture that a rich merchant or wealthy Englishman might have had. It had one center drawer and two large drawers on each side. All were locked. The locks were simple and easily picked by Pat. He pulled out drawer after drawer after drawer. He was careful not to spill their contents, and looked under and on the sides of each one to see if anything was taped to them. Nothing. One drawer was full of the detritus one expects in a desk—a random assortment of paperclips, tape, pencils, pens, binder clips, labels, airline frequent flyer cards, dust balls, and paper shards. Another was filled with files dealing with buildings and factories that Baxter owned.

There were financial records for the money being managed by Brooke. Pat gasped: a billion dollars. Gil bragged about his fortune being worth north of three billion, so he had stashed a lot elsewhere. "We're going to get a piece of it, come hell or high water."

Discouraged, he began to put back the drawers when he noticed that the left drawer was a barely noticeable two inches shorter than the right. He looked into the drawer well. Nothing of worth was there. He tapped the walls. The back wall gave a hollow "thump." He tried again: "thump, thump, thump." A hollow compartment? He pressed on the panel. It didn't open. He pressed hard on every corner and the center of each panel. Naught. He went behind the drawer-well and pounded that panel. No result. Then he spotted one dowel-edge on the desk frame that was raised slightly above the wood. He pressed it. A secret panel sprung open. His heart skipped two beats, and he hurried to dig into the contents.

Inside was a royal-blue velvet drawstring bag cinched with gold ties. He dumped it out on the desk blotter. Out spilled countless, large, sparkling, cut diamonds and a hefty number of uncuts. His heart stopped for a few seconds. He took two deep breaths and called Savannah.

"Savannah, Jesus fucking Christ, come look at this. Pay-dirt."

Savannah arrived and squealed, "Oh my God, oh my God. Must be millions of dollars. We're rich!"

"By now, the police will undoubtedly have found a list of the jewels hidden or in a lock box somewhere." We have to get them out of the country fast, and I have to find a fence." As they left, Pat said, "I have a plan."

CHAPTER NINETEEN

Harry and Amanda were in bed at Harry's place. "Out of bed...*Now*," Harry yelled in Amanda's ear. A very sleepy Amanda said: "what the hell are you doing Harry? It's only 5:15."

"Just trust me. Get into your shorts and be ready to get out of here in ten minutes"

"Why?"

"A surprise. Come get in the car."

She yawned, stretched her arms and said with sleepy eyes: "This better be good Harry"

Harry drove in the pitch black night to the North Sound docks, a mile east of Seven Mile Beach. There was the slightest pre-dawn pink on the Eastern horizon.

The wind was light, warm, westerly and, like most Cayman days, it promised to be stunning. There was a classic 28-foot Erickson sloop waiting at the dock. It had the svelte, sleek classic lines of a racing and cruising boat. But it had seen better days. The mahogany trim and deck paint were faded; there were scrapes on the hull and rub rail. A proud mature lady of the sea. But it looked seaworthy. Well-used patched sails were draped on the boom and foredeck. There were two tipsy-from-the-night-before, unshaven crewmembers in singlets ready to help them on board. Not exactly stewards from the Queen Mary.

Amanda, sporting a broad and winning smile squealed with delight, and said: "Harry, what have you done? How delightful."

"Surprise. Just thought we'd have a little sail and a little fun to start off the day.

They unpacked a wicker basket arranged by a bakery, and picked up for the trip by the crew. They enjoyed the fruit, croissant, and cheese breakfast as they tacked out a half-mile into the ocean to enjoy the sunrise.

The huge flaming orange ball of fire slowly rose from the horizon looking as if it could be touched, hooked, and hauled into the boat. Amanda perched on the bow on the windward side, next to the jib, to take in the show. Harry crawled up beside her, put his arm around her shoulders, kissed her deeply and said:

"Amanda, I love you more than all the stars in the universe. Move in with me. It would make both of us so happy."

"Harry, I love you too. But I don't want to make any long-term commitment. I've been independent all of my life and I don't want to be dependent now. I'm used to going where I please, when I please. I travel with my girlfriends a number of weeks a year, and take trips to Miami and New York frequently and on the spur of the moment as work permits. As matter of fact, we're planning a trip to Paris over Christmas. If I move in, I have to have that same freedom. You should know that I've left several other men when things got boring and I was taken for granted. No warning, no chance to reform, just picked up and left."

"You can have your freedom. I just want to be with you."

"You're sure you want to do this Harry? It's taking a chance that it won't work.

"There will be a lot of hurt if we split."

"Yes. I'll take my chances."

"OK. I love you so much and you need to know how much. Lets go back to the condo, and I'll show you in spades."

CHAPTER TWENTY

Zane is black and shiny as a tar pit in August, and is probably a direct descendent of slaves brought to the island from Jamaica in the seventeenth century. He's tall and thin with angular features and the sinuous muscles and graceful body of a long distance runner. Zane's been around Grand Cayman's tourist and diving scene forever, usually in his standard outfit—a red bandanna around his forehead, white singlet, black Speedos, flip flops and a cigarette dangling saucily from his thickish lips. He always hefts a backpack holding his camera and strobe. He has a Neptune tattoo on one shoulder, a big-toothed scary shark on the other, and a pirate's head and cross-bones on his back—all dimly visible on his dark skin. He uses the tats and bandanna as bait to attract tourists who want to see an exotic, maybe slightly mysterious fake pirate of yore. All he needs to complete the scene is a cutlass and baggy pants. He certainly looks the part.

Zane takes underwater pictures of divers and tourists as a souvenir of their vacations and alleged diving prowess. Tourists and diving prowess are dubious words used in the same sentence down here. He also hits the cruise boat scene taking candid pictures of the unforgettable beauties, the handsome privileged men, the very white and pudgy captains of the universe, and the ordinary tourists out for a good time. He has a world-class personal gallery of fat-fat spandex-clad tourists, photographed from below at Sting Ray City. Their chubby, churning, fat-rippling, cellulited legs dangling in the water, suspended from fluorescent-clad oversize butts are a hoot—like a grotesque floral garden pumped up like a blimp. In reality, he's a fine photographer of people, underwater landscapes and reef life.

The little known dark side of Zane is his felony conviction and ties with the Cayman underworld. Zane spent a year in jail for brutally beating two nasty guys who jumped him for some minor insult in The White Turtle Bar, a well-known, best-avoided downscale joint in backcountry Bowden Town. As light as he his, he packs a wicked punch and plays dirty. Both of the vile characters went to hospital for long stays. One, connected to the island monarchy, managed to see that he got the maximum sentence for assault. Zane, a dedicated extrovert and man-of-the-world, made a lot of friends and acquaintances "inside", and kept in touch when he got out. No one knows where his mean streak came from, or whether he has been doing anything outside the law since his release a decade ago. It's better not to ask. He is, however, one of the island's great characters, knows everyone and is a superlative information source. Zane can be trusted...to a point.

Charlie approached Zane at Seven Mile Beach's public beach. The wide long strip had foot-blistering hot white sand, and eye-squinting glare. It was lined with picnic tables and palm trees, and was a hangout for locals and tourists. Zane was getting off a dive boat with his underwater Nikon rig—a D700 camera with 10-24mm lens in an Aquatica housing sporting two Ikelite strobes—his usual "hunting" gear. A really fine $10,000 rig that would make any underwater photographer drool. He flashed his dazzling smile and white-white teeth, threw his arm around me, and said:

"Where've you been Charlie? Haven't seen you in a long time. You don't like to see your friend anymore?"

"Zane, you look fantastic. I'll bet the tourist ladies are falling all over you".

"Well," Zane chortled, "Still get my share".

"And how's business?"

"Mon, since the cruise boats came to town, I barely get a vacation. These people are hungry for pictures.

I go to Sting Ray City with 'em, take their pictures under water with stingrays swimming around their heads. They love it. Put the pictures on a board by the tender dock for when they come back. Make a fortune."

"Z, I have a problem. I'm looking for a muscular man, 6 feet tall, give or take, who killed Gil Baxter up at Diamond House yesterday. There isn't a clue who the murderer is and don't even know where to look. He was killed, we think with a dive knife around 10:00 on Thursday morning. There was no theft. That's all we know. Hear anything about it on the grapevine ?"

"No mon, nothing."

"Would you keep your ears open for me as you go about your rounds and let me know if there is a hint of trouble or a new guy in town that's suspicious?"

"Sure. You know me though. I don't work without pay. Say $500 for my first pass through the hood and we'll see what I dig up after a couple of days."

"Done. You can reach me a the Ritz."

"Well" Zane laughed, "I certainly didn't do it. Every morning at 10AM I'm up to my ears photographing tourists, so I have alibis, and anyway I wouldn't do anything to upset my market. I'll ask some of my old Island contacts when I make my night rounds in the next couple of days. Word usually gets around fast, at least the rumors do.

"Thanks "Z", you can find me at the Ritz."

"OK, I got to go schmooze the immigration people."

I turned away to go back to the bar at the Ritz. So far, I knew nothing. I've got to get to Thompson and compare notes. We'll find a way to get into Brooke's office and get Baxter's records. I'm sure that Thompson can get in under some Police ruse.

CHAPTER TWENTY-ONE

Amanda, with too many mojitos down her gullet, slipped in the front door as quietly as a "little bit drunk" person could, which was not quiet at all. Harry, stone cold sober, was waiting for her, lightly dozing after attempting to read a ponderous book on forensic procedures. Harry woke up with a start. "God damnit" he said, throwing down the book at a coffee table, crashing an expensive vase, flowers and all, to the floor. "Where the hell have you been? I've been waiting for four hours and you were only going to be out with your girlfriends for an hour or two? You had your cell off. I damn near came looking for you."

"Harry, I'm not chattel. I have a lot of friends and family on this island, and I'm not going to give them up. I'll go out when and where I want to. You're invited if you ever want to go—*if*...you want to put up with girl talk and family babble. If not, shut up about it. "

"You don't tell me to shut up. I'm not a goddamn third grader."

"Sometimes you act like one."

"Bullshit, bullshit, bullshit"

Harry grabbed Amanda, hard, by her upper arms, shook her and said:

"Amanda, I love you and I want to be with you. Fuck the girls and family,"

"Harry, you're hurting me. Take your hands off. "

She shook off Harry's hands and slapped him. She spun around, walked into the bedroom, slammed the door, shattering one of its panels, and started packing her belongings. A few minutes later she stormed out of the front door, head up, eyes blazing, without a word, and carrying two suitcases full of her clothes. Harry slumped in his chair, one hand on his forehead and reached for a bottle of whisky. He pondered how he was going to make this right again.

CHAPTER TWENTY-TWO

Pat said to Savannah: "The police will have undoubtedly taken a complete inventory of the Baxter's condo by now and found the hidden jewels missing. "We need to take a room at the Holiday Inn tonight and figure out our next steps—how to get out of Cayman to a safe place were we can disappear and slowly sell off the jewels."

"Where to now genius?" She sarcastically said.

Pat thought for a minute and said, "Let's go to Little Cayman. It's a tiny obscure island 150 miles east of Grand Cayman. Laid back. No one on the island other than a handful of divers and the local population of 170. I doubt that anyone is going to look for us there for a while. Unfortunately customs is likely inspecting people and luggage, domestic going on domestic, international, and private flights to make sure that the Jewels don't leave the island by air."

"So how are we going to get the jewels in and out of the islands? We have to take them using some 'customs proof' method."

"I have idea. We secure and disguise the spoils by putting them in the bottom of a scuba tank in putty that matches the interior color and texture. No one will know that they're there. Even, in the unlikely event that some one unscrews the valve into the tank, they'll only see an empty vessel."

Pat and Savannah mixed the jewels into the putty until they were invisible and then carefully pressed the mixture into the inside bottom of an empty aluminum scuba tank. They then hustled to the airport.

The two boarded the broad, overhead-winged, guppy-bodied Cayman Airways puddle-jumper that was overloaded with happy, tight and sunburned divers, for the inevitably bumpy flight to Little Cayman. The airline was sometimes called "barf-air."

Once on the Island, Pat and Savannah checked into Sam McCoy's simple lodge. The establishment had been a haven for divers since 1960, and had a small dive operation on the Bloody Bay side of the island.

After they settled in, Pat said, "Lets go for a dive."

"Pat, it's getting dark."

"All the better. Bloody Bay has, for all practical purposes, a virgin reef. Philippe Cousteau considers it one of the greatest dives in the world. At night, you'll see the blooming corals in all of their colored glory."

"That scares me. I've never been underwater at night. What about sharks?"

"Don't worry about it. They're out feeding in deep water. Never seen one at night, and coral doesn't bite. Ha Ha. It's just like a day dive except all of our light comes from our LED dive lights. They're awesome bright and it'll seem like daylight down there. Pat and Savannah left the tanks in their room, picked up their gear, and headed for the dive boat at Bloody Bay.

Immediately after hitting the bottom, Savannah shined her dive light on a school of barracuda slowly swimming in formation with military precision. The fishes' long jaws opened and closed, forcing water over their gills and baring their ominous needle-sharp teeth. Curious animals, but basically harmless. A very large one swam up to her facemask, and peered into her eyes, which were lit by the edge of Pat's dive light beam. Startled and seeing a mouth full of tearing teeth in her face, she started breathing in gulps, using up her air rapidly. Her pulse shot up, she began to sweat, fogging her mask and causing more anxiety.

To make matters worse, she had to flood her mask with seawater to clear her fogged faceplate and then blow air into it through her nose to clear the mask of water.

Her eyes stung from the seawater. She finned herself backward as fast as she could, never taking her eyes off the fish. The silvery animal followed her and wouldn't let her out of its sight. Pat involuntarily laughed, and silvery pods of air bubbles swirled around his head and rose into the black water above. The Barracuda eventually joined its flock, but Savannah was close to being out of air, adding to her unease. She didn't like night diving anyway. Despite Pat's assurances she knew that there were beastly creatures lurking in the dark. Half the time she was looking over her shoulder. Pat and Savannah surfaced and, uncomfortably wet and cold, toweled off and told the boat driver to return to the lodge's dock. "Christ", Savannah said: "Never, never again at night. How did I let you talk me into is shit-eating dive?"

"With difficulty. But weren't you amazed by the variety and colors of coral that bloom at night? One of the world's most beautiful sights."

"No. I didn't even look at them. I was too occupied with my 'friend'." Lets get out of here, change, fuck, and get drunk."

They returned to the Lodge, relaxed-tired and looking forward to a little sex and then a nap. On the way to their room, they casually picked up yesterday's newspaper, *The Cayman Compass*. "Rich American Murdered" screamed the red, bold headlines. The lead story told of the brutal murder of Gil Baxter that took place two days ago. It noted that there were no suspects but that two

Baxter "houseguests," Pat Sweeny and Savannah Lord, were wanted for questioning.

"Christ," Pat said, his throat tightening and hands growing cold. They're going to haul us in. We're not only going to jail for grand larceny but they'll nail us for the murder. Remember, we were still on the island with plenty of time to do the murder and get our plane to Little Cayman. We've got to get out of here. Out of the country. With the loot. Fast."

"How the hell do we get out without getting caught at airport security?"

"Just move fast and hope we're ahead of the posse."

Savannah's forehead wrinkled. A defeated look flooded her face. She, said:

"Where do we go?"

"Cuba. I have a couple of street-smart friends who will put us up until we get settled. Our major problem will be getting through Cayman passport control. We have to hope that our passports aren't tagged and we're not pulled aside for questioning."

CHAPTER TWENTY-THREE

Sergeant Wilson was designated to watch the airport for the couple coming in or out of the country. He had distributed pictures of the pair to taxi drivers, rental car agencies, and security and immigration authorities at the airport. Sure enough, a customs official identified Pat and Savannah and told them that they would have to undergo a thorough search and questioning before they could enter the country. Pat and the official locked eyes.

"What are you, the Gestapo? We're legal residents of the Island. We work here. We're just coming home from a vacation. What's the big deal? I'll have you know that we have connections in Gil Baxter's organization."

"Your friends don't count here. Now come with me."

He firmly put his hands on their elbows guiding them into a cramped windowless interview room. Pat angrily shook off the official's hand and stormed into the room on his own. Savannah followed. The immigration official used a walkie-talkie to signal Sergeant Wilson that he had their quarry. Wilson, with two other officers, took the pair to the baggage claim and grabbed their luggage. Their baggage and diving gear were searched. The tanks were not. Nothing was found. Wilson's crew wasted no time hustling Savannah and Pat to his police SUV to take them into town for questioning.

Looking cold, serious, impatient and imperious, Thompson ushered the duo into his office and started his rapid fire questioning.

"You are Pat and Savannah Lord?"

"Yes" Savannah answered

" Where are you from?"

"Pat chimed in: I'm from Chicago, she's from Connecticut."

"And what are you doing here?"

"We're personal trainers"

"And where do you train?"

"We used to train for the Baxter's"

"I guess that job is knifed to hell," Thompson said making a sick pun. "I understand that you also provided a lot of 'personal services'—like sex."

"No, we were just close friends and partied together."

"Right," Thompson said sarcastically. "Did Baxter take drugs?"

"Yes."

"What kind?"

"You name it. He swallowed, smoked or shot it. He was high on drugs and booze most of the time--pot, coke, heroin, LSD and all kinds of pills—ecstasy, amphetamines, and oxycodone. He chased his pills with shots of single malt scotch.

"Where did he get them?"

" A scruffy guy appeared at the door from time to time with a package for him. After he came we usually had a new pill or drug combination to try. I don't know the guy's name or where he got the drugs. Just a low level runner."

Standing up leaning over the couple, red in the face and putting his nose close to Pat's, Thompson shouted:

"Why did you kill Gil Baxter?"

Savannah and Pat, surprised, instantly shrunk back and answered in unison,

"No, we didn't do it."

Sweating and his face blood-crimson, Thompson pounded the table again with his fist and repeated,

"Did you kill Baxter?"

Pat snapped: "Fuck no. Are you hard of hearing asshole?" Flecks of spittle flew from his mouth, some hitting

Thompson in the face. Thompson pulled back surprised, thoroughly pissed, and wiped the discharge off with a shirtsleeve.

Thompson struggled for a minute to get control of himself and said in a clipped tone of voice:

"Did Baxter have any enemies? Anyone who might have had a motive for killing him? Money disputes; had a fight; jealousy; envy; vengeance?"

"Hey man, he was an asswipe druggie. He played with other people's money. And probably screwed a few. He's bound to have enemies, but I don't specifically know of any."

"Where were you during the day last Thursday?"

"We took the ferry boat out to East End and stayed for the day—eating, drinking, and tending our tans"

"Anybody see you?"

" I suppose boat personnel and waitresses"

"We'll show your pictures around and see if you're telling the truth." Thompson stood up towering over them with a "don't mess with me" look on his face and said: "Don't leave the island."

Pat and Savannah walked out and took a taxi back to the Holiday Inn. Pat stared out of a window thinking, seeing nothing. After a minute, he slowly turned to Savannah with a deadly serious face and said,

"We're going to Cuba. There's a noon flight to Havana on Cubana and we're going to be on it"

"Shit Pat, why Cuba, and not Miami? We don't even speak Spanish for god's sake."

"Simple. There's no extradition to the US or Grand Cayman. It'll be easy to hide. All we have to do is have money and keep our noses clean."

"Won't they know where we are when Cuban immigration scans our passports?"

"No way. The Cubans don't scan or stamp American passports. It's illegal for Americans to go to Cuba but they welcome the tourist dollars. We get a visa on a separate slip of paper. Then we disappear on the Island."

"Bullshit we disappear on the Island. Sooner or later the Cuban Policia will come looking for us when our visas expire. They will throw us out or put us in jail."

"That won't happen. We'll immediately get digs where they can't find us. Besides, if they do find us, we'll bribe our way out of trouble with a few hundred bucks."

"Where are we going to get the bucks to live on? We only have five thousand between us."

"The money will do for a few weeks. My friend, Francisco, will put us up in his house, which is well into the country, and out of the usual orbit for the Policia. He's already got a list of nondescript, out-of-the-way small houses and apartments lined up for us in middle class neighborhoods. He's throwing in a dozen or so chickens so we'll look like another Cuban who has to scramble to put a good meal on the table."

"Who's going take care are of the god damn things?"

"Both of us."

"You baby. You picked this city over Miami, so I'm going to see that you pay the price. What the hell am I going to wear?"

"Francisco will have a bunch of typical Cuban clothing for us. I gave him our sizes. He'll get dark sunglasses, jeans, tops, shoes and sandals, and broad-brimmed hats so that our faces will be hard to see. We'll blend pretty well into the native population."

"I want to buy some dazzling designer dresses, shoes and casual outfits and a portfolio of Bikinis."

"Hold your horses. We have to keep a low profile. By the way, your majesty, he did buy you a passel of the skimpiest see-through bikinis on the island."

"Let me get this straight. I'm going to look like an dull housewife and chicken farmer?"

"Well there are some benefits. First and foremost, the Feds and Cuban Policia won't find us. Then there are the ocean, beaches and sun. Music is everywhere and the clubs are not posh but lots of fun. The people are friendly and helpful. And the Cuban food is great, particularly from one of those hole-in-the wall restaurants in people's homes."

"Yeah. My dream for the rest of my life."

"By the way, Cuba's a really inexpensive place to live when you have American dollars. Before we get short,

I'll find a fence and sell a small diamond or two. More jewels as needed. There's a market for luxury goods among the Government elite and, some rich and powerful Government-protected people. We'll sell them for sure." And I'll bet we can find a compatible couple with a lot of money, drugs and kinky sex habits to live with. You know, Cayman all over again. Sooner or later it'll be safe to find our own more upscale and expansive place to enjoy our booty"

"Skip the live-in sex scenario. I felt like an in-the-flesh on-demand sex movie for the Baxters. We have enough money to live well and have a goodly supply of drugs without prostituting ourselves again."

Before buying tickets to Havana at the airport, Savannah asked: "What about the jewels?"

"We keep 'em in the bottom of the scuba tank. I don't think anyone's going to take a wrench and crank the valve out of a tank and look in. If they do, they'll just see what looks like the bottom of an ordinary scuba tank—hardly an odd commodity on these islands. The jewels are well-mixed in the putty and are invisible"

Savannah said: "I'm very nervous about checking the scuba tank as luggage on an airplane again. What if they lose it?"

"If they lose it, we're screwed."

"Is there a place where we can hide them to take them on the plane?"

Pat thought for a minute; his face brightened and he said,

"Let's take half the jewels, split them between us and swallow them in a condom. Drug smugglers do it all the time"

Savannah screwed up her nose as if downwind from a pig farm and said,

"Christ, I don't believe it. That's fucking disgusting. What if I get diarrhea?"

"Then for sure no one is going to search you."

"You got condoms?"

"Of course," Pat said, and snapped to attention and cocked his right arm with his middle three fingers raised in the Boy Scout salute. "Boy Scouts motto—be prepared."

The men's room in the airport check-in area was empty and Pat disappeared into a stall with the tank. He spun open the valve with a crescent wrench that he carried in his luggage. He fished out the thick putty with a straightened wire coat hanger from his suitcase. He removed the jewels and split them between two heavyweight condoms. Almost choking, he swallowed one with lots of water. *I hope I won't have to take a shit for the next ten hours.*

Pat gave Savannah her condom. She returned to the lounge from the women's room looking sickly and ever so pale.

"OK. Lets go to Havana" Pat said.

Pat bought their tickets and checked their dive gear, tanks and suitcases. In a few minutes they were airborne on the flight to Havana—into unpredictable and unknown terrain.

CHAPTER TWENTY-FOUR

It was dusk and cooling down from 90 blistering degrees to 83 with a brisk westerly breeze. Thompson thought *well no sense in hurrying home. Amanda will be out with the girls tonight. It'll be lonely without her but she won't be out too late.* As he left his condo on his way to meet Charlie at Sunset House he tried, with difficulty, to put the incident out of his mind and vowed to make it right and win Amanda back. Thompson was momentarily distracted by another spectacular sunset mirrored on the still water of a tidal pool—purple-gray clouds shaped like a mountain range hung low on the horizon and fringed in brilliant orange.

He mused: *Truly a scene I never get tired of after years of living on this island. Every sunset is different, every one beautiful in its own way, and what a pull for tourists. A peaceful time and not one to discuss a gory murder with Charlie. But crime pays the bills, so I'll get on with it. A couple of whiskies will lubricate our meeting. I really enjoy the guy. I think we're going to get along just fine. Maybe he'll become a drinking buddy. Nice close to a hectic day.*

Charlie sauntered in twenty minutes late. He was already keeping "Cayman Time," a luxury taken by all but the most fervent business people. Thompson had a gin and tonic waiting for Charlie. During the second round, they got down to business.

Charlie said, "Well, Inspector, what's up?".

"Not much unfortunately. Not to make a bad pun of it, but we're basically clueless. Sweeny and Lord, our only suspects have flown the coop or buried themselves on the island. There is one long shot. Gregory Smith, a relative of one of Cayman's first families, spent a total of ten years in jail for robbery-assault and a number of lesser crimes. He's perpetually in trouble, and his escapades have escalated of late from minor to heavy stuff. Gregory had the mistaken notion that he could rob a wealthy resident way out on the East End and close to where one end of the North Wall reef connects with the island. The wall is dangerous at the best of times, and there was a gale-force wind that night with no moon. So we don't think the perp came in by boat.

The victim, Lorna Applebee, was the wife of one of the rich financial types who fly in on their private jets for the weekend or a week in the sun. The Applebee's live in a huge two-story Mediterranean-style mansion, maybe 15,000 square feet, with an elaborate alarm system and a spectacular ocean view. Smith probably cased the house for a week or so, and decided that it would have lots of valuables, and was vacant. He apparently thought that the seaward patio provided easy entrance and cover from the road and other houses. I have no idea if he even thought of the possibility that the house had an alarm system."

Thompson continued. "Smith broke in at midnight carrying a knife as his weapon. He triggered the alarm and panicked. Mrs. Applebee, who had come onto the island that afternoon, foolishly rushed screaming out of her bedroom with next to nothing on. She went nose-to-nose with him and told him to get the fuck out. He slugged her, knocked her out, and made his escape through the patio where he entered. He didn't cut her, just left her with nasty bruises. As we pieced it together, he worked his way around the back of several houses built on the "iron shore," the part of the island that is ancient hard coral and limestone red rock. He escaped across the main road to Georgetown and into the undeveloped scrubland on the other side. We don't have any patrol cars in East End because the area is lightly populated, and we've never had a serious crime out there. Just petty theft and shoplifting at a local dive shop. It took us half an hour to get there, and Smith was long gone before we could respond."

"How did you catch him?"

"Not being very bright, Smith left a number of incontrovertible clues. He didn't wear a facemask. Mrs. Applebee got a good look at him and provided our sketch artist with a face that was obviously Smith's. We also had fingerprints left at the scene of the crime that matched his on file. We didn't find the knife, which we figure is at the bottom of the ocean. Smith's been in trouble a lot. We picked him up the next day. He was released from prison a week or so before the murder. We'll bring him in for questioning. Maybe he went to Baxter's apartment to burgle some drugs or money, surprised Baxter, and killed him."

"Smith's been hanging around with some of the ex-cons that were with him in Her Majesty's free bed and breakfast. They're a rough bunch. We'll find an excuse to question them as well. Keeps them on their toes or at least out of someone's pockets for a few days. We were particularly interested in a guy named Vargus who we think has been very active on the robbery circuit lately, but he had a concrete alibi.

"I'll let you know if our sleuthing turns up anything else. You go ahead and do your financial stuff so you can get out of here and go home. Let me know as soon as you find something, as will I. Be sure to brief me before you leave the island."

"Will do," said Charlie.

Charlie and Thompson switched to Stella Artois beer and watched the divers come in from their dusk dive, wash their gear in the fresh water tanks, stow it, and head for the bar. Charlie wondered if any of this group could be the murderer given the strong possibility that a dive knife was the weapon. Not likely. Who ever did it is well hidden or off the Island.

Charlie stayed for another beer after Thompson left to put things right with Amanda.

Now I have to get my ass in gear and find a way get information about where the money came from and where it went. I suspect that a lot of it came from dubious sources or illegal activities. It would be just like Baxter. I have to get into his offices alone and riffle his files. There's always a way to break in an office. Illegal, yes, but the only way to get what I want.

CHAPTER TWENTY-FIVE

A tall, electrified fence topped with razor wire surrounded the villa, on the outskirts of the city of Los Gatos in Sinola State. It was guarded by dozens of gunmen, mostly men lured from the Mexican Special Forces. Night vision video cameras swept the grounds. There were motion detectors, ground movement sensors, and Rottweiler attack dogs patrolling the enclosure. Surface-to-air missiles were mounted on the roof, should there be an attack from the air. Not that anyone would be foolish enough to approach the grounds without a reason and an escort. Locals gave the compound a wide berth, particularly at night when the inhabitants were especially jumpy. The local Policia and Federales had been bribed to stay away from the fortress and pay them no heed.

Casa Gonzales was the home and operations center for Miguel Gonzales, the head of the Sinola Cartel, the biggest and most feared in Mexico. Gonzales had ordered the murder of over 10,000 people, mostly rival gang members, uncooperative police, politicians, and unfortunate citizens who got on his turf and in the way of his armed animals. He laundered 25 billion dollars a year, a sum more and more difficult to place as the US DEA and Calderon, Mexico's president, cracked down on banks, drug trafficking, and money laundering. The Sinola cartel sold the bulk of their drugs in Mexico, the United States, and Canada, and had recently branched out to the Caribbean, Europe, South America, and Africa—particularly Nigeria.

Their "business model" was like that of other cartels and drug lords. They bought cocaine in Columbia and transported it through their agents to bulk wholesalers in each country that they served. The wholesalers, in turn, sold to smaller wholesalers who sold to street retailers. All transactions were in cash. The money was passed back to a Gonzales field operative who would wire the money to one of their offshore numbered accounts in Bermuda, Lichtenstein, Grand Cayman, or Switzerland. The money was then transferred to another group of foreign banks under different account numbers, making the transactions almost impossible to trace. The funds were eventually withdrawn and used to purchase tangible goods, such as airplanes, commercial property, gold and gems, land, huge import-export operations, and other legitimate businesses that could then be sold or operated to generate "clean" cash. They were experimenting with Bitcoin, the virtual currency that made transactions impossible to trace—ideal for the drug trade and an anathema to the authoritics.

Miguel Gonzales did not fit the stereotypical Hollywood image of a drug lord— the fat, sweaty, gold-chained, sneering hombre, sporting a pencil thin mustache and surrounded by ruthless picturesque thugs and sensual Latin women. To the contrary, Gonzales was a handsome sophisticated man, about 5'10", gym-muscular, with glossy, styled, raven, swept-back hair. He was partial to Ferraris and Armani clothes. Gonzales often met with high-level officials in the government, Policia and army. Three Chevrolet Suburban's usually accompanied him on his "business trips." The armada bristled with his "soldiers" sporting US Army-issue M-16s smuggled over the Mexican-American border. He didn't personally participate in any hits or territorial warfare, leaving that to his local militias.

Gonzales had been a technological whiz in his life before drugs. The oldest son of a lower middle class family, he witnessed the drug trade and its carnage from the ground up. A brilliant child, he went, on scholarship, to the University of Mexico's Mexico City campus and graduated with a degree in computer science. He saw the privileged Mexico City rich, and was determined to get wealthy as well.

His introduction to the drug trade was through his roommate, Pato, who was the major wholesaler and retailer for the Sinola cartel for the 50,000 students in the University of Mexico system. Under Pato's tutelage and protection, Gonzales took over distribution for the Mexico City campus. His career and the beginnings of his wealth were launched. He never looked back.

Gonzales's prime objective now was to get back his market share of the cocaine markets that he was involved in. He had lost 5 billion dollars worth of business during a war with the rival Juarez and Tijuana cartels and was determined to take a big chunk out of their hides.

The cartel's basement operations room looked like a computer-driven command and control center, which it was. Operations were directed from the basement by seven trusted aides, each gathered around three monitors and each overseeing one of the seven field districts. The system tracked cocaine shipments, bank transfers, bank balances and purchases of tangible properties. It also tracked the location of their agents and firepower and the movements of major competitors so that an overall "military" strategy could be plotted. All of the information needed to run the cartel's business was in this place and from there, orders were given, money ultimately made, and results tabulated.

Major tracking information and a summary of the Cartel's overall operations were displayed on a large, bright LCD screen hanging in the front of the ops room. Gonzales met with his staff each afternoon to study the operations board and other business matters, and make decisions on their next moves. Gonzales's state-of-the-art systems were designed and run by two whiz kids from Mexican investment banks who just didn't feel that twenty-five million pesos a year was enough for their already greedy appetites.

A jewel in his expansion crown was the Caribbean operation, centered in Grand Cayman, and run by a man known only as Zane. Zane was about to make a major move to grow his business in Jamaica and several other smaller islands. Gonzales watched him carefully.

CHAPTER TWENTY-SIX

Harry paced the room. He was dog-tired following his meeting with Charlie and hadn't slept at all last night. He wanted to apologize to Amanda for his outburst, tell her that he loved her, ask her to forgive him, and to move back in. He had left message after message for Amanda and she had not returned his calls. She never picked up even though he knew she was there. He had sent flowers, champagne, and notes. No reply, no thank you. Harry looked for her on the streets to no avail. He didn't see any of her friends who could act as a go-between, or give him a hint about what was going on, what she was saying. But she was not exactly a saint either, he thought, walking out as she did without talking, not letting things cool down. She had a haughty temper. Too independent. On top of it, the drug and murder cases were dragging out and should have been solved by now. Harry was stuck. Depressed and angry about the situation. They needed to talk.

Nervously fidgeting with her fingers, Amanda sat back on her patio with a glass of new-season-just-off-the-plane Beaujolais. She was slightly sick to her stomach and not thinking clearly. Conflicted. The issue was how much Harry and how much of her old life did she want. Was he really the right man for her? What if he didn't want her anymore after the fight? *"He's a pain in the ass,"* she thought, *but I love him; can't get him out of my mind. Not talking is childish. I'm cooler now, and we have to work this out. For my sanity and perspective on life, I want to keep some of my old life. Not all of it, that's not possible, but some of it. What we have to do is work out boundaries without acting like a couple of scorpions circling each other, waiting to strike.*

Amanda picked up the next call. "Harry, let's talk. Your place, 3 PM? I can't get away from a meeting until then."

"Fine."

Amanda drove the short distance from her office to Harry's place. She was still prickly. She knew she'd been out of line too. She greeted Harry with a peck on the cheek and sat down in an armchair opposite Harry.

"Harry, let's try this: You open the conversation by stating what you think our problems are. I'll add my thoughts as we go along. No yelling, no anger, and keep it short. I'll summarize to make sure that I understand your point of view. Then I'll state my points and you summarize them. This is a conversation not a debate. We'll have our 'says' and see where it takes us."

Harry was getting nervous. He didn't like this touchy-feely stuff. Too new age for him. But this was the talk he wanted, so he'd go along with the game and see where it took them.

"Go Harry."

"I'm sorry about my blow-up. I know I have a temper that I try to control. Sometimes I'm not so good at it. It got the best of me Friday. I was drunk. It was immature and uncalled for. I was jealous of your friends who had you for the evening. I wanted you all to myself and that's not right. I should have kept my mouth shut and talked to you about it in the morning. I really love you, Amanda."

"I know you do, Harry, but love and sex don't make a relationship that lasts. So what will make that possible?"

"I want us to live together, be happy together, and be together most of the time that we're not working. We're both used to being very independent—calling our own shots and living alone. We'll have to sacrifice some of our 'single' practices for the relationship. Of course, both of us need time without each other to do some of things that we want and are ours alone. I just don't want to get pissed off because you spend so much with your family and friends—three nights a week is a bit much. I guess they're a lightning rod for my frustration. I know I'm invited to all of your 'girlfriend dates,' but it's your show, not mine. I enjoy your family, but not a couple of your friends, or the conversations about 'women things.' Frankly, I can't stand Monica and Christie—too abrasive, too clinging, too covetous of your time.

"Yes, I know they can be annoying at times, and Monica talks too much. But they're lifelong friends, and I enjoy them."

"Bottom line, I want more time for us to be together," Harry said. "That's the problem." Otherwise things were wonderful. How could either of us replace the nights on the beach, the sailing, dancing, the incredible sex, and the everyday pleasures of just being together? How could we destroy such a beautiful thing? You have the ball Amanda"

"Harry, as I understand it, you're angry and jealous of the time that I spend with others, not you. And my temper is a problem. Right?"

"Right."

"I don't want to walk away from friends that I've had since I was in grade school. They're good people. My family is my family. Always. I think that the problems are my habit of spending so much time with my buddies and family, my determined independence, and my sometimes brash temper. Your judgment is clouded by your jealousy, and your anger about these issues—serious problems that you've had before. So, time and my friends are an issue. The other problem is your temper and outrageous behavior. We have to deal with it. We can never have a fight like this again. It would destroy our trust and relationship."

"So," Harry said, "My problem is my anger, and your time away from me,

"Yes," Amada said. "If this is going to work between two strong personalities, we have to have some ground rules, some boundaries on our behavior—the things that we do together, the life that we build, and the time that we have to do our own stuff. Without personal time, we'll fail."

"I agree," Harry said. "I don't mind the family gatherings. Your family is fun, accepting, and I learn a lot about the island and its culture when I'm with them. Several times a month for dinner is good."

"I can live with that," Amanda said. "What if I cut my time alone with the girls down to once a week. More, if you're busy and I want to get out."

"That will work. I promise."

"Maybe you can find something to do with the boys at work that will occupy you when I'm gone. Why don't you have a night out with Terry and Mark? You know them pretty well. Go out and have 'guy' conversations. How about Charlie? He's interesting and can tell you things about his world and you yours. You seem to be on he way to becoming friends. Getting away from the house will give you something to do, a diversion. Therapeutic. You can talk about work, sports, your female entanglements, the weather—whatever pleases you. Have a couple of drinks, but please Harry, not too many."

"I'll cut down. I don't get drunk very often now, and I'll make sure that it doesn't happen again. The drinking alone was a bad scene."

"Maybe a hobby would be good for you. Ever think about writing about your experiences? They are wonderful, unique and interesting. And your London police years, the serial murders, are a great subject. Why not?"

"Maybe. I'm not a particularly good writer. I can barely get through police reports. But a night out with boys when you're gossiping with the girls would be good for me. I don't socialize enough with my mates as it is. Don't know them well. I'll ask Terry and Mark out for a few beers this Wednesday."

"With these guidelines, we can cut and fit our time and make plans together. I know our jobs suck up a lot of hours, and often there's not time enough for us. Let's make as much space for us as we can."

"As I understand it," Harry said, "we have our own joint turf and then our time alone. The terms you proposed are good. Let's get on with it. See how it works out."

"Fine," Amanda said, "But what about your anger?"

"Amanda, I have to control it. I've tried, but it pops through when I'm frustrated, under pressure, or have a hardened criminal on my hands. The police offer a course in anger management. I promise to take it. What about yours?"

"I'll be aware of my volatile disposition. I'm pretty good about changing my behavior when I want to. And I want to."

"Another thing, Harry," Amanda continued. "We have to find a way to communicate when we're mad or have a serious issue. Let's have a "George" session. Either one of us who has an issue can pull George, dear George, the stuffed giraffe that you gave me when we moved in together, into the middle of the room. That's a signal that there's a big issue and we should talk. That way we learn to fight without damage and work out issues before they fester and blow up. How does that sound?"

"That's what we've been doing, isn't it?"

"Yes."

"Will you move back in, Amanda?"

Amanda stared out of a window for a minute.

"Yes. I want to be with you in the worst possible way."

They hugged and kissed, and Harry helped Amanda move back in, this time with all of her belongings.

CHAPTER TWENTY-SEVEN

Zane's head felt swizzled: Gonzales, Jamaica, the cops, Brooke, Baxter's murder, gang war, new shipment, rumble from another gang, a new safe-house. There was a lot to think about. *White man's burden,* Zane chuckled to himself as he returned to his house on his motorcycle to think in quiet. To plan. To relax if he could.

Zane's house was a typical, quaint late nineteenth-century Caymanian cottage on upper West Bay Road. The house had been passed down through generations from Zane's forbearers. Zane, proud of his heritage, his parents, and his ancestors, kept it in near-pristine condition. It was small, white, with white gingerbread trim on the eves, porch rail painted in Caribbean pink, and topped with a slightly rusted tin roof. The historic house was surrounded by a raked sand yard, punctuated by bushes and several small circular beds of native flowers.

The house had a secret tunnel leading to a watertight door hidden below century-old rusted iron rails that were once used to haul fishing boats out of the water. It was used by Zane's ancestors to smuggle Jamaican slaves to freedom—for a price. Sort of like current day Mexican coyotes that smuggle illegal immigrants over the US border. Zane used it to store weapons, and occasionally, smuggle drugs delivered in skiffs from a larger boat anchored far enough out in the ocean so the it was unlikely to be detected by the authorities. He felt safe. At least for now. It was not the type of house that you would expect a drug king to own.

Zane dismounted his motorcycle and trudged up the front steps. Once inside, he opened a cold Heineken, picked up his laptop, and plopped on his couch to check his mail, email and bills, and relax. There was the usual junk mail—advertisements for Viagra, credit cards and supermarket specials. Email was just routine correspondence.

The encrypted phone rang. It was Gonzales. The relaxation part was not to be.

"Zane, I have Columbian friends, Ricardo and Paula Sanchez, who want to launder 20 million dollars in cash. I'm doing them a personal favor. They want a stash in a liquid form other than cash. Something that they can use in an emergency if they have to escape the country. They'll smuggle the money in on a supposed sailing vacation from Cartagena. They have a forty-five-foot, ocean-racing yacht named Zephyr and will look like a rich couple out for a cruise. The Captain's name is Juan Camilo. Camilo will contact you by encrypted radio with details of their arrival. The code name is 'Congo.' Got it?"

"Yeah. Have them radio me with their ETA when in Cayman waters. They should anchor a quarter mile offshore, opposite my place. They'll look like any other yacht visiting the island. Someone will come out in a Zodiac to get the cargo and smuggle it in through the tunnel—the easiest place for small packages."

"Fine. Then how are you going to launder the money?"

"Easy. Done this before. Jewels. They're small. Easy to hide and smuggle through customs. I'll put them in a safe deposit box and set the account so that your friend can be added to the signature card. I'll give them keys to the boxes later."

"So how do you do this without getting caught?"

"I've used a jeweler, Jared Smythe before. Very reliable, honest with the underground trade, and a no bullshit guy. Has a small jewelry store, Jared Smythe Ltd, on Queen Street. Shows cheap jewelry in his windows but deals with the rich and the laundering trade from his back room. Has plenty of smuggled blood diamonds from the Congo, Venezuelan emeralds, and Burmese rubies and sapphires available. They're salable anywhere in the world. Plenty of gem dealers ask nothing about where the jewels come from. They'll buy them when people want cash. The Caymanian custom guys don't give a shit about Smythe's imports. He brings them in legally and pays the duty. Makes him look legit. Smythe takes the cash to be laundered and gives the customer gems in exchange. They'll put them in safe deposit boxes until they need them. Smythe will buy them back if they want—at a substantial profit to him, of course."

"What do we make on it?" Gonzales said.

"Ten percent."

"How much does he take?"

"Another twenty percent. He'll sell them again for twenty percent above market.

"That's a hell of a commission. Won't that make the price too high for his customers?"

"People pay it and don't complain. They're just happy to get their drug money out of Columbia, washed into US dollars or gems, and hidden in case they have to get out of Columbia fast."

"Fine. One other thing. You have to move a lot more product. We're only on track with last year's sales. I expect a 40% increase. We're sending you another $100 million worth of coke by container ship. You have nine months to sell it. No price cuts, special deals, and for

God's sake, don't start a war anywhere. I'll call you with the arrangements as soon as they're made."

"How the fuck do you expect me to get rid of it in nine months on top of my budgeted sales?"

"I don't give a shit how you sell it. Just sell it." The phone went dead.

Zane lit a cigarette, furrowed his borrow, and walked on the beach by the soothing water to clear his head. *If I'm going to move this stuff, I have to get the Charleston, New Orleans, Baton Rouge, and Galveston markets set up. Shit, not that I don't have anything else to do. I've got to get my organization in shape for my local and Caribbean expansion, much less for the southern US. I only have one proven man that can handle the expansion--Hector. I'll have to get two more experienced lieutenants from Mexico to help him run the US. We'll barely have that market running by the time we need to move these goods. Screw Gonzalez. I have to sell most of it at wholesale and below market price to bust into those cities. No time to get a good retail operation going. Gonzales swill be okay with that if I get results. I've got to sit down with Hector and plan this gig."

CHAPTER TWENTY-EIGHT

It was hot as Hell's frying pan. Sweat rolled off Rat's rodentian face like a dripping faucet. His nose wiggled slightly as he sniffed the odors—sweat, urine and evil on the street of temporary dreams. His pallor almost matched the humid, gray of dusk. It was his shift.

Rat was on the front line for Zane. The key guy. The exposed guy who delivered the drugs to a car or "walk-in". He took the cash from his customers and gave it to a runner, who in turn took it to his distributor, who hid the money temporarily in a stash in a nearby "friendly" apartment house. Rat wore the latest rap-gear: floppy black below-the- knee shorts with his underwear showing at the waist, a NWA (Niggers with Attitude) T shirt, and a light Chicago Bulls jacket. Black as the blackest Jamaican, he was smart, fast and trustworthy. His feet were clad with chunky, black and white $500 "b3 Tumblirs", a favorite on the street. He topped off his outfit with a large heavy gold medallion with the peace symbol on it and was armed with a Sig Saur 9mm stuffed in the back of his pants. Rat was "clean". He detoxed two years ago to improve his chances of moving up a step to become a distributor, a position that ran two or three street crews and paid a lot more.

A white BMW 750iL slipped around the dark corner of King and Victoria streets in one of the few dilapidated, poor, and crime-ridden neighborhoods in Grand Cayman. A Jamaican enclave. The car stopped in front of a dark alley and flicked its lights on and off once. A lookout, a block away from the action, signaled all clear with a laser pen to Rat who was leaning against the wall of a nearby long-closed grocery store. Rat quickly approached the car, scoped the surroundings for danger, and leaned in the passenger side door.

"Whadda you want?"

"A eight ball of coke" the driver said."

"Ours is 99 percent pure. Be careful with it. Ain't like the diluted crap the other dealers are slinging. One sniff'll blow your nose off. That's $300 in twenties or smaller."

Rat was handed a stack of $20 bills.

"You come back to me for the best."

The deal took less than thirty seconds. The car sped off. A scruffy runner in his early teens, wearing, an Oakland Raiders T shirt, and a baseball cap turned sideways, took the money from Rat. He hurried down the street to "deposit" it with the distributor who was holed up in a nearby "friendly" apartment that was changed every few days. He would bring back more drugs for the upcoming evening rush. This was the first of dozens of transactions that night. Customers arrived by car, motorcycle, and on foot. They ranged from rich to poor; from teens to seniors; well dressed to disheveled; clean to filthy. They all had two things in common. First they were hooked—mostly addicts along with a healthy number of recreational users. Good mix for steady business. Second, they would be customers for a long time if treated well with better product and lower prices than other offerings on the street.

The cops cruised by occasionally. They sometimes stopped to talk to a crew or two, but they never made an arrest or tried to get information about the operation. They and their superiors were frequently and lavishly bribed. And so went the night.

Perez's men were watching over this, Zane's hottest street corner.

Juan Carlos Perez, a top lieutenant in the brutal Columbian Norte del Valle cartel, was charged with taking over the lucrative drug trade on Grand Cayman, and establishing a base for transshipping drugs to the

United States and the rest of the Caribbean. Norte del Valle dominated the trade in the Caribbean coastal cities from Cartagena to Barranquilla, with a strong position in Panama. Each year they shipped almost a billion dollars worth of coke to the United States through Mexico. At home in Columbia, Perez was known as Jaguar—a silent, stalking formidable predator. His name was well earned. He had tracked down and cruelly "eliminated" a large number of competitors that got in his way.

Perez was a coffee and cream colored man—half black and half Spanish heritage. He was surly, barrel-chested man, pockmarked and battle scarred and could only be called ugly. He sat on the small patio at his safe house and plotted his strategy to take over Zane's drug business. To be as unnoticeable as possible, Perez dressed as an ordinary Hispanic workman with jeans, a faded, slightly dirty T-shirt with a "I Love New York" logo, and heavy duty, dirty, well scuffed work boots. He appeared aloof and diffident, but his large and wintry eyes and quick mind missed little. He was decisive, coldly calculating and mostly even-tempered. His low-key manner belied his oft-tapped brutal streak. He prized being in top physical condition—his "job" often demanded it. He worked out on weights and a treadmill in the house. He didn't dare run on the road for fear of being killed or kidnapped. A lot of people wanted his head, and the Federales were first in line. His only luxury was a weekly manicure and pedicure. He liked to feel neat and clean.

He would join the outlandishly luxurious life of the other drug lords once he returned to Columbia for good. He didn't like Grand Cayman. Too small, tough living for him, too minor an operation.

Ana crept behind Perez out on the patio, put her hand over his eyes, and kissed him on the nape of his neck.

"Hey", Perez said, "I'm trying to work."

"I have work for you," Ana said as she blew in his ear, put her hands inside his shirt and slowly rubbed her hands up and down his chest.

"Cut it out, I have lot of work to do"

"I have a lot of heavy lifting for you, Alex. Lots", she said, sliding her hands down his stomach.

She pulled her hands free and kneeled in front of him. He fondled her fluid breasts as she leaned over, unzipped his fly, removed a very erect penis, and put it in her mouth. At first, she slowly moved him in and out, flicking the tip and spine with her tongue. As his member engorged and throbbed, the pace quickened. He soon slumped spent and relaxed. Then he returned the favor. They stayed on the patio with a couple of margaritas while Perez went back to calculating his cocaine needs and strategy for the coming three months.

Ana, his mistress of a decade, was a very smart, well-educated, curvaceous, sultry Columbian woman who loved sex. She typically wore tight-tight black slacks; braless in a see-through blouse fitted to show her ample and perky breasts to their best advantage. Her jewelry was expensive and simple with large gold hoop earrings, a solid gold bracelet carved in intricate flower patterns, and a large platinum ring set with a ten caret octagon cut emerald surrounded by flawless diamonds. Gifts from Perez. She held her head high, seemed to effortlessly glide across floors, and had infectious brown eyes that sucked in the current object of her attention. She was almost a dead ringer for Valle Katrine Manchola, the current Miss Columbia. Maybe even more beautiful. She was lover, trophy, friend and occasional adviser to Perez on his personnel choices. She was uncanny, like a mystic, and read people like a book. He frequently asked her opinion on the trustworthiness of his people or view of any negative grumblings in the troops. She had once fingered a lieutenant that was being hired from another gang because she thought him a mole. A subsequent interrogation proved her right.

Perez's current safe house was a cement-cinderblock-stucco structure with heavy slat-shuttered windows. It really wasn't "safe" because the cops and the street people knew where it was. The bribed cops ignored the hideout. From the outside, the house looked like any of the deteriorating bungalows on the block. It was refurbished by a contractor paid to keep his mouth shut and threatened with death if he told anyone about the building's unusual features. The house was in a blue-collar section in West Bay, far from the crime-ridden neighborhoods where he operated. He felt safer being away from the very crime that he fomented.

The building's yellow masonry walls hadn't been painted in decades. Dirt splatters from years of tropical downpours rimmed the base of the building and rivulets of rust stain ran from the tin roof to the ground. The lot was covered with crushed shells and devoid of any trees or greenery. No one could sneak up on the preserve without being seen or heard. There was no cover, and the plot was brilliantly lit at night. There were infrared beam security devices that detected anyone entering the yard and surrounding turf. Night vision CCTV cameras covered the grounds, the buildings, and up and down the roadway in front of the house. There was an escape door in the back wall that led to an alley where two ordinary looking but high-powered and armored GMC SUVs were parked. Inside there was a spartan kitchen, two bedrooms, a small dining area and a large living room. Weapons, grenades, and extra ammunition were stacked beside each window and door. Furnishings were sparse and shabby-cheap like those found in low-grade month-to-month rentals. Underneath the floor there was a large compartment used to hold drugs, and a veritable arsenal of arms and explosives. Explosive charges, that could be triggered by a cellphone, were placed in the space so that the contents and the building could be blown up in the event of a police raid or drug war. The fortress, dug in coral, was sealed to prevent water from seeping in.

There will be, Perez thought, Goddam bloody battles over this this turf. Gonzales's people have it sewed up tight now. They are well armed. Powerful. But I have a seasoned army on my side; fine weapons. Won a lot of battles during the Columbian wars. Kicked the hell out of the Army boys plenty of times. I'll add a billion plus a year in Grand Cayman, including transshipments to some of the other Islands, and the States. Sure, the Mex's know we're here. They just don't know how many of us there are, our plans, and our power. Kicking the shit out of them will be fun.

Perez had imported twenty-five seasoned gang members from Columbia —street hands, money runners, two lieutenants, hit men, a number of soldiers, and a money-laundering specialist. All had temporary work visas as construction workers. They melded into the large number of imported workers needed to support Grand Cayman's building and tourist boom, and formed the core of Perez's army. Perez had quietly approached Zane's street dealers and located a disgruntled distributor. The distributor was bought off for a substantial sum of money and promised a distributor's job in Perez's operation.

Perez's first task was to take over Zane's most lucrative site, the territory around Gibbs Street. At the same time he would assault Zane's in-town safe house. A massive attack.

If Perez failed, his life was on the line; his game plan finished.

It was time to get to work.

CHAPTER TWENTY-NINE

It was one of those beautiful, steady, warm, soothing rains that sprinted and rippled across the surface of West Bay, It peppered the thatch roof on the bar at Sunset House, drained to the ground, and was as calming as the sound of the gentle surf. It was, indeed, romantic if you were there for a prelude to a fling. Being early evening, the stools were stuffed with locals. Smoke hung in the damp air, and the trading of jokes and the mundane events of the day were well on their way.

Thompson and Charlie watched the crowd with selective disinterest. They both nursed an ice cold Corona under one corner of the roof, close enough to the edge to be dusted by the occasional spray whisked in by the wind.

Thompson said, "Well, this is shaping up to be long and tough. I'm at the plodding stage—one step, one interview at a time—as I work my way up the feeding chain of clues. I've questioned the two suspects that I mentioned before, Smith and Vargas, and they've both been cleared. Smith has a long record of misdemeanors and burglaries, but he has an alibi at the time of the murder. He was crew on one of Captain Greene's dive boats over at Bonnie's Arch. Vargas was in a bar in Georgetown. Several people confirmed his presence."

"We picked up no street gossip about who might be the murderer."

"We did pick up one surprising thing from Smith, who still hangs out with his buddies from jail. Apparently, unusually large shipments of very high purity cocaine have been passing through here. We suspect that a good deal of the stuff is headed for Jamaica and the smaller islands east of here. Street gossip has the coke coming in from Mexico and Columbia. We know that the supply of drugs is going up in quantity and quality. A bad combination. We've had several drug-related murders and an increasing number of accidental overdoses with this extremely potent stuff."

"How do they get the drugs in?"

"Most shipments come in on sport-fishermen, high-speed banana boats, specially modified rigid inflatable boats with 1200 horsepower outboard motors called "go-fasts," and occasionally on sailboats and merchant ships. Our shore patrol and American Coast Guard try to intercept the seaborne supply, but it's impossible to plug all of the holes. We're lucky if we nab one in ten. The cartels or big traders sometimes send out a small fleet of half a dozen boats at one time. They know that one will probably get picked up. A cost of doing business for them. It diverts our interception forces and the rest will get through. Private boats can land in any mangrove swamp or secluded part of the island or reconnoiter with another boat near the island and transfer people and goods to shore. We don't know when and where they're going to come in unless we get a tip, or a US or Caymanian Coast Guard patrol boat gets lucky."

"Doesn't customs catch a lot of the imports.?"

"We rarely catch anyone. Our well-bribed customs officials are obviously aiding the process no matter how the drugs come in. Some of them make ten times their annual salary each year by looking the other way when drugs come through."

"So far, so bad. How else would you expect a criminal, who's bent on smuggling drugs, get them in?"

"Some smugglers come in by commercial or private plane. Drugs are concealed in luggage or boxes of legitimate goods like clothes, small household accessories, electronics, and knickknacks. They carry fake papers, and have a reason for being on the island. They claim that they are tourists, residents, or property owners coming in to furnish their homes, or conduct business. They pay the duty due. We don't require visas for most countries, and a temporary stay stamp is issued as long as the individual has a valid passport, no recorded criminal record, and gets by profiling and customs screening. It's a leaky system. The smart ones smuggle in large quantities of drugs, by private yacht, their remarkable "go fast" boats, or fishing boats from other islands or northern Columbia or Venezuela. The most difficult to monitor are the cruise boats because passengers come in mass and we rely on the unsophisticated and sloppy cruise lines to scrutinize passports. If I wanted to bring in small quantities of drugs and come in incognito, I'd probably choose a cruise, bring a counterfeit passport, put my drugs in concealed compartments in my luggage, take an island tour, and disappear."

"All well and good," Charlie responded, "but you have twenty-five thousand people, mostly tourists, landing on the island each week. How would you find out if there were a criminal or suspect among them?"

"With great difficulty."

"Any results yet?"

"No leads from our immigration people."

"To identify suspects, we rely on incoming immigration that has a database of known Cayman criminals or suspects. We have information from the United States, Mexico, and Europe, as well as Interpol, who covers the rest of the world. Of course we do the usual profiling and luggage screening. Very ineffective. Look at it this way. A Mexican national comes in by air, has an apparently legitimate passport, and no criminal record. What do we do? Interrogate every Mexican visitor? No way. Don't have the time and personnel, not to mention the civil rights issue of singling out one ethnic group for scrutiny. Our best source for drugs and financial fraud is tips. Other countries, particularly the United States, have snitch networks that often flag shipments or drug dealers coming our way. Financial fraud? The same way. The IRS tips us off to big tax evaders and investigations of financial fraud that might be relevant. As I said, it's a very complicated system that leaks like a colander."

"We may get a break, however. Assuming that Baxter's murder could be drug related, we might get some 'encouraged' information from a mid-level drug dealer. I have a couple we're going to pick up now. One is named Richard Black, a tough Jamaican that we suspect is part of a much larger gang working here. He has a buddy, Sampson, who hangs with him all of the time. They may or may not be useful. We'll see."

"Do you get anything from the street pushers?"

"No. We watch the street dealers and small wholesalers and pick them up if we can catch them in the act. For snitches, we usually ignore minor drug transactions in exchange for information. This time, we've pumped them for intelligence about their management and supply sources, to no avail. They're afraid of getting killed and would prefer to go to jail than talk. We know that there is a big Mexican cartel behind drug sales on Grand Cayman, and the Columbian's have just moved in. We haven't been able to get a good handle on the bigwigs in either group, and we must if we're going to break up the gangs. Maybe we're a trans-shipment point for other islands. I just don't know. A drug deal gone sour is a remote but real possibility behind Gil's death. We know that he was a substantial user."

Charlie asked, "So where from here?"

"Charlie, we've been too involved in the quick and obvious to thoroughly investigate other sources of information. We need to know more about Gil and Brenda's latest activities. We haven't checked their background. Pat and Savannah need to be questioned. We don't know who their friends are, or what makes them tick. We have no handle on their financial manipulations or their life back in New York. For all we know, this was a New Jersey hit by someone who flew in on the early morning flight, killed Gil and left on the next plane. I have to run down the illusive Brenda Baxter when she returns from her Antarctic trip. I'll grab Lord and Sweeny for questioning as soon as we find them. I hope that our snitches can give us a lead on who supplied Baxter with drugs."

"From my point of view," Charlie said, "I have to get to Brenda and Gil's financial lawyer, Jonathan Brooke. I have an appointment with your financial fraud unit to start to get a handle on the money side of the equation. The IRS, Justice, and the New York authorities had nothing."

"Let's meet as soon as you've finished with your meeting with the financial fraud boys and Brooke. Soon I hope?"

"You got it. Give me two or three days. I'll call you as soon as I know anything."

They clinked their glasses and said in unison, "Good hunting." Then, they started scoping the young, and titillating women in scant bikinis just getting off of a dive boat. Charlie's mind drifted off, thinking about his next step—questioning Jonathan Brooke.

CHAPTER THIRTY

The arresting sergeant manhandled his handcuffed prisoners into the interrogation room. One man stumbled, broke his fall on the table's edge, and said, "You muddahfucker, I'll kill ya when I get out." The other suspect wrestled his handcuffed wrists away from a patrolman and slumped into a chair. His eyes spit venom. The one called Sampson was tall, lean, and physical condition. He had the street-worn look of a pockmarked ferret and smelled like a sweaty weight room in a "heavy lifter" gym. He appeared to be about 25. Sampson wore an expensive Ralph Lauren polo shirt, linen shorts and a Rolex Dive watch. He was the feisty one. Richard was sullen and silent. He was a bit more downscale, but none-the-less, well appointed. Looked like a relative newbie. He was of medium build with a slender angular face and very dark for a Caymanian. There was a thin, red, and ugly scar that ran across one cheek—probably from a knife fight, a badge of honor for him. Richard was a street-savvy eighteen year old. He wore a long-sleeved shirt with broad stripes of Rastafarian colors (red, gold, and green), tucked into tan cargo shorts. He dripped with gold neck and wrist chains and wore a huge ring with Bob Marley's picture on it. Tattooed on one arm was the famous line from the Marley song, "I shot the sheriff, but I did not shoot the deputy."

Richard and Sampson were arrested on the charge of possession with intent to sell. Surveillance photos proved that they were street dealers. They were fingerprinted, photographed, and left to stew for an hour in an interrogation room under blinding, blistering hot lights. Harry slapped each prisoner hard and then gave them a neck-snapping shake and rime enough for them to sweat, dehydrate, get depleted from the heat, anxious, and maybe a bit of drug withdrawal. Both had records for possession of small quantities of drugs and burglary.

Thompson studied the booking photos. He then entered the room, excused the sergeant, slammed the door with a jarring crash, and glared at them silently for five minutes. No one said a word. Thompson threw a bag of cocaine on the table.

"OK, Sampson, this yours?"

"No fucking way, mon. This ain't my shit. You fuckers planted it on me."

"Bullshit creep. You're just little guys who'll be dead before you know it. Someone will knock you off. Trust me. Be a service to society. You had enough stuff on you to charge you with criminal possession. That gets you up to ten years. And three years probation when we'll be breathing down your throat like a hungry cat after a slow mouse."

Harry said, "Now, tell us who's your boss? And who's top dog?"

"Fuck off, mon," Sampson replied.

Red, angry and intense, Thompson turned to the second man and said: "Ok, Dick."

"Richard. My name isn't fucking Dick."

"I'll call you any god damn thing I want, asshole. Now let's try it again. What do you have to say?"

"Nuttin. Same story as his," Richard said, pointing to Sampson. "We didn't do nothing. Nuttin, mon."

"Druggies go to the max-security prison—you know, where the murderers, big-time guys go. You wanna go there? We call it Bunghole Manor. Look around for the biggest guy in the place—he'll be your husband for life. Small fry like you come out with a stretched asshole that you can drive a two-ton truck through. You'll make half the guys in the joint happy. Plus you'll get cut—maybe a little, maybe a lot. On the face. Maybe you'll get the virus."

Thompson felt that Richard was the weaker of the two. He yelled, "Let's have it," swiftly hitting Richard in the jaw and sending him flying flat on the floor. Richard sat up and said: "fuck you pig." Furious, Thompson hit Richard again and dragged him back onto his chair. "Who?" he said, shaking him like a rag doll.

Gray with fear, blood running from his battered lips, Richard cowered in his seat, handcuffed hands in front of his face. He said nothing. Thompson pushed him to the floor again and stood over him threateningly. Richard crumbled into a heap and then went silent. Thompson hauled him back onto his chair.

Thompson turned to Sampson and stood him against a wall, held him by his collar and said, "Your turn. Who? Spit it out."

Another interrogator, Sam Wilkins, who had been watching through a one-way mirror, came into the room on cue. Thompson surreptitiously indicated that the weaker Richard was the one he could break.

"Harry, cut out the rough stuff. I'll take it from here."

Turning to the pair, Wilkins playing the "good cop" said:

"You don't look too bad, so we'll get you some medical attention after this is over. Can I get you a Coke or coffee? I have to say that you're better off with Coke, no pun intended. The coffee sucks around here."

"Cokes for both of us," Sampson said. Harry got the cokes while Wilkins continued:" I'm sorry about my partner He gets out of control from time to time."

"Now, all we want is the name of your distributor and the top dog."

"No way, mon," Richard said. "The cops let out that we snitched, the big man find out, we dead."

"We can make a deal. You tell us what you know and we'll drop charges. That's an easy solution for both of us—you're out, no messy police paperwork or expensive trial or prison stay."

Richard started to say something and Sampson said,

"Shut up asshole. You talk and I'll kill you when we get out, or in the joint."

"Shove it up your ass, you ugly faggot," Sampson said to Thompson. "I know the good cop bad cop routine. It won't work." Wilkins held his cool, though Thompson was on the verge of another assault.

"Dick, you have a wife and three kids. Do you really not want to be with them for ten years? The kids will be grown up and out of the house when you get out. Your woman will be with someone else. They usually are. They need sex as much as you. You're going to be jerking off, getting raped, or enjoying a blowjob from some toothless animal."

Silence.

Wilkins threw a bunch of photos on the table. "We have surveillance photos of you both selling drugs. Have you dead to rights. This is simple. Give us the name of your distributor and his boss and you walk."

"No deal," Richard said, "Better prison than dead. And when we get out we'll still have a job."

Thompson had had enough of the soft stuff. He stood up, face sweating and flushed, eyes blazing. He walked around the table twice, stopped in front of Richard, bent over him, and put his nose inches from the man's bug-eyed face. He stared into his frightened eyes and said, I'll beat your sorry ass until you talk. Now. Last chance."

Richard stared vacantly at the wall behind his tormenter.

Thompson, his anger barely contained, took a towel out of the table's drawer. "See this? I'm going to force this down your throat inch-by-inch until it reaches your stomach. When you start to digest it, I'll yank it out, taking your stomach lining with it. It's very, very painful. You'll be eating baby formula for months. If I screw it up, you may just gag to death. Pity." Harry had no intention of following through with his grisly threat, but threatening to use the technique had worked many times on recalcitrant criminals.

Harry barreled on with a carnivorous smile. He started by stuffing a small piece of the towel into Richard's mouth. The prisoner's eyes bulged in their sockets. He sweat torrents and distorted his red face trying to scream. He couldn't. He could barely breathe through his nose. "Give me his name or you'll be arraigned for drug trafficking tomorrow — if you're not dead. Just admit to the drugs that you had, tell us your boss's name and we'll let you go." Sweat poured down Richard's face and he slumped further into his chair. He trembled like a sad, battered, exhausted losing boxer in the final round of a brutal prizefight.

Wilkins, as part of the deception said, " Don't do it Harry, You almost killed the last guy you did this to."

Thompson, clutching Richard's shirt, said, "Again, just tell us the names and we'll let you go free. No hard feelings. Otherwise, you'll get arrested. Or maybe we'll let you go and put your name out on the street as snitches. You'll live for about a week, if that." The prisoner's face turned red-blue. Thompson yanked out the towel and said, "*Now*."

Richard, gulping precious air, slumped further into his seat, then said: "Pokey Anderson. He's the guy we buy from. He's the big distributor. Don't know who his boss is or where he gets the drugs. All I know is that big shipments come in all the time. Part of it hits the streets, the rest gets shipped on to some other place."

"Where do I find him?"

"He hangs out at the Royal Crown Bar."

"One final question," Thompson said.

"Any street talk about the murder of a guy named Baxter?"

Sampson spoke up. "We don't know. He bought lots of drugs. Maybe he owed somebody money. That don't go well on the street."

"What did he buy?"

"Everything. Coke, Pot, Ecstasy, heroin, Meth, Vicodin, glass, ruffies, LSD, you name it. A supermarket.

He partied all the time. Bought a lot for his friends here and in the States."

"How do you know?"

"People brag all the time. Best customer on Grand Cayman they say."

"Who're they?"

"Just street talk."

Thompson unlocked their cuffs and said, "Out of here, both of you. If we catch you again, we'll throw the book at you."

Sampson and Richard fell all over each other rushing for the door.

CHAPTER THIRTY-ONE

Amanda was steamy, hot, and dripping water. She dried off after her shower and went to Harry's bedroom to get ready for their dinner date. It was going to be good—at least the exquisitely prepared Caribbean food at the Grand Old House would be. She was not so sure about the rest of the evening. She pulled on an ecru sheer blouse over a tiny, matching bra, and a pair of well-pressed tan linen slacks, over beige alligator-strapped, high-platform sandals. Amanda put the finishing touches on her flawless skin—a matching tan foundation, a little blush to give slight color and shape to her cheeks, mascara, and beige eyeliner to emphasize her fluid brown eyes. Dangling, dazzling, gold earrings completed the picture.

She looked in her full-length mirror, pleased, and thought, "Damn good package head to toe." She knew this from the way men's eyes scanned her and threatened women stared icily at her when she entered a party. *Harry ought to really like this rig. He loves the see-through stuff. The question is, what's going to happen with Harry and me?"*

Amanda's parents had plenty of money. Her father was heavily involved in the family businesses. But his real love was politics. He was politically ambitious and dealt in a world where money and connections were valued above all. He wanted to become a minister of state and be part of the Chief Minister's inner circle. Amanda never wanted for anything—except a family. Her parents just plain didn't want to have a child but in a moment of careless passion, spawned her. They fought like hell all of the time—most often about her father never being home, never helping with Amanda, usually at work, cruising with his political buddies, or cavorting with one of the many mistresses he was rumored to have had over the years.

When Amanda reached ten, her parents had had it with their children and their marriage. They separated and shipped Amanda and her brothers to boarding schools—she to St Andrews Episcopal School in

Boca Raton Florida, and the boys to Admiral Farragut Academy in St. Petersburg.

The co-ed boarding school was definitely upscale, college prep, and assuredly not for Amanda. She thought it too confining; not laid back like the island. And, besides, she missed her friends. But her parents agreed on one thing: she would be well educated, would get into a good college, and would get the discipline that she would never have in their fractured home. She took a liking to science, particularly Biology, and graduated with solid grades without a lot of effort. Rather than go to college immediately, Amanda returned to the island she loved to get a job. Surely her father's connections would land a good one for her. And surely they did.

Her job was with Cayman Under Sea Environmental, a private company surveying Cayman's reefs, documenting the extensive damage being done by divers and global warming. It made great use of her skills in science and biology, took her outdoors, and did good work for the community. She didn't know what she wanted to do in the future and was quite content to live in the present and let life's eddies take her where they would. As it turned out, the extended family persuaded her to join their businesses. She took a middle-management job in the supermarket chain and found that she liked it. She was good with people, a fine manager, and destined to rise quickly in the company.

Thompson and Amanda had drinks at a candlelit table in The Grand Old House's bar—he, gin and tonic; she, Chardonnay. Their heads were together, talking quietly so that others on the crowded patio could not hear them. Almost all the locals knew each other, and they didn't want any gossip about their conversation.

Thompson leaned over the table, took Amanda's hands in his, kissed her and said, "Will you marry me?" Amanda hesitated and thought for a minute and said:

"I'm not ready for that yet. I love you like I've never loved before. But we need more time living together, getting to know each other better before I can be comfortable with marriage."

Harry's heart sunk. He felt insecure about their relationship again. Deflated.

Later that night, a disappointed Harry and a subdued Amanda drove east up Church Street, past Smith's Cove National Park, and along a deserted band of thick brush, stately palms, and casuarina trees lining one of the most beautiful and secluded beaches on the island. Halfway up the mile-long strand, Harry pulled off the road, parked, and they made their way through a small breach in the undergrowth to the pristine white beach. They were invisible to the world.

The light from the full moon broke into shimmering, zigzagging shreds that danced across the water. They could see each other clearly as they stood in the soft silvery light. It seemed like a winking man-in-the-moon smiled favorably on them. A cruise ship, with its white carnival-like lights hung from the superstructure, slowly slipped by like a giant glowing ghost walking on water. The water was calm, warm, clear, deserted, inviting, irresistible.

Harry took Amanda into his arms, breathing in her ear, and moving his hands to caress her breasts. He quickly unbuttoned her blouse, pulled her bra down, and flicked his tongue around her hardening nipples, a hand slowly massaging between her legs. Amanda, laughing, suddenly pulled back, stripped off her clothes, threw them on the sand, and ran, splashing into the shallows. She yelled for Harry to hurry up. She was ready. She was a nymph, a goddess of the sea, a free and soaring spirit. Harry blushed.

Harry screamed, "What the hell are you doing, Amanda? Someone might see you."

"Who gives a shit? This place is as quiet as the moon. Come on in."

A reluctant Harry peeled off his clothes and first walked slowly, tentatively, into the water as if it were studded with ice and bristling with biting things. The water quickly became a sultry, beckoning, erotic force, and he plunged in. Amanda pulled Harry to her in waist-deep water, tongue-kissed him, touched him until he was extended, big, hard. She floated on her back in the water. The moon kissed her exposed face, breasts, and thighs. Her dark pubic triangle invited Harry. She put her legs around him, guided him into her and they made love gasping and thrashing in the water.

When they were finished, spent, Harry put his arms around Amanda and said, lets go home and cuddle.

CHAPTER THIRTY-TWO

Pokey Anderson took over the Royal Crown Bar from his father some twenty years ago. The bar was a decent looking establishment decorated with the usual neon and LED beer signs. It was in Bodden Town, a short distance down a local road from the popular tourist attraction, Pirates Cave. The bar was popular with the blue-collar trade who lived in the area—the waiters, cooks. mechanics, drivers, and construction workers. It had made a good deal of money for his father who retired at 65 to spend time fishing and tending to grandchildren. Pokey, a confirmed bachelor, had no children that he knew of. God knows he frequented plenty of the fairer sexes bed, but never stayed with one for long.

Pokey was tall and slender to the point of being scrawny. Though he towered over most of his patrons, he never appeared threatening or dominating. He moved slowly and gracefully like a fine basketball player and gave the impression that he was never in a hurry and had plenty of time to talk or listen to everyone. For this, he was called Pokey. He had a well-trimmed salt and pepper beard that gave him a fatherly look; the look of a wise and experienced man. His brown eyes were both sympathetic and searching at the same time. There was a casual and confortable way about him.

Pokey's patrons were mostly locals. Everyone knew everyone else. The after work and evening trade was pleasant and rarely out of hand. It had been months since George Jones slammed Jose Fernandez into the bar and they started to wail away over a woman across the room at a table. Both thought that they had a date with her. Pokey didn't think she was worth fighting over—kind of a well worn, flabby, going-to-seed tart. *But,* he observed, *no accounting for taste. Particularly in women.*

Pokey kept a baseball bat behind the bar, and all he usually had to do was bang it on a table to break up a fight. Occasionally, when feeling frisky, he would swing on a row of bar glasses and let the crack and sound of shattering glass get the miscreants attention. He was strong, far stronger than his slight frame indicated. He was perfectly capable of bashing a bad guy over the head, which he did one night when a couple of strangers came in and tried to break up the place. The nameless intruders both took a bruising home run swat on the back of their legs. Embarrassed, limping badly and defeated, they took their disagreement outside. The woman never found a date that night. At least not at Pokey's.

Sometimes there were a handful of men from Georgetown that came in to drink or hook up with some willing patron. Maybe they didn't want to be seen on their home turf for one reason or another.

Then there were those who cane to Pokey for advice. Pokey would lean on the bar and listen to the joys and problems of his customers. He dispensed practical advice—helping with martial problems or dealing with girlfriends, or sympathizing on losses, or figuring out how to handle a problem on the job or in a business.

Behind all of this was a shrewd, business-savvy mind. He also used his manner and chats with and patrons to build a business far more lucrative than alcohol—drugs. He turned trading information and its exchange among people to his advantage.

The drug business started when Jackie G came into the bar and confided to Pokey:

"Pokey, can I talk to you confidentially about a tough problem? If our conversation ever gets out the they could put me away for a long time and I could get myself killed."

"What in hell have you gotten yourself into that could get you killed? Must be women or drugs or both. Talk to me."

"I'm into drugs. I mean I don't take them; I import them and sell to distributors who sell them to men working the streets. My problem is that I have 20 kilos of Coke that my regular customers don't need. I owe my supplier a lot of money. Have any ideas where I might unload it?"

Pokey said: "I just happen to know someone who might buy the stuff, or knows someone who would. I take 20 percent. If that works for you, I'll negotiate a deal, and the two of you can make the transaction without me. I expect to get my commission within a day. I'll get back to you tomorrow."

"Alright. Don't let me down man."

They slapped palms and his patron left.

As result of this transaction, word got around. Pokey was the man to see if you had a problem selling or buying drugs. He was discrete and no one ever got into trouble dealing with him. In fact, he was so good with business advice that he virtually turned into a management consultant to the usually streetwise but business dumb Cayman drug industry. Thus, Pokey's real job became that of a drug broker. As his clientele grew, his network spread. If someone needed drugs, he'd find out who had them and negotiate a deal with the seller. If someone wanted to sell drugs, he'd do the same thing in reverse.

Pokey went back to wiping the bar knowing that he would get his money when his patrons made a deal. He knew too much about almost everyone in the drug trade. Cross Pokey, and you risked your name being leaked to the police or, perhaps fatally, a drug gang that had a beef with you or wanted your territory.

As far as Pokey was concerned, he had the best of all possible worlds. He had a nice little drug business and the cops looked the other way. Some time ago he was arrested for distributing cocaine. He was helpful in giving the names of some important dealers to the police. The Police viewed him as a very valuable information source and dropped charges against him in exchange for future information on the drug trade. As long as he didn't begin importing drugs, they guaranteed that he could continue to conduct his business as usual. They didn't care if drugs moved from dealer to dealer. They were going after the big guys where they could shut down major importers of the stuff. They might raid his bar or arrest him from time to time for show and to keep him a trusted "one of the boys." But he would always get off on a technicality such failure to read his rights or lost evidence or a raid without a warrant.

Thompson walked into the bar, went over to Pokey, slapped him on the back and said:

"Hi Pokey, my friend, how you be?"

Pokey leaned back slightly, and said,

"I think I'd be a lot better if you weren't here." Pokey said with a smile, but his voice and body language projected a reluctance to engage.

"Well, have you appreciated he protection that we've given you on your little drug deals?"

"Absolutely"

"Beer"

"No thanks. I'm on duty."

" What can I do for you? Hope I can help,"

"You know that Gil Baxter was murdered?"

"Of course. Who doesn't? Nasty man. Lots of money. Do you have any idea who did it?"

"No, but I hear that he was really into debt to the Mexican Cartel boys. That's not a good place to be. They take no shit from anyone. They're quick to act, even on minor slights. Their general answer to being stiffed is to create a stiff out of the fool that stiffed them. Any surplus bodies you find around here likely belong to them. Remember Rico the Runt?" He was a street guy for them. He got caught skimming small amounts of drugs and cash. He was never seen again after that. Fish food. "

"Who heads up the gang?"

"I don't know. Honestly. It's a tight-lipped group and none of the big-boy Mexicans come in here. A few of their Caymanian street dealers or distributors do, but they know nothing about the management of their operations. I occasionally get a higher-level field distributor, but never one of the top guys. Rumor is that the top dog is Caymanian."

"Can you ask around for me? I need to know who the top guy is, and where he hides out."

"I'll do my best. That's a tough job. Maybe even fatal. What little extra incentive can you giver me to make it worthwhile to put my neck on the line?"

"How about you make sure that the drug cops pay no attention to me for nine months?. I've got a lot of deals in the air, and harassment would put off the guys I'm trading with"

"I'll see to that, if you'll get the name and address of the head guy here."

" I'll try."

They shook hands, and Thompson walked back to his car thinking: *one more seed planted. I still have a very large garden to plough.*

CHAPTER THIRTY-THREE

Michael Moreno, a former member of the Columbian Army, and a top enforcer for Perez's gang, balanced his AS 50 Navy Seal, sniper rifle on a pillow placed on a windowsill in a house opposite Zane's hottest corner— the site that moved the largest quantity of drugs each night. He centered his target in his night vision scope, breathed in, held his breath until his pulse dropped, and slowly squeezed the trigger. He fired. Crack-swish. One drug dealer fell dead on the street. Another crack. A second dealer's head exploded like a pumpkin, splattering blood and brains on the front of a house. A third shot. The watchman, crumpled to the ground before he could run. The rest ran. Perez's ground troops drove by in a armored white Honda SUV, poured onto the street with automatic rifles, and chased down and killed the remaining members of the street gang as they tried to escape. Several buyers were cut down. The street was littered with bodies and drenched in blood as the gang boarded the SUV and sped off to a new safe-house. The Mexican Cartel's hottest corner was wiped out.

Simultaneously, Perez's second crew pulled up to Zane's in-town safe-house. Half a dozen men jumped out of a van and spread, two on each side, two in back and two in front. Alarms covering the property sounded inside. Before Zane's men could defend themselves, an RPG was fired. It blew a hole in the façade, killed four occupants and set the interior on fire. Two other men were gunned down as they fled through the back door. Only one of Perez's men was badly wounded by return fire, and left on the battlefield. Zane was not there. He not only lost his house and men, but at least 30 kilos of coke. His men were completely surprised. It was a shooting gallery. It was carnage.

In his country safe-house, Zane said, "Jesus Christ. We had it all. Now that motherfucker Perez is starting a war. He won't win."

"Call out the troops," Zane said to a lieutenant. "Double the guns here. Send enforcers to every one of our corners. Protect our trade. M-14s all around. Take RPGs' and grenades. We'll deal with Perez later."

The lieutenant rallied Zane's troops by cell phone and ignited their defensive plan. Enforcers appeared at the unscathed corners to protect the trade. The periphery of the in-town safe-house was guarded for one block in every direction. Coke from another in-town stash was transferred to the country house. There were two vans on the street each with four of Zane's gunmen roving his territory, ready to descend on any firefight with Perez's men. All in all, Zane had twenty armed and dangerous soldiers defending his turf. His job, after the defensive move was over, was to get Perez.

Thompson's cell rang. He was roused out of Amanda's warm embrace at 12:10 AM. He blinked his eyes open, rolled over, tangled himself in the sheet, and woke up an irritated Amanda fumbling over her head to reach his phone.

"Jesus Christ, who is it?"

"Sir," the desk sergeant, a graying veteran close to retirement said, "it's happened. We have a drug war on our hands. A Mex street gang was hit on Kings street and a house blown up in West Bay. We assume that it was the Columbians trying to take over the Mex's turf. Uniforms, ambulances, and a SWAT team have been dispatched to both scenes and street patrols doubled in all of the drug trafficking areas."

Horrible, he thought, *but this might be the break we're looking for. The bastards are chasing each other out in the open. They'll save us a lot of trouble if they just kill each other off.*

Thompson kissed Amanda, threw on his uniform shirt, shorts and boots, strapped his Ruger 9mm on his side, and hurried to his car.

He ducked under the blue striped police tape and surveyed the scene. There were six bodies lying in anguished positions, soaking in their own blood, and strewn over the entire length of the block. They looked like torn, discarded, straw dust-leaking rag dolls in the deep shadows thrown by dim streetlights. A few packets of dropped coke and handfuls of one hundred and twenty dollar bills were scattered helter-skelter on the asphalt. Hundreds of spent brass shell casings were spread like fallen soldiers after a massive battle. Street urchins battled with the police to get the scattered money and coke.

The detective in charge of the scene approached Thompson. " Six of the gang are dead. A wounded Perez man was left behind and is on his way to Tomlinson Memorial. He'll live, the medics say. As soon as we get medical clearance, we can question him. We've finished the canvas of bystanders and people in the houses"

Thompson said,

"Anybody see anything?"

"No, and they're not telling us anything either. This is not a neighborhood where people say much to the police or outsiders. They keep a very low profile and stay in their houses after a gang incident."

"What about the bodies?"

" Look at this guy. Chest ripped into hamburger. There are three like this. Automatic weapon fire at close range. See how far apart from each other they are? They were running. Their legs are splayed apart like open scissors."

Moving to another body, the sergeant said, "Look at this guy. What do you see?"

Thompson bent over the carcass. "Clean shot to the head. Must have been a sniper. Why in hell would they use a sniper when they sent in a tank full of gunners to mop up the rest?"

"My guess is intimidation. Shows they can kill off anyone, anytime, anywhere. Obvious warning to the big shots. The possibility of complete surprise creates nagging fear. If the Perez's men show their faces in public and are stupid enough to follow predictable routines when they are outside their lair, they can be popped."

"Ok, as soon as you finish here, give me what you've got. And the forensics of course. I have to go in and interrogate this guy in the hospital. The guards at the hospital just texted that he can talk"

Georgetown became an armed camp ready to explode in violence. Cruise boats stopped calling. Planes arrived almost empty. The population went about their business only in daylight, sticking to heavily traveled routes.

CHAPTER THIRTY-FOUR

Thompson's cell rang. He was roused out of Amanda's warm cuddle at 12:10 AM. He blinked his eyes open, rolled over, tangled himself in the sheet, and woke up an irritated Amanda fumbling over her head to reach his phone.

"Jesus Christ, who is it?"

"Sir," the desk sergeant, a graying veteran close to retirement said, "it's happened. We have a drug war on our hands." A burrito street gang was hit on Kings street and a house blown up in West Bay. Uniforms, ambulances, and a SWAT team have been dispatched to both scenes and street patrols doubled in all of the drug trafficking areas."

Horrible, he thought, *but this might be the break we're looking for. The bastards are chasing each other out in the open. They'll save us a lot of trouble if they just kill each other off.*

Thompson threw on his uniform shirt, shorts and boots, strapped his Ruger 9mm on his side, and hurried to his car.

He ducked under the blue striped police tape and surveyed the scene. There were six bodies lying in anguished positions, soaking in their own blood, strewn over the entire length of the block. They looked like torn, discarded, straw dust-leaking rag dolls in the deep shadows thrown by dim streetlights. A few packets of dropped coke and a handful of one hundred dollar bills were scattered helter-skelter on the asphalt. Hundreds of spent brass shell casings were spread like fallen soldiers after a massive battle. Street urchins battled with the police to get the scattered money and coke.

The detective in charge of the scene approached Thompson. " Six of the Mex Cartel's gang are dead. A wounded Perez man was left behind and is on his way to Tomlinson Memorial. He'll live, the medics say. As soon as we get medical clearance, we can question him."

"We've finished the canvas of bystanders and people in the houses?"

"Yes," he said.

"Anybody see anything?"

"No, and they're not telling us anything either. This is not a neighborhood where people say much to the police or outsiders. They keep a very low profile and stay in their houses after a gang incident."

"What about the bodies?"

" Look at this guy. Chest ripped into hamburger. There are three like this. Automatic weapon fire at close range. See how far apart from each other they are? They were running. Their legs are splayed apart like open scissors."

Moving to another body, the sergeant said, "Look at this guy. What do you see?"

Thompson bent over the carcass. "Clean shot to the head. Must have been a sniper. Why in hell would they use a sniper when they sent in a tank full of gunners to mop up the rest?"

"My guess is intimidation. Shows they can kill off anyone, anytime, anywhere. Obvious warning to the big shots. The possibility of complete surprise creates nagging fear. If the Columbian gang show their faces in public and are stupid enough to follow predictable routines when they are outside their lair, they can be popped."

"Ok, as soon as you finish here, give me what you've got. And the forensics of course. I have to go in and interrogate this guy in the hospital. The guards at the hospital just texted that he's can talk"

Georgetown became an armed camp ready to explode in violence. Cruise boats stopped calling. Planes arrived almost empty. The population went about their business only in daylight, sticking to heavily traveled routes.

CHAPTER THIRTY-FIVE

It's a territorial war, Thompson thought. Smoke rose from the crumbled ruins of Zane's safe-house. The scene was scattered with yellow markers to indicate evidence for forensics to examine. Chunky cinderblock fragments of the house covered the yard and the street. Only the jagged walls of the house remained. Windows were broken in surrounding houses. Three shattered, burned, and bloody bodies lay under sheets waiting for the medical examiner. More than one hundred whispering neighbors milled around the tape fencing off the scene. The lone survivor of the gun battle, a member of the assaulting gang, was captured in critical condition and transported under guard to the hospital.

Thompson arrived at the detainee's room for an interrogation after the prisoner was able to talk.

Two muscular constables guarded the man's hospital room. He looked like a mummy with his head swaddled in bandages. Only his mouth and eyes poked through. Blood seeped through the gauze. IV's dripped into both arms, and a group of monitors blinked numbers and wrote squiggly lines on their displays. His leg was in a cast and elevated. Nervous eyes peeked through the dressings and stared at Thompson. He was sedated and giddy.

I may be in luck, Thompson mused. *Maybe the drugs have relaxed him enough to spill the beans.*

"What's your name?"

"Jolice."

"Who were you fighting for?"

"Let's have it, Jolice. I want to know who did this."

"I don't know. I'm just a wholesaler. I take orders. Nobody tells me nuttin' but how much drugs I have to move, who we're gonna sell them to and where. They've only been 'round a few months."

"So who's your boss?"

Silence.

An angry, over-the-top Thompson, fed up with evasion, looked to see if anyone but the guards were in the hall and shut the door. He "accidentally" leaned on Jolice's battered leg.

"Ahhhhhhhh," screamed Jolice."

Thompson leaned again. Harder.

Jolice started moaning, hyperventilating, and on the verge of passing out.

Thompson stared bullets into his prisoner's eyes, baring his teeth, and put his nose close to his captive's.

"Once more. Who runs your gang?"

Silence.

Thompson sauntered to the foot of the bed and bent back Jolice's toes. There was a crunch and the toes turned white. The prisoner screamed like a banshee. His eyes bulged and flicked from side to side. His wounded leg thrashed.

"I don't know. Wouldn't tell you if I did. They'll kill me if I talk. Maybe they will anyway because you're here."

Furious anger driven by mental images of his wife's brutal murder, his impatience and hatred of violent criminals led him to say:

"Talk or I'm going to give you a pedicure that you won't forget."

Silence.

Thompson pulled out a pair of needle-nose pliers and tugged on Jolice's right, big toe nail. Enough to hurt, not enough for serious damage.

"No man. No. Don't do this."

Thompson slowly increased the pressure and the pain and then yanked the nail out with one hard, swift pull. Jolice shrieked. For a long time. Blood drizzled from the wound painting the bed sheet bright red. Thompson held the dripping, yellowed nail in front of Jolice's face and said, "More?"

Silence.

Jolice just stared at Thompson with terrified and pleading eyes. Thompson, stone-faced, glared back at his captive.

"You son-of-a-bitch. Talk."

Jolice hesitated. Thompson wasted no time with toothless threats and pulled a nail from the other foot. Jolice howled. His eyes rolled from side to side in pain and panic. From what Thompson could see of Jolice's face, it had turned to a putrid gray. Thompson began to pull on another nail. Jolice wailed like an ambulance siren and sobbed, "Stop. Stop. I'll talk, I'll talk. Don't do it."

"Who's the boss?"

"Perez. He brought the gang over from Columbia over the last couple of months. Snuck them in under temporary labor visas. They worked construction jobs for a while. Some still do during the day. Most don't work the streets but serve as wholesalers, enforcers, lieutenants and the like. The street vendors were recruited from gangs here. They hang out and sell—day and night."

"Where do I find this guy?"

Jolice said nothing.

Thompson grabbed Jolice's arm and twisted it until it was on the verge of breaking. The captive gasped.

Thompson put his pliers on a fingernail and tugged. "Want more?" Talk and you get off easy. We'll deport you back to Columbia. You can hide there. If you don't, I'll put you in jail for ten years or throw you to the dogs on the street. Then you're a dead man. Drug gangs just love snitch meat," Thompson lied to Jolice. He had no intention of making a deal. He had only circumstantial evidence that Jolice was involved in the drug trade, not enough to get a conviction. But for Thompson, all the rules went out the book in interrogations, and the prisoner was "voluntarily talking."

"No, no, no. He hangs out in an apartment on Aspiration Way—a blue bungalow on the left-hand side as you turn down from Fairbanks. That's all I know."

"Where does he keep the drugs?"

"In a couple of apartments and a house. I don't know where they are. A man gives the drugs to me and takes the money I make back to one of the stashes."

" How does he get the drugs in?"

"They come from Columbia by way of Venezuela by boat or plane."

"OK. We'll get you fixed up and on your way back home. I hope you have someone there that'll hide you. Gangs have long arms."

Jolice closed his eyes and shuddered.

On his way out, Thompson said to the guards, "Tell the nurse they missed a couple of wounds that they might want to dress."

CHAPTER THIRTY-SIX

About eight on a Wednesday morning, Harry rapped on Amanda's office door. "Lets go."

"Let's go where? What sort of game are you playing now, Harry?"

"I'm pooped. Fuzzy. Taking the day off. We're going to Havana in time for dinner and a night out on the town. I have two tickets on the noon flight, so you'd better hustle. I've packed a bag for you."

"Harrrry," she said with her eyeballs rolled up into her head like a disgusted teenager. "How am I supposed to get any work done with you and your spur-of-the-moment ventures?"

"Ever been there?"

"No."

"Havana's smashing. It sings—there's music everywhere, and the people are warm, welcoming and happy. Sunny personalities."

"My friends who have been there love it."

"And we're staying at the historic Saratoga. One of the best. The place to be if you want to experience old Havana with the new. Five star. Great restaurant and bars. Phenomenal service. Hemmingway used to drink with friends in the Palm Court."

"So what's the game plan?"

"Do what we want. And sex, sex and more sex," he said as he breathed in her ear and put his hands under her breasts, lifting them slightly. "Tonight, maybe a couple of mojitos, a good restaurant for dinner and some music. Should be terrific.

"Yeah, with any luck, we'll climb out of bed a few times to eat and take in some food and culture. I'll love, love, love it with you."

"Just come."

"Sounds like a blast," she said, standing up and giving Harry a long, deep kiss with a full, body press.

"Let's move before this turns into something else and we miss our plane."

The rackety, old, Cayman Airways Boeing 737 all-too-slowly struggled off the runway at Owen Roberts Field and headed for Havana, thirty minutes away. Once at cruising altitude, Amanda reached for Harry's hand.

"Love you. More than I have ever loved anyone before. Love me too?"

Harry leaned over and kissed Amanda and softly said, "Of course."

"Thank you for planning this. I think it's sensational. All the better to be there with you."

Amanda put her head on Harry's shoulder for a short nap. As the plane began to descend for landing, Harry unconsciously patted his inside coat pocket to be sure that the ring was safely tucked in.

After clearing tourist-friendly immigration and customs, they rolled their bags out of the terminal and hailed one of the ever-hovering, proud, ancient pre-Castro taxis. It was a beautifully maintained, shiny 1953 Oldsmobile Rocket 88, tricked out in sparkling re-plated chrome, fancy wheels, and the original paint scheme—dark green with a light-light green accent swish going from the front fender to the trunk. They rolled the windows down for the only air-conditioning they were going to get on this blistering, 89-degree, smothering-humidity day.

Their chariot trailed a thick stream of blue smoke behind it and creaked, groaned, and clattered a bit, complaining about its ancient body. There were a smattering of cars and trucks on the 1950s highway, most of them old, with a few Toyotas and Nissans dispersed in the mix. Well-tended, small, white-washed houses were interspersed between clumps of royal palms, farmed and unfarmed fields. From a distance, Havana looked like a city of two-story buildings punctuated by a few short skyscrapers and apartment houses. The old city was dominated by low, pastel-colored, Spanish-colonial-style houses with ornate wrought iron railings on their balconies—not unlike those in New Orleans. Many were in a state of decay with moldy, cracking, peeling stucco facades. A reflection of Cuba's sad economy.

The hotel was at the intersection of Paseo del Prado and Dragones Street, one of the busiest, honking, clattering, and congested areas in the city. People crowded the sidewalks and parts of the street. They moved with the exuberant pace of a heated conversation in Spanish—slow to move forward, animated as they went. The area had lots of shops—cigars, fruits and vegetables, books, souvenirs, afro-Cuban dolls and statues. There was Venezuelan and Cuban art, and clothing from the ordinary to the expensive—at least by Cuban standards.

The neoclassical 1890s Saratoga was the coolest hotel in town. It could only be described as a huge decorated limestone wedding cake, with stories one and a half times the size of ordinary buildings. It is an eclectic potpourri of architectural and decorative styles—neo-classic, art deco, beaux-arts, and modern, overlaid with a Spanish-Cuban flavor. Harry and Amanda entered the hotel through the brass doors crowned by the iconic, floridly ornamented and dazzlingly polished brass clock with a sculpted blue angel prominent on its front. A massive modern mural of multicolored lizards, dragons with flickering tongues, and striated trilobites dominated the lobby. The front desk was crafted from dark, veined mahogany with bright brass trim. After registering, they went to their room, and Harry opened the door to a cascade of warm, afternoon light coming from the ceiling-high arched windows cut into the opposite wall.

"Smashing," Amanda said, spreading her arms out to embrace the scene. "Harry, have you ever seen anything like it? That four-poster must have held mosquito netting in the early 1900s. I hope the damn mattress isn't that old. And look at the claw-footed bathtub. It's got spray heads all around and big enough for the two of us. I hope there's plenty of hot water."

"We can pop in anytime," Harry said with more than a slight glint in his eyes and a lilt of his head.

The rest of the room was luxurious and oddly decorated. Prints of paintings by the famous modern Cuban artists Carlos Guzman and Miranda Ibraham hung on the walls. They stood in stark contrast with the room's eclectic furnishings--art deco lamps, a modern glass coffee table, yellow-mustard striped, plush armchairs, and a small couch. There were two small palm trees and a vase overflowing with exquisitely perfumed white ginger flowers, Cuba's national flower.

Ordinarily, the disparate decorations would be a visual nightmare, but, for some reason, they really worked together and mirrored the personality of the quirky hotel. A bottle of chilled Cava, ordered in advance by Harry, was on the coffee table with two fluted Champaign glasses. Harry and Amanda put their feet up on the table and toasted to their good luck and to their stay in Havana. They agreed to head to dinner around nine when the city slipped into darkness and nightlife began to peek out from clubs, large and small.

Harry sat down on the edge of the bed and looked up at Amanda standing in front of him unbuttoning her blouse.

"Down boy," she said to Harry. "This is my treat." She slowly pulled off her sundress, and let it slip to the floor. Then she teased off her bra. She seductively moved toward Harry, caressed her breasts; erect pink nipples peeking through her fingers. Harry's eyes scanned up and down her body almost not believing what a luscious sight; what a beautiful woman she was. He quickly shed his pants and underwear. She dropped her panties. Now, very wet, breathing deeply, she straddled him, guided his wanting penis into her. She ever, ever so slowly moved her body up and down, up and down, almost teasing herself and Harry. As she felt him swell and throb and as she needed more, she went faster, then faster. Their breathing grew rapid and deep. She moaned. When she felt Harry about to explode, she gave four quick deep thrusts and cried out as they both came together.

The pungent smell of sex filled the room and they slept.

The club, La Zoora y el Cerro, recommended by the Saratoga's concierge, was located downstairs on a non-descript residential street. A couple of typical street guitar player-singers lounged out front. They were hardly expecting to be discovered, but playing, like so many others, their brand of song and rhythm for whoever walked by. The club was known for booking up-and-coming musicians who might, as many had, become major stars. The room was small, with a circular stage in the middle of an intimate circle of about twenty-five tables. Laughter and eye-stinging cigar and cigarette smoke filled the room like fog rolling in from the ocean. The drink of the patrons seemed to be beer, mostly Bucanero Max and Palme Cristal. Harry and Amanda had strong mojitos, with double-shot of white, potent, Cuban rum.

The ten-piece house band, sweaty and spirited, brightly lit with warm stage lights, was just finishing a rousing set of up-tempo Afro-Cuban tunes. They gave way to the next act, Luis Felipe Garcia, a new talent and guitar player was backed up by an acoustic bass, drums and subtle Latin percussion. He sounded a bit like Jim Hall, sparse, bell-like, with unusual chord changes, progressions, and intriguing melody lines. He launched his set with a medium tempo version of "The Song is You" and then settled into a sensuous ballad, "When I Fall in Love."

More than mellow after a couple more mojitos, Amanda kissed Harry hard, and said, "What a neat trip. It's wonderful. I'm so glad you thought of it." She looked Harry in the eyes with love and admiration, and he returned the favor. "In spite of your extraordinary quiver of faults, I love you."

Harry retorted, "Compared to you, I'm flawless," and laughed. Before Amanda could reply, still looking into her eyes, he said, "I want to be with you forever." He slipped the ruby and diamond engagement ring on her finger.

Flustered, breathless, eyes glistening and without hesitation, Amanda said, "Yes, Harry, Yes," and broke into happy tears. She kissed Harry again and again, and put her head into the notch of his shoulder and held him tight as he stroked her hair. "Harry, let's do this right away. We'll have about sixty people—your friends, mine, my family, and a few must-invite dignitaries. How about in a month or so, before it gets outrageously hot?"

"I'd love it. I half expected you to turn me down again."

"Not a chance. I was waiting for a second chance. Let's skip tomorrow and get back. We have plans to make. There'll be plenty of travel time later."

They returned to Grand Cayman the next morning.

CHAPTER THIRTY-SEVEN

A snitch told the cops about one of Zane's trusted top distributors, Roberto. He was yanked off the street and brought into police headquarters. After three hours of intense questioning by Thompson and two other detectives, he was cut loose. They had nothing on him, and they got zip about Zane's operation. Zane would kill him—literally if he thought he'd given him up to the cops. He knew that he would be watched and would be useless on the street after this. Maybe he could stay in the action as part of Zane's militia or be transferred to another island's operation.

Roberto had first been afraid that the police would nail him on a second drug trafficking charge and throw him into Her Majesty's smelly Northward Prison for five years. The prison was next to the island's landfill and held the most hardened criminals on the island. Some said that the pungent smell of damp, sun-drenched steaming diapers, decaying meat, orange rinds, and unidentifiable garbage, was a torture worse than the prison itself. He got lucky.

But, he thought, *Thompson will get on to Zane soon. The fucking shit will hit the fan. Maybe Zane should get off the island and set up a base somewhere else. At any rate, he needed to up the defenses; be more careful. The cops would be looking to hunt everybody down, slug it out.*

Roberto bolted from his car and ran toward Zane's home like the Roadrunner on jungle juice—feet practically off the ground, and spinning up a cloud of dust. Disheveled. Breathing hard, and bush shirt drenched, Roberto stumbled up Zane's front porch stairs and slumped in an armchair opposite Zane.

"Roberto," Zane said, with a puzzled look, "what's the hurry? You look like you've seen a ghost or are sampling your own stuff and fell out of bed on your head. Want some water or a beer?"

"Beer," looking guiltily and dejectedly at his knees. "It's bad, real bad," he stuttered.

Zane brought two Iron Shore Bocks, handing one to Roberto. "Calm down, get it together, tell me what the hell is going on."

Roberto sighed. "We have big-time trouble. Thompson hauled me in for questioning. Three hours worth. Some goddamn snitch fingered me. If I find out who, I'll kill him. To give the bluebottles something to chew on, I gave up George Saunders, the little Colombian turd cutting in on my downtown dealers. Saunders's eating into us too much to let him stay around. A little time in Her Majesty's dump would be good for the little shit and us too. When he gets out maybe he'll have sense enough to carve out his spot outside of our territory. The cops are hell bent for leather to find out who the top dog is on the island, and that's you. Better beef up the troops. Maybe lay low for a while."

"We can't. We have a major load coming in by ship from Cartagena on November 1 and we have to get that into the country and redistribute it. Otherwise, Jamaica, Cuba, Barbados, Trinidad and Tobago, and a lot of the smaller islands will go dry. That's 75 million worth of business. We'll be armed to the teeth and if the Cayman's Special Operations team shows up, we'll make them look like kids with firecrackers."

"Who's working the case?"

"Detective Inspector Thompson. He's the top CID man from London who retired to Cayman and took this job to keep his fingers in the pie. Nasty. A real son-of-a-bitch. Tough questioner. A bulldog. We've had little contact with the guy so don't know more than that. He has a girlfriend. She may be useful in getting our way with him."

"Have both of them followed until we know their patterns well. Then we'll pick a place to grab him. Beat the hell out of him. See what he knows. Find out as much as you can about what Thompson knows about our operation. Leave the girl out of it for now. We'll use her later as a hostage if we can't get the information that we want from Thompson. We'll tell Thompson that we'll release her when we get our questions answered. Come to think forget the kidnaping threat. When you're finished questioning him, feed him to the sharks so there's no evidence left behind. It'll send a message to the cops and anyone else thinking of messing with us to leave us alone."

"Done."

CHAPTER THIRTY-EIGHT

DRUG MASSACRE CONTINUES...16 DEAD
Caymanian Compass Monday 11/11/ 2000

Sixteen people were killed and seven injured during massive explosions at two residences in Georgetown. Two additional victims, George Fairbanks and Sammy Locum, both drug dealers, were assassinated in their sleep in their homes. Their families were left tied-up and gagged but unharmed. Police attribute the carnage to retaliation by an unidentified drug gang for the murder of several street dealers and the destruction of a house two weeks ago that took ten lives. Heavy weapons such as RPGs or small battlefield missiles destroyed the homes.

Inspector Harry Thompson of the Cayman Police Force commented, "We think that the perpetrators were members of a Columbian gang that just started operating in Grand Cayman. They appear to be attempting to take over the territory of an established and dangerous Mexican drug organization. To date, the gang has shown no signs of violence. We are intensively investigating this scourge with little result. This attack may open the door to discovering the higher-ups in both the Mex and Columbian gangs, and their destruction."

"The assassinations were simultaneous with the bombings. The assassins smashed down their target's doors, quickly subdued the occupants, and shot the victims twice in the head with a large caliber weapon."

CHAPTER THIRTY-NINE

The southern lights flashed and swayed, blushed in and out, like an old Wurlitzer coin-operated jukebox. The Antarctic display was spectacular, Brenda thought, as she peered out of the panoramic window of the toasty passenger lounge of the Arctic Explorer. They were cruising in -40 degree weather and 50 miles an hour winds, just off the Larson 2 ice shelf. All she could see was a ceaseless expanse of gray sky and endless white-capped, stomach-roiling water dotted with icebergs, giant and small. Brenda had taken the trip to give her time to think over how and when she would leave Gil and make him pay for all of the grief that he caused her. Whatever method she used, she wanted it to be quick and as painful for Gil as possible. She had to figure out how she would find the money that she was certain that Gil had buried in secret spots somewhere in the world. It should be a princely sum, she thought, not that he was a prince—far from it. And, how much was there? She had to calm down, squelch her murderous emotions and be cool, cold, and collected as she sorted through the mess and developed a strategy.

The elite, 200-foot ship held only twenty passengers—luxurious, fine food, large attentive crew, exceptional guides, and classy, wealthy, passengers. It should be. It was a $15,000 Abercrombie and Kent 12 day tour, and she had the largest suite on the boat. They had hit the "usual" spots, seen the obligatory things. Always present were the magnificent, treacherous icebergs. Backlit, the sun penetrated the ice monsters, turning them into translucent blue and white gems. The bergs had deep blue channels and ridges slashing their face, with splashes of sunlight careening off the edges like the reflections from a fine diamond. All she saw was the tip of the iceberg. Kilotons of ice were under the water. At evening, when the sun no longer played on their surface, the icebergs reminded Brenda of her marriage—underwater, fractured, dark, and the sparkle gone.

The other sights were fascinating to most of the passengers—glaciers, hundreds of Adelie penguins sunning themselves on shore; speedy leopard seals heaving out of the water taking a penguin for lunch; stunning sunsets;

endless fields of intriguing, sometimes beautifully sunlit, sometimes scary, gray-white glaciers. She couldn't imagine the hardship and courage of explorers like Peary and Ross who crossed and mapped part of the continent. She saw orcas and pods of blue whales. Occasionally, there was a magnificent, lone, soaring albatross and flights of amazing Arctic terns migrating from some 20,000 miles away to breed on their home ground.

The scenery and animals were of little interest to Brenda. She took none of the trips to shore to view the flora and fauna, glaciers and animals, close up and personal. She would fly to Grand Cayman on her return, consult a divorce lawyer, and try to pry some information about Gil's money out of Jonathan Brooke. He managed a multi-million dollar account for her. She felt he owed her something for the exorbitant $200,000 fee she paid him each year for his perfunctory services. Then she'd deal with Gil.

Halfway through the trip, the captain asked her to come to the bridge. A tour of the ship she thought. Others had taken the tour and found it interesting, so Brenda decided to go. A little diversion from her dark mood.

When she reached the bridge, the captain asked her to sit down. "Brenda, there's no way to say this except to tell you that your husband was murdered yesterday."

A bolt of emotional lightening braised her body. She put her ashen face in her hands. Her heart beat like a hummingbird's. She was shocked, confused, and surprisingly sad. After a few deep breaths, however, she raised her head and found that she was actually happy. *Rid of the bastard at last,* she thought. *Solves a lot of problems. He's gone. No hassle over the divorce. I get my money now. I should thank the murderer. Probably one of the drug dealers that regularly supplied him. He was always late about paying for his drugs, sometimes so late that the beaners had to send along an "enforcer" to get their money. Maybe an investor who lost his shirt in one of Gil's funds that went bust.* All she could think of was that she was free of Gil, and Pat and Savannah.

The captain interjected, "Please accept my condolences. We'll be back in port in Ushuaia in five days. In the meantime, you have complete use of our communication facilities, and we'll do as much as possible to make the remainder of your trip comfortable. You'll eat at my table from now on. You tell me personally what you need."

"Captain, please get me Charlie Braun on the satellite telephone. 212-445-2020."

"I'll take you to your cabin so you'll have privacy and put the call through to you. Will you be OK alone?"

"Better than you can possibly know."

The phone quietly buzzed, and Brenda abruptly said, "Charlie, what the hell happened?"

"Gil was murdered yesterday in the condo. I am so so sorry."

"Don't spare me the details. I want all of them."

"His throat was cut in the living room. There was nothing stolen as far as we know. It wasn't a break-in. He must have let the murderer in. Likely someone he knew. No suspects. I'm going to keep close to Inspector Harry Thompson—the man who's personally handling the case. How are you holding up, Brenda?"

"Just fine. Ecstatic. Actually, this solves a lot of problems, and you know that. Charlie, get to work on finding the money. We'll be in port in a few days, and I'll let you know when I'll be back in Cayman. I'll call you from time to time to get the latest scoop. Probably be in in a week or so."

"Anything I can do for you?"

"Yes, take care of the funeral. Burn him to a crisp, and have him scattered to the wind over the Black Swamp before I get back to the island. I don't want a vestige of the bastard around. Bye, Charlie." Click.

Brenda asked the captain to get plane reservations for her and retired to the bar for a celebratory bottle of Dom Perignon.

The captain booked a flight for her to Grand Cayman via Miami.

CHAPTER FORTY

Brenda walked into Brook's office, across a rich Persian rug and pulled up a chair in front of an obviously antique and very expensive English carved oak desk.

"Jonathan," she said, "let's get right to it. Gil's dead. I don't care, but I want to know where he's hidden his money and how to get it. His will leaves me a puny $150 million, a couple favorite charities $25 million, and $20 million to his sister, Anne. Anne will be really pissed for getting what she will consider a paltry sum. I suspect that there's a whole lot more out there, and I want it."

"Brenda, what on earth do you need more money for? You have a huge fortune and everything you could possibly want now. What will another house, another household full of servants, another lock-box full of jewels, do for you?"

"I want the money because I want it. I guess you haven't figured out the primordial attraction of money. With me, it's genetic. It's power. It's glorious. I'd like to roll naked in a mountain of it. I'd never have married the jerk and lived with him for thirty years if it wasn't for the money. You figure out where it is and how to get it and I'll figure out what to do with it."

"Where do you think the money came from if not from his hedge fund?" Brooke said.

"I don't know, certainly not from his incessant gambling. On the spur of the moment, he would take his plane, to Las Vegas or Macao, and spend days at the tables. Back room, by invitation only poker was his favorite game and he turned to baccarat when he liked to back off the intensity a bit. He loved taking risks—look at the business he was in—betting billions of other people's money on the stock market and business ventures. He was always a loser at the tables and usually came back a few million poorer. I guess he got as high on gambling adrenaline as he did on booze and coke. Now what the hell are you going to do for me?"

"Brenda, go take care of the funeral arrangements. I don't have a solution for you. Money's hard to trace which is why Grand Cayman is so prosperous. I'll get back to you in a day or so."

"You slimy son of a bitch," Brenda screamed. "I know you're dirty as hell. You'd better come through for me. Fast. If you don't, I'll get the goods on you and sink you to the bottom of the Cayman trench." She plucked a large brass nautical barometer off of a nearby shelf and slammed it on Brooke's desk. The glass faceplate shattered and left a sizable dent in Brooke's precious desk. She glared at Brook and huffed out of the office.

CHAPTER FORTY-ONE

Having been unable to obtain any information about Gil's finances, Brenda turned to Ruth Schneider for help. She wanted a tough, under-the-radar, trustworthy investigator to help her get her money. If anybody could help her find one, Ruth could.

Ruth and her husband Sam, a former Navy diver and underwater photographer, had come to Grand Cayman in the early 1970s, when only the most ardent and knowledgeable divers came to the island. Those were the halcyon days of diving on the island – virgin reefs, a mediocre Holiday Inn and hot bed joint, no stoplights, two cops, and no tourists except hardcore divers. It was a place where three well-known stray dogs would sleep, unperturbed in the middle of West Bay road, and drivers would carefully maneuver around them. Cayman then, was a far cry and decades away from today's overbuilt, over-touristed, cruise-shipped island. Ruth and Sam, a rotund, warm and fuzzy man, opened the first underwater photography store in the Caymans—cameras, instruction, film, and a lot of sassy talk. Ruth ran the business, and Sam, the teaching and technical side.

A sixty-year-old Jewish woman from Queens, Ruth stood about five foot three. She was thin, gray-haired, well wrinkled, continuously scoping the store, like a hawk hunting for prey. She was a smart-as-hell, feisty, and calculating woman, but strangely, given her tough personality, helpful to those that knew her. Her interests, in rank order, were her grandson, her store, and her Caymanian lover, a man she had been with for twenty years and the cause of the breakup of her marriage to Sam. The first thing that she did on seeing a friend or acquaintance, or even a stranger, was show them the latest handful of pictures of her six-year-old grandson. She would tell grandmotherly stories of the funny things that he did and how he was going to be a famous surgeon. She was infinitely curious about people and knew just about anything and everything about the island and everyone on it. Little of importance went unnoticed by Ruth. When she and Sam split in the mid 80s, and he returned to the States, she dumped the unprofitable photo business and started "T" shirt stores in two of the large resort condominiums that had recently been built.

As tourism grew, the stores became very successful, and she, a serial entrepreneur, used her earnings and her great love of books to establish the island's first large, full-service bookstore. She stocked everything from children's books to classics to best sellers, and the store became a focal point for intellectuals, tourists, and residents. She also ran reading circles for children and sponsored readings and book signings for local and visiting authors. Ruth was also a font of information—news, gossip, whispered secrets. She traded story for story, confidence for confidence, inside information for profitable tips about people and island commerce.

The laws of the land required her to have a Caymanian partner owning at least 49% of the business. She found one in Clifford Pryce, an influential lawyer in Caymanian practice, who became her silent, uninvolved partner. As a result of her business and Clifford, there were few influential people that she didn't have access to.

Ruth immediately recognized Brenda when she walked in the door and came out from behind the cash register to give her a hug.

"Brenda. How horrible. I was so sorry to hear about Gil. Do they know what happened, who did it?"

" No one has a clue. I understand that the murder was bloody and brutal. I'm sorry that Gil is dead, no one deserves that, but I really don't give a damn. The marriage was on the rocks and it was just a matter of who filed for divorce first. But frankly, Ruth, I need your help in figuring out the mess that Gil left our affairs in. He never told me anything about his money and business. I think that a lot of the stuff that he did was not on the up and up. I'm completely in the dark and mad as hell. I had a telephone conversation with Inspector Thompson, the CID man. on the case, and a meeting with Jonathan Brooke, Gil's local lawyer and finance man who did God-knows-what for him. They would not give me the inventory because the police wanted no more meddling in he case. I think that's bullshit. They were about as useful as a plugged up toilet."

A list indicated that there were gems that they didn't find in the first search of the condo and safe deposit boxes. The cops did an all-out second inventory. They tore the place apart—ripped out the walls and ceiling, pulled up the floorboards, destroyed the furniture, and left the appliances in heaps of torn metal. Nothing turned up but an open metal lockbox next to Gil's desk that wasn't there at during the first search. They also found a empty secret compartment in the desk. They suspect that the box was in the compartment. They're sure that someone had been in the place and riffled it for the jewels. The obvious suspects were Savannah and Pat who had a key to the condo, but disappeared off the radar."

"Just say the word and you know I'll help any way that I can. Let me show you Simon's pictures. Isn't he a handsome little kid?"

Brenda quickly said the expected oohs and aahs. "Let's go into your office. This is something I want to discuss away from the public's ears."

They squeezed into Ruth's office. It was the size of a small broom closet and cluttered with papers, stacked books, the usual computer, scanner, phones, fax machine, copier, and two tiny chairs. Brenda and Ruth had to sit knee to knee when the door was closed.

"So, tell me already," Ruth said.

Brenda continued: "I've been stiffed. Gil's estate lawyer, a man called Charlie Braun, told me little. He claims that he knows nothing about Gil's money. I'm sure that he's lying. I'm certain that my dear departed spouse had a lot of money salted away in some numbered bank accounts in Cayman and other countries. There are undoubtedly a lot of off-the-books real estate and business ventures somewhere. I just came from a meeting with Jonathan Brooke, Gil's lawyer and financial adviser. He was 'Gil's boy' and told me squat. He doesn't particularly like me—probably for good reason, because I detest him. Basically a haughty legal asshole. Bottom line: I want Gil's money and will stop at nothing to find it. Brooke and Braun were about as useful as a stuffed up toilet."

"I know just the man. Peter Lopez. He's half Caymanian, half Cuban. But you have to be very, very careful with him. He keeps a low profile, is tough, and not beyond pushing the law to get what he wants. The police know him, of course. But he's always been able to toss them a few tidbits of valuable information so that they overlook his little excesses and help him a bit. In short, he's very good, but is always walking the thin line between the legal and illegal."

"How do I get in touch?"

"I'll arrange it. Where are you staying?"

"Eunice's Bed and Breakfast. Off the beaten track. No one will see me there."

"How about I arrange a meeting today?"

"Ok by me. Anytime."

Ruth, dialed, waited a moment until the phone was picked up and said: "Peter, I have a potential client for you. Very classy. Can pay your ridiculous rates. Can you meet her at 2 at Eunice's? She's an important woman and an old friend. I can vouch for her. Known her for twenty years.

"Thanks, she'll be there. I owe you one."

Ruth hung up the phone: "You heard the conversation. You're all set."

CHAPTER FORTY-TWO

*B*usiness *sucks.* Lopez thought. *The goddamn, screwed up, hands-in-pockets government. Trying to save money. Chopped off my business with them. And the who's-screwing-who marital stuff and corporate racket is tanking too. Perfect storm.* He snuffed his cigarette in a stone-cold cup of oily coffee, already floating with dead butts, and called to his secretary-assistant, all around pain-in-the-ass sister, Jessica.

"Get me another cup of coffee!"

"Fuck off, Peter," she said, momentarily pausing "Grand Theft Auto III" on her Xbox. "Get your own damn coffee. And, by the way, you still owe me a month's salary. I'm not your slave."

"Yeah, yeah. I know. Next case you get paid first."

"I've heard that before. By the way, Ruth called. Some broad named Brenda wants to see you at 10 at Eunice's B&B. Apparently this is a big hush-hush deal, so keep your head low. I said yes because your calendar is practically blank for the whole month."

Peter grumbled, put down his paper, squeaked his dirty white-sneakered feet off his desk, heaved himself out of his wobbly office chair, tripped over a dying miniature palm, shuffled into the outer office, and gave Jess the finger. She returned the favor. He got his own hours-old, acrid coffee.

Peter, a round-faced, balding, medium height, a few-pounds-too-many, Cuban-American, came to Grand Cayman from Miami. His grandfather, Francisco Lopez, and grandmother were trapped by the Castro revolution in Cuba in 1959. They were vehemently anti-communist and escaped to the US on one of those rickety boats cobbled together to make the treacherous ninety mile trip to Key West. Detained by US authorities, the couple was eventually released and given asylum under a general amnesty granted to Cuban escapees by President Kennedy.

Francisco Lopez had owned a clothing store in Cuba, but had to walk away from his store, house, and savings to get out of the country, leaving him impoverished. In Miami, he found work as a salesman in a shoe store in the large and growing Cuban community. The job paid enough money to feed and clothe his family of four, but with little left over for luxuries. A night out at the movies with popcorn and coke was a big deal.

Peter's father Alejandro Lopez became a cop and married a reasonably prosperous American real estate agent. Peter wanted to follow in his father's footsteps and become a policeman too. He attended the Miami Dade School of Criminal Justice. Following graduation from the Police Academy, he started as a street cop on the Miami Police Force. Peter moved up quickly to become a major crimes Detective and led the investigations of some of the toughest, hardest-to-solve murder and drug cases in the city's history. He became a master at working with state authorities and the FBI on inter-state cases.

Lopez solved more murder cases than anyone in the department's history. For this he received a commendation from the mayor, and added that to the bundle of honors that preceded it. He was promoted to lieutenant.

At forty-three, Lopez was still a bachelor and restless. After twenty years on the Miami force, he had earned his pension and figured that he could pretty much do what he wanted: start a new life. Looking for a quieter place to live and play but still within reach of his Miami family, he answered an ad for a Spanish-speaking detective for the Royal Cayman Islands Police. Apparently they were short of trained detectives and a Spanish-speaking officer would be a great asset given the number of Hispanics visiting and settling on the island.

After a decade of working in Grand Cayman for an inept, self-aggrandizing boss that he called a "rat-faced buffoon" behind his back, Peter decided to become a private investigator. He'd investigated plenty of major crime cases in Miami and Grand Cayman. He therefore knew the local culture and people inside and outside of the government, which he needed to know to run a tidy little under-the-radar business. He got his start by taking outsourced investigations for the Caymanian Government—mainly finding people suspected of financial fraud, and consulting with the department on major and difficult cases. Of course he was not beyond taking any other business he could pick up. All he had now was a couple of adultery cases—the usual surveillance work that wasn't even interesting anymore.

Once he'd planted a few video cameras, shot a few stills of lovers in various settings and physically improbable positions, and recorded the heavy breathing and sweet nothings, his voyeur's thrill, and the adventure of the chase, was gone. Besides, dealing with vengeful husbands and wives—the crying and histrionics, the murderous thoughts, the handholding, their disbelief, was tiresome. Same-old, same-old. Guy meets gal. Gal meets guy. Pheromones, booze, coke, or just plain vanilla lust sweeps them off their feet and into bed. Promises of wealth; adventure; happiness; a new, exciting life thereafter. Mostly short-lived after the injured mate finds out. Typical routine—find the beds, the 'secret spots' for assignations, take photos, document the venture. Hairy reconciliation or divorce. Finding the beds was simple. Just follow the steamy, starry-eyed couple. A few days of collecting the evidence and he was done. Got paid. Mostly up front. Then out of the picture. Not big money deals, nobody shooting at him, but pretty good petty cash.

Peter, dressed in his usual jeans, sneakers, rumpled safari shirt, round-framed tortoise- shell English glasses, and Panama hat, walked into the sitting room at Eunice's. He was greeted by a stunningly attractive, slender, auburn-haired woman, dressed in expensive casual slacks, a silk blouse, minimalist jewelry, and designer sunglasses.

Big bucks, he thought. *Nice body. Very delectable. Reminds me of a sultry hot fudge sundae with nuts, rum, whipped cream, and a cherry on top. She can pay big. Unless she's one of those rich-bitch tightwads I occasionally get in the find-out-who-my-husband-is-fucking business. And wants a platinum job for a 'tin bracelet price'*

She stood up and introduced herself. "Peter, I'm Brenda Baxter. And I have a big problem. Ruth Schneider recommended you, and her endorsement is good enough for me. She told me all about you. We can skip the preliminaries, so let's get to the point. I need to find out how much money and property my dead husband has hidden, where it is, and how to get my hands on it."

Brenda filled Peter in on the whole story from marital strife, to Gil's murder, to being stiffed by Thompson and Charlie Braun when she tried to get Gil's financial information. She concluded, "The key to the money puzzle is Jonathan Brooke. He handled a lot of Gil's business affairs. I'm sure he knows where the money is and what I want is all of it.

"Whew." Peter emphatically exhaled, slumping slightly, and said in a sarcastic tone, "You want me to find the secret accounts and how to get into them? That's about as hard as getting a peg-leg sailor to rap dance on a high wire. Well, I want to start with Brooke."

"What good is it going to do you? He's not going to give you a thing"

"It's always important to talk to a key player. I want to size him up. I need to know anything I can see, hear, smell, and touch—what he looks like, how he walks and holds himself, thinks, his mannerisms, his office layout, what kind of people he employs and what they claim to do as a firm. You never know what you'll find out that will be useful later. Sometimes people say things that they think are unimportant but really are. It would be nice if he just handed me a spreadsheet with all of the bank names and account numbers. Unlikely. The information is buried deep somewhere. Probably on a computer with the data encrypted. However, most people keep a written record somewhere in case their computers have a fatal crash."

"Well, I'll set you up. At least Brooke will have to see you. After all, he handles a ton of money that Gil gave to me, and I pay him megabucks in fees. It won't hurt him to know that I've hired a PI to work on Gil's case. So what else?"

"I'll talk to the police about your husband's murder. Find out what they know; if they know about the money motive, have any suspects. My buddies will keep me informed as the investigation goes along. I'll talk to some close friends in the government, banking and financial fraud sections and approach some contacts in the big banks, and financial firms. Again, unlikely that I'll find out much, but I'll at least find out about Brooke and what his legitimate business is all about. "Then I go where the clues lead me."

"OK. Your fees?"

Figuring that he could make a lot more from Brenda than his usual $1,200 a day, he said, "$2,000 a day plus expenses with a $20,000 retainer. The hooker is," he said, "There may be additional 'fees.' Some of my information sources may cost you—say, $10-20,000. Without the fees we won't get very far."

"Done. What's your first step, and how soon will you report back to me?"

"Give me four days and I'll have a preliminary report for you and a game plan."

"Don't fuck this up. There's a $25,000 bonus if you lead me to the money."

Lopez stopped breathing for a second while the penny dropped. *Holy shit*, Lopez thought, trying not to appear too wide-eyed. *I can buy the Mercedes with that down payment.*

"Ciao," she said as she turned on her heels and sashayed out of the room.

Peter admired the rear view…and the prospects of the money even more. *Now to snooker Brooke.*

CHAPTER FORTY-THREE

The cellphone call came minutes after the butchery dealt by Zane's army to Perez's troops. Perez picked up on the first ring. *It can't be good news.* He heard the distant crackling sounds of fire, the scream of sirens, the yells of first responders, and the pleas for help from his wounded men. The panting, angry, almost screaming voice of Diego, Perez's enforcer, blared through the speaker.

"Man, the Burrito gang just took out our safe-house. Rocket propelled grenade. The place is destroyed. Rodriguez, Gomez and Martinez are dead. They hauled Jolice off to the hospital. Rest escaped. Couldn't do a thing."

"Where are you now?" Diego said

"In the SUV about half a block away. "

"Are you ok?"

"Yes, but what do you want me to do?"

Cold as an ice cube, Perez went silent and thought about his people and options.

"Who survived?"

"Cristiano, Julian and Ricardo."

"Get as many men as you can on the streets now. Well-armed. Protect what we've just won. Gonzalez's people will go hell-bent-for-leather to take back their territory now that we're weakened. The cops will be on a full-scale campaign to run us off the street. Watch out for the cops, but get us back in business."

"Isn't that risky? Won't the fuzz hand us our heads? Shouldn't we lay low?"

"Don't be so stupid, man. Think. That's what I supposedly pay you for. I told you, if we show weakness, the Gonzalez's gang will be all over us like maggot on a rotting body. We may lose a few more people. So be it. There are lots more where they come from."

Worried, Diego said, "Hombre, you sure you wanna do this? We're probably outnumbered and out-gunned."

"Go now."

Perez thought for a minute. *We need to hold our ground and prepare for all-out war or we're going to fucking lose this island. I have to get more troops and arms, much less explain to the boss, how I let this happen. Our street spies should have known about this or our sentries should have seen the raid coming. How the hell they found out where our headquarters was, I don't know. Snitch maybe? Followed some of the gang? Mole? Not much you can do when a truck with an RPG pulls up and lets you have it. The security system sucks. We'll relocate and split operations between a couple of places.*

Perez and Ana left Roberts Field for Caracas on a private executive jet an hour after the explosion. He was going to consult with his boss, Higgins, and then prepare for the next war.

CHAPTER FORTY-FOUR

The wind was a cruel gale force at 40 miles per hour with bursts to 75. Twenty-foot waves broke and careened over the bows of the twin-hulled eighty-foot catamaran, sloshing over the deck, and inundating skipper Santiago with blinding sheets of water. He was clipped to a lifeline, his feet planted on the stern deck. He and another crewman wrestled, white-knuckled, with the slippery wheel, attempting to keep the boat on course. Three others, armed muscle, were below deck fighting seasickness. The boat practically skied down the side of the waves into the trough like an Olympic downhill skier. The windward hull was so far out of he water that it felt as if the boat would capsize any second. He was making a blistering 40 mph on a tight reach and had to keep this course and speed to make his 0200 rendezvous at Grand Cayman. He had only an hour and a half window with which to unload and put back to sea.

The hulls of the smuggling boat were modeled after America's Cup yachts, but much more stable. It was equipped with two rigid, movable, computer controlled aircraft-like wings instead of a sails. The main wing was as big as that of a 747, making it one of the fastest and most maneuverable sailboats in the world. The angle of the main wing and the smaller jib-wing, and the space between them, determined the boat's speed and direction. The sails were trimmed for maximum speed even though that made the boat unstable and hard to control. The hooded control panel in front of the steering wheel housed the latest navigation, radar, communication gear, and boat management systems. The twenty-five million dollar rocket looked, as was intended, like another moneyed man's toy. It was equipped with buttery leather furniture in the salon, mahogany paneled staterooms, small "gourmet" galley, teak deck, and shiny brass fittings. Each hull was double walled so that drugs could be stashed inside them in virtually undetectable compartments.

The yacht carried Caymanian registry and had white hulls with a thin gold stripe running from stem to stern. Ironically, and with Gonzales' brazen tongue in cheek, the name "Smuggler" was emblazoned in gold script on the transom. If spotted during the day, the authorities would be likely to pass it off as another of South America's "rich, rich" on a cruise. Smugglers don't usually use sailboats. To avoid detection by radar, the craft's hulls and wings were constructed of military-grade, stealth carbon fiber, the same as used on the Air Force's F22A Raptor. The position of the wings was computer controlled, allowing the sails to be trimmed for maximum speed and help hold the catamaran on course.

Jason Whitney was Jonathan Brooke's co-conspirator. He was English and a lawyer in his mid-forties, who had settled in Grand Cayman a decade ago. Brooke took Whitney on as a "regular" lawyer and he was soon corrupted by the substantial money that Brooke offered if he would "cut corners a bit." He loved cutting corners and handling the money even more. He did the "dirty work", transferring funds and making sure that smuggled drugs were safely landed and handed over to Zane's people for storage and distribution.

Whitney yelled to his assistant and co-conspirator, Alice, who was in the outer office: " Radio the yacht that we'll be waiting for them in the inflatable at Foster's cove. It's a good protected and remote area where the water is rough, and the reef passage difficult enough to discourage other traffic. They should anchor just outside the reef and signal us by flashing their mast light three times. Then we'll go out and pick up the cargo. The wind is heavy and the seas around 4 feet inshore--not the best night for our purposes, but we'll deal with it. Quick in and out. Tell them not to worry about the harbor patrol. I've arranged for them to be on the east side of the Island from 0100 to dawn. Alice, I want you to go with me. I'm taking Roberto and two of his men, who will be well armed. We'll move the cargo to Zane's boat at Rum Point. Zane will meet us there and we'll split out the Jamaican gang's share of the coke, which Zane will take to the waiting Jamaican "go-fast". They'll take off post-haste to the north shore of Jamaica."

"What's in it for us this time?" Alice said.

"The take is big money—$50,000,000 on the street in New York and the cost is only $4,000,000, delivered. My commission is $5,000,000. As usual, Jonathan gets seventy percent of the commission, I get thirty, and you get your normal $20,000 bonus. We don't want to miss a beat on this one. Plus, there's $20,000,000 in cash to launder." With a wry and cynical look on his face Whitney said: "We'll skim our usual cut for a bit of additional spending money just for you and me." With my creative accounting, they'll never know the difference"

Alice picked up the radio receiver and tuned it to the boat's frequency for an encrypted conversation. There was a beep and squawk-crackle of storm interference that sounded like the opening screech from an ancient AOL Internet connection.

"White horse to dark horse, do you copy?"

"Dark horse to white horse. Copy"

"What is your position and ETA?"

"We're about a hundred miles out and on course. Gusts up to 75 now. Barely in control. We've had to slow down to 35 mph to keep upright. It looks like a late ETA of 0230 now. How's the weather there?"

"Weather radar shows the gale breaking about twenty miles in from your current position. Forecast here is 30 mph wind gusting to 45 and five to seven foot seas. Should be calmer sailing for you shortly. You're going to hit the same gale force winds again on your way back to Columbia. The front's about a hundred miles wide."

"Merida. Thanks lot Alice"

"Confirming destination coordinate are: 19.333°N—81.2167°W. You've been there before. Anchor well outside the reef. It's treacherous, particularly in high seas like you're experiencing now. You can be blown into the reef fast. Do you read me dark horse?"

" Affirmative white horse."

"Expect you at 0230, Keep us posted. I suppose you don't want us to have the Coast Guard escort you in do you?" she said with a smile and a sarcastic lilt to her voice.

Usted punde meterio, sexy. Over and out."

Whitney moved to Grand Cayman ten years ago. He had answered an ad in London's "*Legalweek*" asking for an attorney with experience in financial law and willing to live in Grand Cayman. It was an ideal opportunity for him. He was basically unemployable in

England. It seems that his prior firm had used some client escrow funds for their own purposes and Whitney got a minor piece of the action. His partners took the rap for the scheme. Whitney escaped prosecution by testifying against them and his reputation was forever tainted. Brooke, knowing his background and thinking "once a felon, always a felon," eased Whitney into the real business of the firm—money laundering and handling some drug shipments. Zane preferred leaving the detail and dirty work to Brooke's firm. Whitney would also handle legitimate business that served as a front for the firm--applications for residency, wills and estates, divorces, large bank accounts, and the affairs of corporate offshore banking. From Whitney's point of view it was an ideal fit. Besides, he wanted to get away from London's miserable weather and he, an expert diver, could dive to his heart's content.

Santiago felt the lessening of the wind, though the seas were still very high. He checked his instruments. The wind was westerly at a blustery 25 mph, the "Smuggler" making an easy thirty. The island was the truncated tip of a volcano that sloped down from he beach to 120 feet at about a quarter mile from shore, then dropped down precipitously into the 26,000 foot Cayman Trench--for all practical purposes into infinity. The depth finder showed only occasional pelagic fish, likely tuna, marlin or wahoo, but no bottom. As he approached the Island, he knew that the bottom would instantly jump up on the scope. He would have little time to slow the boat to avoid hitting the reef and find a spot outside of the inlet to rendezvous with the pickup boat.

"Dark horse to White horse"

"Copy dark horse"

"We've just cleared the storm front and the sea's dropping. I expect to make the reef and be anchored by 0240 just west of the breach in the reef. Aircraft radar shows no bogies. Surface radar nothing but the island. Any bogies on shore?"

"No, 'Smuggler'. Who the hell would want to be out on a night like this? Lousy weather; good night for us. We're ready for pickup. Four men will be waiting to unload the merchandise into the inflatable and there are two onshore vehicles for transfer, and two for diversion in case there are cops or nosey islanders around."

"Keep you posted. Over and out"

Santiago intended to anchor the boat in about 40 feet of water. He would run up to about 200 feet of the breach in the reef, and turn the boat directly into the wind to stop it dead in its tracks. He would then throw out an anchor, and signal that they were moored. They should be able to get the cargo unloaded in about half an hour, and be on their way. That quick, and supposedly that simple. A classic drop.

Santiago watched the depth finder. It suddenly jumped to 120 feet and he could see the furious waves breaking on the reef and throwing water in the air like a geyser. He began laying off the wings, slowing the boat down to 20 knots, and readied the crew for anchoring and unloading. The numbers on the depth finder began to spin like a slot machine, decreasing quickly to 200, 100, 70, 60, 50, 40 feet. Santiago yanked the wheel to starboard, pointed the boat into the wind, and dropped anchor a hundred feet from the reef.

There was a sharp, loud, bang-whine, like that of a high-power rifle. Santiago flinched. The steering wheel spun like a roulette wheel. The cable from the wheel to the rudder had snapped. The boat lost steerage and was uncontrollable. Santiago desperately tried to pull the emergency tiller from its compartment under the deck. The compartment jammed. The boat sped at 30 knots straight toward the reef.

There was a sickening crash. The two bows hit the unforgiving reef. The fiberglass shattered. Chunks and small pieces of the once proud yacht fall into the sea. The waves and wind quickly pushed the starboard hull under the water, beginning its fatal battle with the sea. The wings, now tipping toward the reef, push the hull further down into the water. Seawater poured into both hulls and the boat slides forward preparing for its final slide into the sea. Santiago told the crew to get the two lifeboats inflated, in the water and into shore as quickly as possible. Santiago and half the crew got away in the stern life raft, and were able to start their engine, and fight their way to the cut in the reef toward shore. The other raft was not so fortunate. Two of the four crewmen, attempting to board during the drenching confusion, fell in the water. They were eaten by the surf and bashed against the reef. The remaining crew eventually struggled to shore in the two rafts.

Whitney assessed the damage with Santiago and radioed Zane saying:

"I've got bad news. The Smuggler hit the reef and sank. We lost two men, and the cargo is in about 50 feet of water."

"Jesus Christ almighty, motherfucking son of bitch. What did those imbeciles do?" Zane asked, throwing a lamp to the floor; smashing it into bits. "Where the fuck is Santiago?"

"Here He's damn near catatonic."

"Tie him up and get the bastard over to me. Now. I want to get to the bottom of this. He has sailed and maybe lived his last"

"Yessir"

"One more thing. I damn well mean ASAP. Remove any traces of our presence. Be sure to rub out tire tracks in the dirt. We're abandoning the drugs. No time to recover any before dawn. Get the crew over to the North Side mangrove dock, and see that a go-fast boat gets them back to Columbia. Move, move, move!"

"Shit," Jason says to Alice, "we lost our commission and our 'skim'. But there'll be another day...soon."

CHAPTER FORTY-FIVE

There were no lights on in Branford House where Brooke's office was located. Lopez thought and hoped that no one would be there at three in the morning. Dressed in black, he parked his car in the pitch-dark parking lot behind the building and listened. No sounds--only the occasional car on West Bay Road. Probably revelers after closing down one of the island's after-hours joints. Satisfied that the place was unoccupied, he casually walked from his car to the corner of the building where the phone and cable lines entered the basement. He noiselessly put his backpack of tools on the ground and pulled on latex gloves.

Lopez was about to remove his tools when he thought he heard faint footfalls. He went silent and listened again. The person was coming closer. Lopez stopped breathing for a moment and tensed. Goddammit, there's a night watchman. This is all I need. He took a lead shot filled sap from his kit and flattened himself against the wall. The steps came slowly at a shuffling pace. Probably drunk, he thought. The man rounded the corner. There was a sharp crack, like a bullwhip hitting its target, when the sap connected with the side of the man's head. He collapsed to the ground, unconscious. Looking at his handiwork, he thought, *Stupid fake cop uniform these "rent-a-cops" wear. Dumb asses; trying to look like the real thing—big phone on hips, arm patch, small satchel on their belt that appears to be a gun. Pathetic.* Lopez made short work of the man, gagging him and tying his hands and feet together with his ever-handy duct tape.

Lopez quickly turned to the work at hand. He cut the phone and Internet cables to the offices, slicing off burglar alarm signals to the police. *Fools*, he concluded, *anyone with any sense would bury the cables so that the alarm to the police couldn't be disabled.*

Brook's office was exactly where he remembered it to be—on the left corner of the back wall and on the ground floor. He would go in through the large window. Like all of those on the ground floor, the window was fitted with thick safety glass, set into a staunch metal frame, and supposedly burglarproof.

Not so, Lopez knew. He could easily remove the pane. Taking a large-handled suction cup and diamond wheel glasscutter out of his backpack, he attached the cup to the window so that the pane would not crash to the ground when cut out. The glasscutter sounded like the faint crunching of rolling tires on frozen snow as he traced around the edge of the rectangular window. As he finished, the plate broke free; the suction cup lost its grip, and the glass plate crashed to the ground with a loud clank, almost like a garbage can lid hitting concrete. *Christ,* Lopez thought. *A lot of noise and already behind schedule. Risky.* He pulled his night-vision goggles from his backpack, strapped the device over his eyes, and switched them on. He scanned the interior. It was like looking through a green-gray haze, like fog lit by a green neon sign. But the objects in the room were crisply outlined and details visible.

There was little in the room: Brooke's desk, chair, a non-descript, fake Oriental rug, one file cabinet, two bookshelves, and a desktop computer. He tossed the desk first, strewing papers on the floor. There was nothing of interest--routine company correspondence, personal notes from people, and social invitations. There was the usual collection of paper clips, pens, purchase receipts, and detritus that's found in anyone's desk. He removed the hard drive from the computer for later examination.

Lopez pulled all of the books off the shelf and rifled their pages. He tore the paper off backs of pictures to see if anything was pasted there, or a safe hidden behind them. Nothing. He examined the walls for secret compartments. He rolled up the rug to see if there was a concealed hiding place under the floor. Again, nothing.

The formidable fireproof file cabinet was more interesting. It was made of heavy gage steel and had a supposedly unbreakable industrial-strength combination lock. A challenge, but not impossible. Peter took a Voight-Johnson autodialer from his tool kit, attached it to the lock, turned it on, and let the small specialized computer go through tens of thousands of cycles until it displayed the lock combination on its LED display. He carefully opened the drawer and ransacked the files, throwing useless ones on the floor. There was a printout summarizing the status of each of Brooke's dozen clients. Brenda's was there and he took it. Nothing in the files to do with any secret accounts. Nothing to do with Gil.

On his way back to the window, Peter noticed a picture on a wall that he had missed in his search. It was of a moored yacht preparing to sail. Brooke and his wife were on board with a number of people he couldn't identify. Nice party. Likely Brooke's yacht. He was known for his luxurious tastes and lavish spending. The name, "Hedge Me Baby," was on the transom. *What a place to hide stuff. Has to be moored with all of the luxury boats, close to Rum Point near the deep-water channel in the North Wall. I'll check it out.*

Lopez crawled out of the window, walked back to his car, and headed home.

CHAPTER FORTY-SIX

There are maybe two degrees of separation between residents of Grand Cayman. Everyone knows everyone else, or at least knows someone who knows someone. And Lopez was no exception. As soon as he arrived on the island some ten years ago, he quickly made a lot of friends, including Sam Witt, the bartender at the Lone Star Café. Witt liked Lopez's frequent patronage, gift for gab, and iconoclastic sense of humor. Of course, being a bartender, he knew just about everything that was going on, and everybody who was doing it.

Lopez sauntered into the Lone Star dressed in his casual, trolling, don't-mess-with-me outfit: black cowboy hat, black Ralph Lauren polo shirt, black AG designer jeans, black hand-tooled Tony Lama boots, dark Ray-bans and a thirsty look. He scanned the bar for entertainment prospects for the evening but found only a couple of frumpy women that looked like retired schoolteachers thinking they were in paradise. Not the blond of his dreams that he had been searching for most of his life. Not even the promise of a good time and a guiltless thrash on the beach. *So, move on*, he thought. *So much for adding a little heat to the beach tonight.*

Lopez sidled up to the bar and slapped the slick, varnished mahogany surface twice with his hand to get Witt's attention. Witt gave him a whimsical "Christ, here we go again look" and said,

"What'll it be, Iron Shore Bok?"

"No, a Jameson's on the rocks. I'm feeling pretty Irish tonight. Can't you tell by brogue?"

Lopez, a few blond and tourist jokes, Lopez asked, "Who can give me the poop on the yacht 'Hedge Me Baby'? It probably sails out of the North End."

"Why, you thinking of chartering it?" Witt said with raised eyebrows and a "come off it" smile.

"Sure asshole, I'm going to take a hundred of my closest friends on a booze cruise, but you're not invited."

"Why not?"

"It's only for the upper crust. The island's most beautiful people. Did you look in a mirror lately?"

"Okay, wiseass, we can brutalize each other later. So what do you need to know?"

"As much as I can get. First, who owns it? I think it's Jonathan Brooke, but I need to confirm that. Where's it moored? When's it usually taken out? Who's normally on board? Who's the skipper? The whole nine yards."

"Whoa, this sounds like pretty serious stuff. What kind of trouble has Brooke gotten himself into to warrant a PI?"

"Can't say. You know, detective-client privilege. But I can tell you this, he lied. It's about who's playing hanky panky with whose wife. You know my drill. Follow 'em, photograph 'em in the act, give the offended victim the pictures, watch the fur fly, collect the rest of my money and disappear."

Witt leaned over the bar, conspiratorially cupped both hands over Lopez's left ear and stage whispered: "Have I got a deal for you. It'll cost you a date with your sister, but I'll really make it worth her while. Trust me. You will make that happen, won't you?"

"Horseshit, Jessica doesn't date worn-out senior citizens with tobacco-drizzled beards."

"Okay, you'll owe me one. I have a name for you. My cousin, Alden Witt, is dockmaster at the Rum Point Marina. Been there for years. The man is a treasure trove of information. He can tell you just about anything you want to know. He's a bit of a talker. He'll ramble on and on about anything and tell you lots of stuff you could care less about. But he's reliable. Just buy him a couple of beers, and he'll tell all. I'll call him and tell him that you're a slimy old taco, but a good man all the same."

CHAPTER FORTY-SEVEN

"The Plastered Puffer," an overpriced tourist trap at Rum Point, looked more Hawaiian than Cayman. Tiki torches belching black Kerosene smoke lined the crushed coral pathways. The comely, young, barefoot waitresses wore flowered South Pacific sarongs with skimpy halter-tops and a red hibiscus over an ear. The drink menu featured lethal rum drinks made with a combination of fruit juices, sugar, and unnamed spices. Cute, little colored umbrellas topped the drinks, and the stirring sticks featured a tacky cutthroat pirate's face. Their specialty was the "Cayman Crash," a rum, vodka, and grappa fruit punch that could burn in a Tiki lamp in a pinch.

Lopez scanned the crowd. He expected to find the stereotypical dockhand—wizened, sun-wrinkled, and wily, sitting back and cynically viewing the passing, or in this case, sitting scene. Dockhands were usually semi-retired older men who earned a so-so living, docking, cleaning, fueling, and provisioning boats. They were often former island-to-island drifters, aged-out divemasters, or sea and boat lovers whose ship had never come in.

A man saluted him from a small table at the corner of the patio next to beach and away from the crowded and noisy bar. Lopez squeezed through a raft of tightly packed tables and shook the man's hand.

"I'm Peter Lopez."

"I know, you're the only Tex-Mex something-or-other in the place."

"And you're Captain Crunch?"

Alden Witt laughed. "I think we're going to get along just fine."

Alden did not look like the typical dockhand that Lopez had in mind. He had a handsome Kirk Douglas face, complete with thrust out and dimpled chin. His intelligent, quizzical, and confident eyes, locked on Lopez's for a moment. He had white skin rings around his eyes, obviously from constant use of sunglasses on the sun-splashed docks and boats. What was really surprising was his body. He wore a sleeveless "muscle shirt" and shorts that displayed his heavily muscled anatomy. He took pride in his body and worked out frequently. Alden had a large anchor and coiled anchor chain tattooed on one arm, and a large rooster on the other. The rooster, Lopez knew, was a centuries-old totem of sailors who believed that the tattoo of a rooster would help save them from drowning if their ship went down. Ancient mariners believed that chickens usually survived a shipwreck when men did not. There was no substantive evidence to support this, of course. A drowned chicken is a drowned chicken, but the superstition and practice survived until the era of sail ended…and for few, never.

Lopez sat down. They ordered a couple of beers. Alden and Lopez were shortly inundated by "no-see-ums," those tiny, black beach flies that bite, creating an instant rash and itch. Fighting a predictably losing battle, they swatted at the invaders for a while before getting some Deet bug spray from Alden's bartender buddy. Asked why he liked such a dump, Alden laughed and said, "My brother-in-law owns it."

"I understand that you want info about 'Hedge Me Baby.' Wadda you want."

"Everything. Let's start with who owns it and where is it kept?"

"Well, a 'piece of work' called Jonathan Brooke owns it. It's been based in North Sound for about five years. I see a lot of boats and a lot of people, so I'm a pretty good judge of character. I know with certainty that Brooke is a secretive, slimy, arrogant bastard. He treats dock personnel like shit. Doesn't tip and demands a lot."

"Where's the boat moored?"

"In a secluded cove about half a mile southwest of Rum Point near the mangrove swamps. He changes its location from time to time, but I'm pretty sure that that's where it is now."

"How does he get to it?"

"He keeps a motor launch at the marina for transporting passengers to and from the vessel."

"How often is it used?"

"A lot--almost every weekend but occasionally out for 7-10 days—long enough for a round trip to Jamaica or Venezuela."

"Who takes care of the boat?"

"A friend of mine provisions it with cases of champagne, tins of caviar, and the usual assortment of steaks, lobster, and fish. He's paid to clean the vessel, keep it fueled, act as a crewman on occasion, and keep his mouth shut. There is always a healthy party crowd aboard, but they are secretive about where they are headed and when they will be back."

"Brooke sail it himself?"

"No, he has a crew of three including a very young Swedish beauty as cook. She parades around braless in a tight, thin "T" shirt. Worth a visit if you're in the area when she's ashore," Alden said smiling.

Alden and Lopez had a few more beers, talked local politics and the available female population and called it a night.

Lopez decided that he would go "yachting" the next night.

CHAPTER FORTY-EIGHT

Dressed in his black "visiting clothes," Peter Lopez sat quietly in his small, stolen Zodiac by the edge of the black mangroves lining the shore opposite the "Hedge Me Baby." There was some light from a quarter moon but Lopez was, for all practical purposes, invisible. Nudged by the wind and light swells, the boat swung lazily on a narrow arc from its anchor line. The white hull was barely visible in the thin light. It looked like the slice of moon over it, floating on black velvet. But Lopez watched the boat for half an hour with his 7x50 large-aperture Zeiss binoculars. There were no lights on the boat. There was no movement. Maybe there was someone sleeping on board. If so, he'd just have to be prepared to hastily abandon ship or get in a fight. But the boat had not been provisioned according to Alden, so it was probable that no one was on board. It was unlikely that he would be seen in open water if he moved slowly with little wake.

Lopez quietly maneuvered his Zodiac next to the sleek, 70-foot ocean-going yacht moored at a secluded area southwest of Rum Point. He quietly clambered over the side of "Hedge Me Baby" at 0200. He had three hours before dawn. Lopez tied up on the side away from shore, so he wouldn't be seen if someone should be on the beach at this most ghostly of hours. The boat was dark on this sliver-mooned night. There were no sounds, save the gentle lapping of waves. Nothing moved onboard. Perfect.

Lopez put on his balaclava and night vision goggles, quietly jimmied open the locked salon door, and stuck his head through the opening. From what he could see with the green-gray image of the goggles, it was like a rich man's den with a nautical theme.

The room was paneled in wood and had a fine-carpeted floor. Against the port side was a tufted leather sofa with a coffee table with a driftwood base and hinged top, folding out for serving food, he guessed. There was a door in the front bulkhead leading to the sleeping cabins and head. On the forward wall to the left of the door to the staterooms, was a panel of basic instruments in circular matched brass cases—thermometer, barometer, anemometer, compass, and wind direction gauge. To the left of the door was a computer workstation that monitored the status of the boat's systems and provided satellite communications. There were two wing chairs against the starboard forward wall. There was a small galley with a two-burner gas stove, small oven, refrigerator, and sink toward the stern. The fittings on the circular ports had a high sheen. Probably gold plated, given Brooke's penchant for spending money. *The best-equipped yacht I've ever seen. Swanky. Enough Gawking. Get on with it.* He decided to start his search below in the master suite and sleeping cabins.

He stopped at the head of the ladder leading down to the salon and listened. No sounds. As he took his first quiet step down, then his second, his peripheral vision picked up slight motion. A rustling sound. He unzipped his tool kit and reached for his Glock 45. It was under a tangle of tools and he couldn't get it out quickly. A formidable hand reached around the side of the ladder and yanked him off his feet. With a gasp and a loud "mierda," he tumbled down the ladder and fell to the deck, flat on his face. The breath whooshed out of him. He momentarily blacked out. A great weight, a man, fell on his back, like a lion on prey, pinning him to the ground and furiously hitting him on the side of the head.

His strength waning, bleeding from his mouth, Lopez arched his back, flipped over with a yelling grunt, heaved the man off his back, and stood up. As the man rose, Lopez kicked him in the ribs, throwing him against the galley stove. A dozen dishes and plates crashed to the floor adding to the din. His opponent propelled himself off the stove and threw a karate side-kick at Lopez. He missed. Lopez grabbed the goon's leg as it went by, smashing his opponent against a wall. The man picked up a fire extinguisher and hurled it toward Lopez. In the instant that the extinguisher was thrown, Lopez ducked the missile, and countered with a brutal foot kick to the leg. There was a snap, like a dry tree branch being broken over someone's knee. A scream. The man went down. Lopez quickly pinned him and slammed his head with his fist until he was unconscious. He was breathing hard, covered with his own blood and that of his assailant. *I really didn't need this shit.* He examined his body and concluded, nothing broken. *A little blood here and there. I'll look like a human punching bag when the bruises come up in their blue-black glory, but nothing serious that can't wait for attention. One goddamn sore fist.*

To make sure that his opponent was going nowhere for a while, Lopez went down into the sail locker tucked under the prow of the boat where he knew he would find tools and rope. He took duct tape, thirty feet of Dacron line, and a jib, the smallest sail on the boat, returned to the cabin, and taped the man's hands together behind his back and immobilized his feet. Lopez gagged him with tape. He then wrapped the man in the sail, with only his head sticking out, and tightly spiral-taped the package closed. He laughed at his handy work. The enemy looked like a mummy. *I'm running out of time. I'll start searching in the sail locker and work my way back.*

An hour later, Lopez had tossed the entire boat, looking for hidden compartments and safes. He ripped open the furniture upholstery, scoured the engine compartment, and even probed the fuel tanks. Nothing. *I hope to hell he didn't bury the records somewhere because we'll never find them. Kidnapping Brooke and interrogating him under sodium pentothal is a last resort move. I'm out of here.*

Lopez hauled the "mummy' up on the stern deck and tied it to a cleat. He'd be discovered tomorrow when the boat is serviced or he doesn't come home. On his way to get on the Zodiac, he spotted scuba equipment and an underwater dive light. *Could the records be hidden under water? The mooring? The boat's hull? Worth a look.*

Lopez donned the scuba gear, checked the pressure gage to insure that he had adequate air, clipped on the weight belt, strapped on the mask and knife, picked up the light, and carefully slipped into the water. He knew it was risky because a dive light moving underwater could be seen on the surface as a bobbing blob of white light through the crystal clear water, potentially bringing the curious. Without light, he quickly descended down the mooring line in thirty feet of water where the boat was tied to a cylinder block of a big, probably truck, diesel engine. He carefully probed the oily cylinder casings.

A sole octopus jetted out of a cylinder hole, squirting black ink. A spotted moray eel bared its serrated teeth. Zip in the mooring.

To examine the hull, he ascended the mooring line quickly, scanning the light along one side of the boat and keel. Zilch. Then the stern. Nada. Then, swimming past the bow, on the other side of the boat, he saw something. Attached to the hull where it joined the keel was a small protuberance about the size of a book. Lopez turned off the light and surfaced by his Zodiac. Finding a screwdriver and a pair of pliers, he returned to the strange pod.

The pod was glued to the hull. He tried to pry the pod off but couldn't get the edge of the screwdriver under the lip. He tried again. No dice. Finally, frustrated, he put the screwdriver blade at one corner of the enclosure and banged it with his hand until a small tab of the cover peeled back. He pried three more times, and a corner came loose. Attaching the pliers to the loose corner of the pod, he ripped back the cover. Underneath was a sealed, metal, waterproof box. He took it and returned to his boat. He threw the box in the boat, and took off the scuba gear in the water.

He quietly piloted the dingy parallel to the beach, and when out of sight of the sailboat, back to shore. As he left, he heard the sound of a boat approaching the yacht at high speed. Out just in time.

Lopez plowed around Rum Point and through the rough, wind-tossed waters of the windward side of the island and ditched the boat on a secluded stretch of iron shore where he had left his car.

He quickly returned home and went to work on the metal box, hacksawing off one end and dumping out a plastic-wrapped object. He unwrapped it. It was an IPad. He turned it on. It was unlike any iPad display he'd ever seen. Absent were the icons for Google, Safari, calendar, and e-mail, and all of the other tiles that you would expect. Instead, there were four icons marked "Gil," "Brenda," "Cartel," and "Me." Pressing on the icons brought up a screen asking for a password. Nothing he could do about it without a computer nerd to decode the iPad contents and computer drive that he had stolen from Brooke's office.

Stymied, Lopez locked the iPad in his safe and figured he'd better give Brenda the good-news-bad-news and then hunt for a world-class hacker to figure out what was on the iPad.

CHAPTER FORTY-NINE

A month after the Havana trip, Amanda stepped out of the shower and thought: *My god, this is really going to happen…I'm giving up my freedom…what about the Wednesday and Friday night cocktail club…the laughs, the stress relief, the raucous humor, the comfort of being with old friends you can talk to about anything…Sally's recount of the week's gossip…going where I want, when I want. That will stop…it's OK…Harry and I will do some things together… With our schedules, how much time will we really have together…shit…sure… Harry said 'go ahead and take the time to be with your friends'…doubt it…we'll have some time but not a lot…won't be able to do what I want, when I want…will I lose my verve…last chance to bail out…no…love this man as much as the universe is big...think it better to lose a little freedom and gain a lot of Harry.*

Amanda's maid of honor, Sally Walton, helped her slip into her wedding dress, a spaghetti-strapped, rich ecru, scoop-necked sheath made of raw silk. It was tight in the waist and bust and was form-fitting to just above her knees, showing off her elegant figure. It felt as silk should —sleek, sensuous, delicate. A New York designer made it for her, and it was obviously expensive yet not ostentatious. She put on a double strand of her mother's classic large pearls with a diamond clasp. Amanda slipped on a pair of Jimmy Choo medium-height heels that matched her dress, touched up her makeup, and was ready.

The governor's chauffeured, white Rolls Royce Phantom picked up Amanda and Sally at 33 Silver Sands at precisely 5:00 in the evening. Grand Cayman was a British protectorate where they took care of foreign affairs, defense, monitoring the Caymanian Parliament, and had the power to stop any legislation deemed inappropriate, and the right to call for new elections. The governor's position was mainly diplomatic and ceremonial. The wedding was to begin at 6:00 PM in the cool of early evening at Government House, the home and office of the governor. The two fender flags-- the Union Jack on the right and the Caymanian flag, with its symbolic sea turtle, on the left, were sheathed, signaling that the Governor was not present. They would be unfurled, flying impressively, only when the Governor was in the car. Amanda felt like royalty. It was rare to have a private function presided over by the top dog on the island. It was only because Amanda's father was an important member of the Cabinet and a good friend of Governor Duncan Taylor, that she was accorded such an honor.

The car took the short trip down West Bay Road and turned right into the broad, iron-fenced, palm-lined driveway of Government House. The seventy-year-old, one-story structure, the focal point of the British Government on the island, was unique. It was fashioned after an important civil servant's house in Colonial Nigeria and was set on two acres of a spectacular tropical landscape designed and tended by the group that ran the island's botanical garden. A green, well-watered and groomed lawn, where the wedding would be held, swept down to the shaded beach, which was considered the best on the island. The home and office were large, but not huge. They were about the size of a house that a reasonably wealthy Caymanian would build. Certainly very small compared to the over-the-top mansions that the hyper-wealthy built. The structure was situated and its windows situated for cross-ventilation from the ocean breezes, as, during the colonial era there was no air conditioning.

A valet in tails opened the car door. Amanda demurely got out and felt her heart thumping, her mind racing, her throat tense, and her legs a little wobbly again. *Here we go.*

She was greeted by her father and Governor Duncan in the circle in front of Government House.

The governor welcomed her, saying in his pure, classic Eton accent: "Welcome to Government House, Amanda. How absolutely lovely you are--the picture of a happy bride. And it's such a pleasure to have you here. I haven't seen much of you in the past few years, so I hope that you will allow Mrs. Duncan and me to entertain you and Mr. Thompson privately, after you return from your honeymoon. We'd very much like to sit down, have tea, and get to know you and Harry better."

"Thank you," Amanda said. "We'd love to see you. You are so good to host our wedding in such a beautiful and important location. We're very grateful."

The handsome, distinguished, and graying-haired governor was in a white Royal Navy dress-uniform with rows of medals lining the left side of his blouse, gold braid draped from the right, and a ceremonial sword with a handle covered with woven gold hung from his right hip. From what she could glimpse, this man had been awarded a CBE, Commander of the British Empire, the highest honor that a person can get from the Queen before a knighthood, and one personally awarded by her. This was the same uniform that he wore to open parliament each year as the queen's representative.

The governor took her arm and led her, Sally, and her father, through the central hall that ran from the front to the back of the house, to a small waiting room next to the exit to the back lawn. Her mother awaited her in an anteroom that was decorated with a large vase of white lilies.

The wedding guests included sixty-five close relatives, friends of the bride and groom, and Amanda's family. The crowd, salted with some of the socially and politically important people on the island, was dressed to the teeth and way outside the usual norm of casual clothes. The men wore black tie or dinner jackets with an occasional bon vivant in a white "Tom Wolf" white suit and Panama hat. Most of the older women wore long cocktail dresses in a prism of colors; the younger, wore stylish, up-to-date shifts or the ever-present-always-in-style "little black dress." A few appeared in flowing, modern African dress including the unique, wound and layered cloth headdress common among Nigeria's Yoruba. The proud and approving "cocktail club" was there in force—and a bit tight and happy, for they had met for "warm-up" drinks before the wedding. A number of Harry's police colleagues were present in their dress uniforms. A reporter-photographer from the Caymanian Compass, Cayman's daily rag of news, gossip and local happenings, was there to capture the prominent event for the public.

Amanda's parents were civil, though on close observation, guests could see the hostility in their eyes when they exchanged glances. They sat on opposite sides of the aisle. Harry's best friend, Colin, a bachelor from

London, had flown in on the morning British Airways flight, to see his old friend off on his new adventure and to meet the bride. He was the sole groomsman, and approved of Amanda in the most hearty, heart-felt, and maybe a bit envious, way.

The late, warm, golden April afternoon sun washed over the scene. The temperature hovered around a reasonable seventy-eight degrees. There was a light breeze coming in from the west to refresh the crowd. The setting for the wedding was simple. There were two sections of chairs facing the beach. Those on the two aisles were decorated with tasteful arrangements of white roses and white satin-ribbon bows. Set to one side, for the reception, all-white tables were covered with fine linen and set with sterling silver, Baccarat crystal, fine porcelain china, and candles, garnished with the same lilies as the anteroom. A string quartet played Bach's "Air from Suite in D."

Harry looked like a diplomat, dressed in morning clothes—black stripes on dark gray trousers, black long-tailed coat, light gray waistcoat, and white tie. He and the best man waited by the minister at the front of the congregation. His heart fluttered a bit, but he was happily anticipating the ceremony. He turned and waited for Amanda and her maid of honor to walk down the aisle. The flower girl appeared, sprinkling red rose petals in front of Amanda as she, trailed by her maid of honor, confidently poised, and stepped down the path toward the minister. *"God,"* Harry thought, *"what a wonderful woman."*

Amanda mused, "*Shit, this is it.*"

The Anglican minister said, "Harry, do you take this woman to be your lawfully wedded wife, for better or for worse, in sickness and in health?"

"I do," said Harry, in a confident, loving voice.

"Amanda do you--..."

Amanda, ever impatient and anxious to get on with things, cut the minister off, and said "Ditto," to the amazement of the minister, who jumped to the concluding part of the ceremony, slightly ruffled.

"Please exchange rings, and you may kiss the bride."

There was loud and sustained applause from the now standing congregation.

Harry laid a very long and deep kiss on Amanda. She pinched his ass.

"I now present you with Mr. and Mrs. Harry Thompson." The

The bride and groom put up with the obligatory reception line. They did the expected first dance on a portable dance floor, slow dancing to a superb jazz quintet that played their song: "Where or When," by Rogers and Hart. It was their favorite ballad because they thought they had been together before in another life, somewhere, somehow. They really believed it. Harry, with a surprise romantic streak, whispered the lyrics in

Amanda's ear: "and so it seems that we have met before, and loved before, but who knows where or when."

The reception was short. With lots of champagne. The dinner featured artichokes stuffed with shrimp as an hor d'oervre. This was followed by charcoal-grilled Cayman lobster with garlic butter garnished with mango for the main course. Desert was a traditional English raspberry trifle—that eccentric concoction of custard, cake, fruit, white wine and sherry, served in a large dessert glass. Pleasant chatter accompanied the meal, and a few aspiring socialites and politicians "worked the crowd." Harry and Amanda dictated that there be no more than four toasts, so that often dull or embarrassing part of the ceremony whizzed by.

Sally caught the bouquet of flowers tossed by Amanda and squealed, as she was most anxious to nab a man.

Amanda and Harry connived with the governor to sneak out early while the party was still in progress and before the traditional flower petal throwing sending the couple away to their honeymoon. They had better things to do. They were whisked to the airport, in the Governor's Rolls, to a private jet lent by a friend of Amanda's father.

They made exhausting, athletic love twice in the passenger cabin during the four-hour trip to their honeymoon in New York.

CHAPTER FIFTY

At dusk, the white stretch limo whisked Amanda and Harry from New Jersey's Teterboro Airport, through the Lincoln tunnel and into the heart of Manhattan. Neither had been to New York before, and Amanda wanted to see the Mecca for tourists-—Times Square—right off the bat. They drove up 7th avenue, east on 50th street, and south on Broadway, entering the awesome "canyon of blazing light" that is Times Square.

Millions of multicolored LEDs, flickered, streamed, flashed, and beamed messages from dozens and dozens of companies and events, including Coca Cola, Toyota, The Lion King, Samsung, Calvin Klein, Beyoncé', M&M, and ABC News. Some signs were mammoth—seven to seventeen stories high. Others were mid-size to small, maybe two to five stories, stacked one upon the other and jammed in beside their neighbors. It was an animated electronic quilt of massive proportions stitched in every color in the world—a show playing to an audience of fifteen thousand sardine-packed tourists every day. The crowd pushed slowly and happily through the square, laughing, joking, taking pictures, corralling teenagers and children, and sharing their experiences with their friends and families. They craned their necks in awe, ate their sandwiches, drank their drinks, bumped elbows with the crowd, and admired their "I Love New York" T-shirts or little snow globes containing tiny Statues of Liberty swirling in miniature blizzards of plastic snow.

As the limo pushed its way down Broadway, Harry leaned over and deep kissed Amanda and said, "Welcome to New York." He slowly ran his hand all the way up her thigh, barely touching and almost tickling her skin. The driver discretely raised the opaque window separating the driver and passengers in the dark-windowed limo. Harry and Amanda didn't see much of Times Square.

Exhausted from the wedding, trip, and the Times Square tryst, Harry and Amanda checked into the iconic, quirky and very, very expensive, Algonquin Hotel on 44th Street between Fifth and Sixth Avenues. They were greeted by a traditionally, slightly rumpled doorman and the fluffy Persian hotel cat, Matilda, who eyed them from her perch on the doorman's luggage cart. A fixture, she seemed to say in her jaded way: "What are you doing in my place?" They were not sure that they passed muster.

The modest-size lobby-lounge was configured for conversation—rich leather chairs with tables for two, a number of larger round tables and banquettes for bigger, but still intimate groups. Small palms in planters interrupted the groups of chairs. The walls were oak paneled as were the pillars holding up the high, turn-of-the-century, cream-colored, articulated ceiling. A brass plaque on the wall by the desk explained how the hotel became a haven for artists, actors, journalists, and other intellectuals and free thinkers. Soon after its opening in 1902. In 1919, it continued; the Algonquin became the home of "The Vicious Circle," a group of intellectual giants that included Dorothy Parker, Robert Benchley, George Kaufmann, Edna Ferber, and Harold Ross. The "circle" was known for its sharp, sometimes nasty wit, and the mentoring of authors such as F. Scott Fitzgerald and Ernest Hemingway. They founded "The New Yorker" magazine with Ross at its head.

Checked in, and having their fill of history, Amanda and Harry found their room, undressed, and exhausted, fell into deep sleep.

The noonday sun perched in a blue, white-tufted sky and dazzled off the glass facades of the mid-town skyscrapers. The light crept across their room and flicked into Harry and Amanda's sleepy eyes. They stretched, got up, and decided to have breakfast at the Yale Club where a friend who was a member got them dining privileges. They quickly dressed and wandered down 43rd Street by the New York Yacht Club and the Harvard Club, across Madison Avenue, to the Yale Club adjacent to Grand Central Station. The imposing club, the oldest university club in New York, served an awesome brunch buffet on Sundays. At the rooftop dining room, they gorged on smoked salmon, shrimp, eggs made to order, brioche and bacon, topped off with luscious chocolate mousse. They went downstairs to the half block-long sitting room on the second floor. The classic 1900's room was outfitted like a London club with leather arm chairs with tables lining the walls and tables and chairs for small groups arrayed around the center. The center table held a variety of morning newspapers: The New York Times, The Daily News, The Post, The Wall Street Journal, and The Financial Times. In a hall outside of the room, a Bloomberg financial terminal held sway. The magnificent off-white room was two stories high with a delicate, articulated medallion-patterned ceiling and the original floral cornices. The banks of soaring, twenty-foot windows looked out on Grand Central Station. It was salted with men and women from young graduates and guests to the elderly, talking, reading papers or books, digesting a good breakfast with tea, coffee, and the occasional day-starting or hangover-quenching cocktail.

Harry and Amanda took their coffee to an open pair of chairs and staked out their two days. First, there would be that grand dame of transportation, Grand Central Station, across the street. The vast station's sky-blue ceiling, decorated with the constellations, and the light streaming through its famous, soaring windows were worth the visit alone. Then there would be a short walk to the shiny, stainless steel, art deco landmark Chrysler Building, just around the corner. They'd hike over to 34th Street and Sixth Avenue to see the Empire State Building and its 360-degree view of Manhattan. Next, a trek up Fifth Avenue past Rockefeller Center and St. Patrick's Cathedral, along the rows of overpriced luxury stores, and then up to Central Park for a carriage ride through the park. Their timing was perfect as the park in the spring was stunning in all of nature's glory. It boasted hundreds of varieties of trees, giving every shade of green, every color of bloom, every texture that nature could offer. There were azaleas, lavender, daffodils, roses, and tulips that added their own glow to the scene. The happy park was always filled with kids, adults, and lovers, basking in the sun, sauntering along its vast paths, or taking in the lakes and fountains. The evening would be topped off by a dinner-dancing cruise around Manhattan on the Viatour line.

On an unusually clear and moonless night, with bright stars poking through a black velvet sky and a light, warm wind wafting, the boat circled the Statue of Liberty in New York Harbor. Amanda's head was on Harry's shoulder, slow-dancing to a jazz quintet playing "Where or When," at Harry's request. Harry held her tight, swaying on the dance floor, kissed her, and said, "I love you. It'll be forever." Amanda returned the vow as they squeezed as closely as two human beings could be.

Later, Harry held his arms around her waist on the port rail as the boat swung up the East River by the sparkling lights of lower Manhattan and then the midtown skyscrapers and apartment houses. The Twin Towers were gone, but the Woolworth Building, Empire State Building, Met Life Tower, and Citibank offices stood out like beacons among the sea of glass, steel and concrete. Amanda wondered who was behind those hundreds of thousands of windows, those portals, those veiled eyes into the hidden and undecipherable lives that they led, ants in a colony of eight million. Overwhelming.

They took a taxi back to the Algonquin. Upon entering, the cat eyed them with the bored expression that only a cat can give, and a man at the desk hailed Harry. He handed him a note that crisply said: "Back in New York. Must see you tomorrow. 10:00 AM. My office. There are developments. Charlie."

So much for tomorrow, Harry thought.

Before bed, Harry gave Amanda the bad news about the meeting, and promised to meet her at 12:30 for lunch at Masa, the $500 fixe prix Japanese restaurant that some critics called the best restaurant in New York.

Amanda took the news with equanimity. "I want to sleep in anyway and maybe do a little "girl" shopping.

"That's good," Harry said. "I hope that the meeting won't last too long and then we can get on with our honeymoon."

CHAPTER FIFTY-ONE

Harry and Charlie patted each other's shoulders and hugged like long-lost brothers in arms and, indeed, they had a long march, if not a battle, in front of them. Charlie's phone rang. His secretary signaled that it was an urgent call, so Charlie motioned Harry to sit down and indicated that he would be only a few minutes.

Harry scoped out Charlie's large, corner, 50th floor office. It had floor-to-ceiling glass and a spectacular view of Central Park, reflected in a large mirror framed in ebony and carved with modern African images. The office was posh. Reeked of money. It was not the stodgy, typical lawyer's office dripping in the traditional flavor:

oak, leather, and wall-to-wall carpeting, and cute engravings of the legal profession's ancient inhabitants —something Harry had expected given Charlie's conservative dress and demeanor. Instead, it was starkly modern. His custom-made desk was a semicircular sheet of glass, supported by two custom-made Iroko end panels, and intricately carved in Nigeria in the style of an Ibo chief's house doors. There was a picture of his wife, who had died at fifty, and two daughters posing in front of a ski chalet--probably in Switzerland, a favorite haunt. *What a lovely family; what a wife; a stunner,* he thought, noting Harry's wife's auburn hair, glowing green eyes and everything else important, beautifully streamlined and incased in skin-tight Lycra ski clothes. *The daughters looked exactly like their mother, thank God.* Charlie looked like a white, bushy eye-browed, aging cherub.

A rich, dark red, khaki and blue antique Mashhad Persian carpet from Iran covered the floor. A comfortable, soft-leather sofa and chairs were arrayed in a circle around a coffee table carved in the same Iroko wood and pattern as the desk panels. In a bookcase on one wall, there were the obligatory law books, more for show than use. Computer searches had long displaced paper. The books shared a small, private, eclectic library of first or early editions of Shakespeare, Capote, Melville, Fitzgerald, Whitman, and a raft of other famous writers. The walls were adorned with rare, traditional, carefully labeled African art that included a Benin bronze,

Senufo facemask from the Ivory Coast, and a Luba female figure from the Congo. Harry knew that all were collected during Charlie's many photographic treks to Africa over the decades. *What a deal. And I have that lovely 12x12 hole, called an office, with a grey, steel desk, a couple of hand-me-down, scuffed, wooden chairs used by many owners before me, no windows, glaring florescent lights, and walls as bare as a newborn baby's ass. Maybe I should have been a lawyer…or a top-dog drug king, though my life expectancy might be a little low.*

"Goddammit," Charlie said with a red face as he slammed down the phone. "I'm handling a huge estate. Three sisters, who hate each other, are fighting over who gets the New York duplex, the Palm Beach estate, and the mansion in Rio. I've told them the hell with it. Get the damn thing settled. The government wants its money, and so do I. Sell the lot and buy something. Whatever you want. They all have many millions and are sucking my time dry. Hate the petty stuff.

"So, how was the wedding?"

"A blinding success. Amanda was stunningly regal, radiant as the brightest star, a true princess. The Gov. officiated. About seventy-five people. The Cayman social and political register dressed to the teeth. I was dressed like a bloody toff—tails, top hat, starched shirt, studs, and those damn shiny shoes, and the lot. You'd think that it was a coronation. But Amanda insisted on going all out—after all, this was forever and will last until we see the last sunset and dance forever into the beyond. The police commissioner and a few of his top brass were there. Good to see the old boys loosen up a bit. The Friday Night Club followed us to the airport blowing horns, trailing streamers, and generally acting obnoxious. Flew private to New York courtesy of the Carter Empire. So here I am. Enough about the wedding. I want to get on with the honeymoon. What's happening?"

The nutty, rich smell of coffee drifted into the office. Charlie's assistant quietly came in and served them steaming espresso and biscuits.

"Well, I think I've made a lot of progress," Charlie said with a self-satisfied smile. "I know that there are billions of dollars' worth of stock and cash, as well as less liquid, real estate, financial instruments, and titles to legitimate companies, stashed throughout the world and managed in Gil's personal investment fund. And, guess who is controlling the money—Jonathan Brooke, the lawyer in Grand Cayman, who's an expert in global financial management. I know what companies and real estate he had, but we don't have a clue where the money and securities are--I suspect in secret numbered accounts throughout the world."

Harry interjected. "Brooke? Jonathan Brooke? I wouldn't trust the man as far as I could throw him. A rogue. Underhanded. Secretive. Probably a crook, but our fraud unit can't prove it. He was under investigation for allegedly trading client securities for his own account. And the very tight financial community in Cayman doesn't know what he really does—a rarity on that small island. Secret accounts for rich people and Private hedge funds? Probably. Regular stocks? Real estate holdings? Purchase of companies? I certainly don't know."

The fraud unit discovered that he was suspected of being involved in a pyramid scam in England some twenty years ago. Beyond the statute of limitations now, so he can't be tried, but worth watching in case he gets any smart-ass ideas on Cayman. We'd better be careful. We don't want to run afoul of the fraud unit and get them tampering with the investigation. We have to be strictly below the radar. Secret. Like MI 5 stuff."

Charlie continued. "Yes, we'll be cautious. Brenda is certain that the money was funneled from Baxter's legit hedge funds into secret, private funds to hide it from her and the tax authorities. As you mentioned, it wouldn't surprise me if he siphoned off some of his client's money as well, to supplement his fortune." Charlie shrugged, interlacing his fingers in front of his chest, looking a bit smug and raising his overgrown bushy eyebrows.

He relaxed, took off his shoes, casually put his feet on his desk, and continued. "Things get very, very complicated and dangerous. Bet-your-life type dangerous. The drug cartel's Cayman operation is involved. Brooke handles a second hedge fund that launders money for the Cartel. Baxter was the brain behind the scheme, picked the investments, and advised on when and what to buy and sell for both funds—for a substantial fee of course. Baxter and Brooke established a secret company in Zurich that manages both accounts. The funds buy the securities and other assets such as real estate and established corporations and sell them later at a substantial profit. The cash and proceeds from investments are stashed in secret bank accounts. They operate in about ten countries, including Russia, The Ukraine, Brazil, and China, who don't care about illegal deals as long as someone important gets a cut. Aside from legitimate investments, I gather they're involved in some pretty unsavory, but hugely profitable ventures, like rebel-controlled blood diamonds from the Eastern Congo diamonds from Sierra Leone, Liberia, and Angola."

Harry, interjected, a bit tired of all of the confusing detail. "I have a million questions, but let's start with how you found all of this out."

Charlie leaned forward in his chair, smiling, and looking proud of himself. "I just hired the best hacker in the world—Sam Goldman. At the age of 16, Goldman was considered a genius in computer operations, architecture, and programming. He developed the original programs for searching the web, for Google. He taught at Stanford when he was 18. He's a hard-core hacker and, like most, believes in the hacker's code developed at MIT in the early 1980s when computing power started to become readily available. Dedicated hackers believe that they should have free access to anyone's information, that hacking is an art form and sport, and that all authority is to be resisted. Goldman was hired by the Department of Defense, Homeland Security, NSA, and the CIA to try and break into their computers and obtain top-secret information. They wanted to see if their systems were 'hack-proof.' They weren't."

Among other things, he obtained the strategic and battle plan for the Afghan war, the personnel files of the Joint Chiefs of Staff, and the CIA's list of covert agents in Eastern Europe. At NSA he hacked into the program that spies on citizens through the capture of their e-mail, phone and cellphone traffic. He shut it down for 24 hours until they figured out how to patch the software. They all were shocked and had to revamp their entire computer security systems. He got nailed and charged with computer fraud when he hacked into Cal Tech's internal network, and for the fun of it, stole files from the president's office. He also snatched some valuable research records. He hacked into the R&D secrets of a number of corporations and even stole the formula for Coca Cola's syrup and sold it to Pepsi. He was charged, released on bail, and fled the country to Bulgaria."

"Sounds like science fiction."

"There's more. He's freelancing in Sofia, protected by the Bulgarian Mafia, and penetrating various government and private computer systems throughout the world. There's no extradition treaty between Bulgaria and the US. His major clients are Russia, Israel and China, but he'll take on any client if the assignment promises to be challenging and lucrative enough."

"How did you find this guy?"

"Old school tie. Have a roommate at the CIA who found him for me at no little risk to his career. It gets even better. Goldman found a link from Brooke's financial control system to the cartel's system in Mexico. He can find the destinations, dates, amounts, and value of shipments to Grand Cayman and a lot of other places. Quite a find."

Thompson shifted in his seat and with a concerned look on his face said, "Can we trust this guy? Who says that he won't feed us fake information or sell it to others or blow our cover and put us on a cartel hit list?"

"There are no guarantees. It's like honor among thieves, if you believe in it. I suppose the only holds that we have on him are the money and the fun of the hunt. That's not to say, that he might not expose us or stop giving us information when he gets some of his payoff or he gets bored after he initially cracks the system. After all, his history says that he does this for fun, a test of skill, and thumbing his nose at the establishment. Money seems to be a handsome byproduct of his efforts. He's accumulated plenty."

"Of course, we could use the implied threat of contacting the cartel and leaking to them what Goldman's done," Thompson interjected. "My well-connected drug snitches on the island have a pipeline to Mexico and could take him down. If the cartel gets wind of it, he's a dead man. And maybe us. They reach far into Eastern Europe and their drug and criminal contacts would eventually lead them to him."

"Bottom line," Charlie said, "I still don't know whether we can trust him. We have to take the risk. He's all we've got. Realistically, his failure would only leave us where we are now, which is nowhere."

"So how do you contact the guy?"

"Easy. The initial contact information came to me via my CIA buddy who received it in an encrypted message. Goldman said he will set up a devilishly scrambled satellite signal for safe and direct communication to and from us when needed. The system will transmit voice and data back and forth between Bulgaria, New York, and Grand Cayman and anywhere else in the world we have to operate. The link "rides" on and is mixed in with conventional signals. It's virtually undetectable and unbreakable. He learned the technique when he consulted with the NSA, has improved it, and now beats them at their own game."

"So, what kind of trouble can we get into if we get caught? I know I'd be drummed out of the police force for sure. I may never get another job and would probably lose my residency status and be kicked off of the island."

Charlie said, "We're rolling the dice and getting stolen information and that makes us part of a conspiracy to commit fraud. I don't think there's a danger of getting caught, as the information we're stealing is from criminals who have a strong motivation not to get nailed. It's unethical, but it's the only way to get the bulk of the money back to Brenda and minor sums to other family members."

"But Harry, we'll have to involve the Caymanian Mexican, Columbian and US authorities sooner or later. We'll be heroes if we turn the gang over to them, or criminals if we don't tell them before they catch onto our scheme. We'll break the news to the authorities when we get the money back. You can then complete your investigation and get your arrests and indictments. I hope the courts will be kind to us for committing a crime to get the information. I think so. We can probably get immunity from prosecution for our testimony against the bad guys."

Thompson's face clouded. He stared out of a window for a minute. "We have to act ASAP. I have to coordinate a force to intercept drugs and trace them to the dealer in Grand Cayman. You have to deal with the money stream. We have to find out through Goldman when and where a large shipment will be smuggled into Cayman. That's the beginning of our ability to bring down the Cayman drug network. The information will be stellar for the DEA who may be able to interrupt the flow of drugs into other countries. But how are we going to pay for this? The police are having trouble buying paperclips, much less a rogue computer guy who gets megabucks from foreign countries."

"Simple. I figure that there's five to fifteen billion dollars hidden out there. Goldman gets 1% of the recovered fund money, say ten million dollars, for cracking the case. Actually, he's more interested in the challenge than the money. He's never hacked into worldwide investment and banking systems before. I'll share the initial setup costs with him. We'll get paid back from the stolen money before it's distributed to its rightful owners." With a wry smile, Charlie said: "I won't even take my usual $ 600 per hour or traditional five times markup on expenses that lawyers customarily charge."

"Now, here's the best news. Brenda's private eye, Peter Lopez, recovered an iPad and hard drive of Brooke's that she believes has important information on it. She won't tell me how she got it. Not legally I'm sure, knowing Lopez's methods, but I have it in my safe. It's encrypted and I can't get into any files. We have to take it to Goldman and see if he can crack it. We need to get the cartel information first-hand anyway. You'll meet the little genius in Sofia."

"Sofia? You've got to be shitting me. That's a three-day trip into one of most miserable Eastern Block countries in the world. For Christ's sake, the place is gray even when the sun is shining."

"Relax, Harry. There's no choice. You want that drug bust, don't you?"

"You win. When?"

"We leave tonight at 7 PM. The meet's set for tomorrow afternoon. My secretary's already booked us on a flight from Kennedy, and a hotel in Sofia."

"I don't know where Baxter's murder fits into the money part of the puzzle, if at all. We have to find out."

Charlie smiled and raised his eyebrows and said, "Ten to one, murder follows the money."

"Probably. On the drug side of the equation, my sources say that a major shipment of drugs is coming to Grand Cayman directly from Mexico. But I don't know when and how. I need to nail the gang that picks up the drugs on the island. We need him to tap into the cartel systems and get all of the shipment information that he can."

"We'll ask him."

They shook hands, and Harry returned to his bride and their abbreviated enjoyment of New York.

CHAPTER FIFTY-TWO

Demarion Bailey, called "De," handled Zane's drug trade on Jamaica and the smaller islands of Antigua, Guadalupe, Montserrat, and Grenada. De called his gang "Normandy," after the invasion of Europe during WWII, signifying the incursions that he intended to make on Jamaica's drug trade. Kingston, Jamaica's capital, was particularly lucrative and where he focused the efforts of his 90-person organization. There was wholesale corruption on the island, from top to bottom, in government, the political parties, and society in general. Normandy was affiliated with the two major political parties--The Jamaican Labor Party and

Peoples National Party. So buying police "protection" for his business was easy.

The market for drugs was immense given the misery of its three million people who were looking for anything that would give them relief, even temporarily, from wrenching poverty and unemployment. De's gang was dominant in the government, university, upscale, and residential markets. He was weak in "street" sales and, being the largest drug dealer in the country wasn't good enough for De or Zane. There were twenty other gangs sharing the drug trade, and he had ambitions to take over a considerable share of the markets that he did not have. Laundering money through Jamaican banks was no problem. The corrupt banks were masters at washing political and drug money—for a significant fee of course.

The Renkers, the island's second largest gang, and a formidable force, was moving to takeover some of De's most lucrative territories. The whole name of the game was holding and gaining market territory, block-by-block, tenement-by-tenement, neighborhood-by-neighborhood. De had by far the largest, best trained, and experienced army in the field. It was salted with former Jamaican Defense Force Special Forces veterans. They persuaded smaller rivals with weak defenses to join them. Or they pushed them out by selling the purist coke available in their territory at prices lower than the competition could meet. Sometimes they killed the rival's leadership through street fights, assassinations and drive-by shootings. But to really gain a lot of business they would have to take it away from the Renkers, the second largest and well organized gang on the Island. To top it all off, the Renkers had brutally murdered three of De's best field people in an unsuccessful attempt to take over one of his most lucrative territories. This alone, as a matter of course, required revenge. Anyway, he couldn't let the proverbial camel's head under the tent. And he wanted a large piece of that camel.

So, De had a defensive war developing to protect his territory on one hand, and an offensive battle to gain territory on the other. There would likely be a blood bath. He would make it worthwhile.

Growing also meant strategically expanding his Caribbean business beyond Jamaica. If De did well, Zane said he might recommend that he play a major role in the Cartel's expansion into Europe. Money, power, territory, lifestyle and beautiful women were the scorecards by which successful wholesalers judged themselves. De wanted it all. A healthy Caribbean operation and a cut of the European business would give him more money, more power and make him a major drug king. Maybe he would buy his own plane. He would make immense profits. After all, he could get drugs cheaply through Zane—maybe even cheaper if he bypassed the Cartel, bought directly from Columbia and sold drugs in Europe directly. A life-threatening move, but worth thinking about. Prices and margins were very high over there and drug enforcement relatively weak. Recruiting expatriate or illegal Jamaicans in Europe would be easy after sending several trusted aides to the old country to recruit.

De had the typical organization of a drug lord efficiently equipped to conduct business and war. First was headquarters management: his buyer ran imports; his treasurer kept the books and laundered money; his enforcer took care of discipline and managed necessary violence and wars; his operations man handled field operations and the Cartel's computer system. In the field were twenty foot soldiers who distributed drugs to smaller dealers, and seventy rank and file who sold the drugs to individual buyers.

A cool, calm, calculating man prone to extreme violence, De came up through the ranks as a dealer, a key staff member, and then head of the operation when his prior boss was murdered. He was a mulatto: coffee and cream-colored with a full face and a handsome mixture of the genes of various tribes of the African slaves brought to Jamaica in the 1600s. He also had a healthy dose of Irish, English, and Spanish blood. These ethnic layers were added since a slave woman had an illegitimate child by an English plantation owner over two centuries ago. De had a muscular, medium build, with several knife-fight scars on his face and arms, and a healed gunshot wound on his shoulder. His lips were taut lips signaling his intensity and his demeanor standoffish.

De spent four years in the Jamaican Defense Force before returning to the streets. To blend into the background and in, the rare instance that he went out into the "field," and because of his rebellious pride, he wore traditional "Rasta" garb of black pants; green, yellow and red "Bob Marley" T-shirt; and black New Balance running shoes. He drizzled shoulder length braded dreadlocks and judiciously avoided the flash and fancy clothes of the other successful drug merchants. He was smart enough to avoid personal use of drugs, a sure way of getting killed one way or another. De lived in a fortified mansion in Ocho Rios, a protected beach haven where all of the tourists rented their two weeks in paradise.

To complicate matters, Zane ordered De to murder a man named Whitney who laundered money for the Grand Cayman operation. It appeared that he had skimmed millions of dollars' worth of the Cartel's money into his own accounts. This man couldn't be left alive and still preserve the discipline in his troops and his reputation among the drug lords and the Cartel. It was the law of the business. Zane thought it best to use an outside assassin who could unremarkably slip in and out of Cayman. De sent Kquewanda Dixon, a mean, heartless woman handy with a knife, who had pulled off many "policing" duties of various sorts before. Though the knife was her preferred and silent weapon, she was equally proficient in all of the tools of her trade tools: silenced pistols, sniper rifles, explosives, breaking necks, strangling and garroting.

A skilled scuba diver, she once blew up a rival's yacht by placing a limpet mine on its hull,

Dixon left for Grand Cayman via Havana, a hard-to-track air route. She was spoiling for action.

CHAPTER FIFTY-THREE

Dixon, tailed Whitney for a week. She had his routine down pat, noting when he went to bed and rose, where and when he worked with his associates, his favorite haunts, his girlfriends, and his work associates. She had a notebook full of the critical details of his life—when he got out of bed and when he went to sleep. His office routine and favorite restaurants and bars and a visit to an apparent girlfriend. The only time that she lost him was when he sailed on yachts to points unknown, but apparently local trips, because he was always back in town the next day. He went diving three or four times a week with dive guide George Savage with no regular pattern except that he took one night dive a week, armed with his underwater camera gear. Whitney had incurred Zane's wrath, apparently for skimming drugs off the top of shipments. Tallies didn't match with records of shipments from Mexico, and he trusted his Mexican colleagues.

After considering a number of options, Dixon knew exactly how and where Jason Whitney would be killed. Only the time and day were left in doubt.

On a pitch-black, moonless night with calm seas, Savage maneuvered his dimly lit boat over the wreck of the Balboa, the finest night dive in the Caymans. The Balboa, a freighter that sunk during a hurricane, was dynamited to pieces to clear Georgetown. The twisted and broken wreckage, the rudder, engine room, and inverted pieces of the hull, harbored a divers guidebook full of night creatures. There were octopuses, anemones, enormous crabs, and parrotfish in their filmy white sleeping cocoons, free-swimming moray eels, and corals that bloomed and fed only at night. Eight eager photographer-divers splashed over the side of the boat and quickly dropped through thirty-five feet of water to the wreck sitting on the sand below. The canvas of brilliant color and movement unfolded like a painter's palette, illuminated by the bright LED dive lights.

Shrouded in darkness, Dixon put on her black wet suit and hood, buoyancy compensator, and other scuba gear. She was careful to see that her air was on, her regulator firmly attached, her weight belt clipped on, and her long, sharp dive knife securely strapped on her leg. Her dive light was off but ready. She took a bearing with her lighted compass to the spot where she saw the diver's lights glowing, bobbing, and weaving under water. The phantom figure slipped silently into the water from the iron shore just southwest of Georgetown Harbor, submerged to the bottom of the harbor, and navigated to the spot where the divers were enjoying their underwater exploration led by Savage. When she reached the pod of divers, she maneuvered, undetected, into the back of the pod of the group and turned on her light—just another diver in the pack.

Jason had always wanted to photograph an Orange Ball Anemone, a rare, shy and prized species. An experienced diver-photographer with thousands of photographs under his belt, he was determined to get his trophy on this excursion. George led him alone to an inverted piece of hull far from the other divers where he had recently spotted the anemone. He rarely told anyone where this rare animal lived and warned Jason that there was barely space for one diver under the funnel-like structure and to be careful not to wedge himself in, as the hull rapidly narrowed to a dead end. He could well get stuck if he went in too far, and to be prepared to back out of the space, as there was no other exit. George left to join his charges, some distance away.

Jason skooched his way under the hull. There was his quarry, anchored in a narrow spot between the hull and the sand bottom. A perfect place for a fine photograph. The anemone was a finely articulated, little animal about five inches tall with a dozen translucent tentacles topped by delicate orange balls and arrayed like the spikes on a king's crown. It looked like an underwater fireworks display. It swayed back and forth in the slight underwater swell, feeding on plankton that floated by. The orange tips sparkled like faceted jewels in the intense beam of her dive light. Jason juggled his cumbersome underwater camera and strobe into position, concentrating intensely, almost mesmerized, as he began to take photo after photo.

He sensed a presence. He felt something brush his legs and couldn't turn his head to see what it was. Then a hand roughly and forcefully grabbed the neck of his scuba tank, shoving him forward, pinning his arms against the wreck, immobilizing him. His hair was suddenly yanked back exposing his throat. He couldn't move to protect himself. He struggled. The last thing that he felt was the edge of a dive knife tracing his throat from one side to the other. His blood pulsed from his jugulars. The hull's cavity filled with swirling eddies of blood. The diver wedged the body into the space so it wouldn't move. It would not be discovered for at least three quarters of an hour when the divers returned to the boat and a head count was taken.

Dixon navigated in darkness back to shore. The black figure quickly packed the diving gear into a battered black pickup truck, and headed back to Zane's Bowdon Town safe house. The mercenary's mission accomplished, she would be back in Jamaica the next day.

Savage took a count of the divers once they were on board. He was short one diver. Whitney. He saw the beam of a dive light in the water some distance from the boat and was annoyed that one thoughtless diver would hold up the entire group. Besides, he was chilled from a long dive and wanted to get his boat on his trailer and haul it home. He donned his scuba gear again and went down to get the recalcitrant diver. He found two barely visible dive fins sticking out of the wreck, blood streaming, dissipating in the slight current. He pulled Jason out by his legs and swam him to the surface. Once Jason's limp body was pulled up the dive ladder, it was obvious that he was dead. No dive accident this. He had been murdered. Maybe by one of the other divers.

Savage called the Coast Guard by radio. They took the body to shore to be met by an ambulance and Inspector Thompson. Thompson had another murder on his hands. Murder aside, this would not be good for the tourist industry.

CHAPTER FIFTY-FOUR

Charlie and Thompson, iPad and hard drive in hand, connected in London for their Bulgaria Air flight to Sofia. The 737-800 descended over the snow-capped 7000-foot Vitosha Mountains that exquisitely framed Sofia, and landed at Sofia Airport. It turned out to be a very humid 40-degree day in Sophia.

"Miserable," said Thompson. "Just like London at its worst."

They cleared customs, and immigration and, pushed their way into the terminal through a mob of yelling school children returning from abroad for their spring holiday. Charlie spotted a tall, lanky man casually leaning against a post with his arms across his chest like an oriental potentate.

The man was intensely scanning the crowd through steel-rimmed, John Lennon glasses. He was dressed in a black mock turtleneck, black jeans, black New Balance running shoes, black socks, and a black plastic watch. A Steve Jobs outfit.

"There," Charlie said, "That has to be Goldman."

"I expected some scruffy teenager in a Rolling Stones T-shirt and torn jeans."

"Guess not."

Charlie approached the man. "Goldman?"

"Yes"

"I'm Charlie Braun and this is Harry Thompson."

Goldman guided them to his battered twenty-year-old Volkswagen Beetle and whisked through the center of the city. "We'll be there in fifteen minutes. I've cracked into Brooke's network and broken into the Mexican cartel's system through it. I have a ton of information for you."

Charlie and Harry breathed a sigh of relief, relaxed a bit, and said almost in unison, "Thank God."

Charlie added, "Any trouble getting into the data?"

"No, duck soup."

"What are the chances that they'll know that they've been hacked?"

"Almost zero."

Goldman stepped hard on the accelerator. "I'll let you enjoy the sights, and we'll cover details when I can show them on the computer." He went silent.

Charlie, being thorough as usual, had studied travel and history books about Sofia and went into his intellectual lecture mode.

"Harry, look at that beautiful, old church. It's called the Boyna Church, and parts of it dates from the early 15th century. You know, of course, that the city was the crossroads for trade between The Middle East and West and has been run over and occupied by everyone in sight, almost since the beginning of recorded history—the Persians, Romans, the Huns, the Ottomans, and the Russians, to name a few. Bulgaria was a punching bag for all and sundry."

"Yeah sure, Charlie, we covered all that at the police academy."

"Oh, come on, get a little culture, see a few sights, you'll never be back here."

"Thank God."

Charlie continued, "The people are Slavs. Tough. Don't like outsiders. Lots of Russian-style corruption.

The city dates from 420 BC, although evidence shows that the site may have been occupied 43,000 year ago. The modern city was mostly built after 1900. Only sights worth seeing are a handful of churches and a Roman temple. See how new the buildings are? The city was bombed into oblivion during WWII and rebuilt with those low, unattractive, little, red tile-roofed buildings, some bland pseudo-modern, glassy office buildings, and the colossal, horrid, crumbling, gray cement apartments thrown together during the Russian occupation.

"Look, there's the Roman Rotunda. Notice the red brick silos and…"

"Enough, Charlie, for Christ's sake. Calm down and focus on the job at hand."

"Ok, Ok, enjoy the ride for tomorrow we may be in jail."

Goldman whisked them to his non-descript row house in the city's center. The houses on his street were ill kempt and dreary. They were post-WWII construction, and the stucco facings, window trim, and roofs were patched and showing their age. Plants in planters were morbidly brown, dying or dead with a few green spots indicating that there was some caring life in the neighborhood. The street and sidewalks were devoid of pedestrians, traffic, kids, and toys. The parked cars, a mixture of Czech, German, Russian, and French, were as old and disheveled as Goldman's. It looked like a blue-collar community inhabited by older or retired people. An odd place for a vital young man to be, but maybe the best for someone who doesn't want to be noticed and is operating outside of the law.

Goldman ushered them into his living room, which had walls covered with faded and stained wallpaper printed with small once-red roses. Overhead was one plastic globe with a low wattage bulb. The furniture looked like it came from the Sofia equivalent of The Salvation Army. A sagging, lime-green sofa, with an off-center Metallica poster over it, slumped against one wall. There was a coffee table with a few computer and video game magazines scattered over it and two armchairs that looked sturdy, but the worse for wear. A couple of floor lamps completed the shabby array.

"Would you like a drink?" Goldman said.

"No thanks," Thompson replied. "We had a couple on the plane, and we want to get down to business. So tell us what you have."

"Better yet, I'll show you. Welcome to my own personal electronics store—all of the latest goodies and some the world doesn't even know about yet. Sometimes I have to build my own stuff."

They were led into a climate-controlled room with plywood-blackened windows and greeted with the ear-splitting noise of Metallica's "Creeping Death," spewing from a pair of hyper expensive Langertoic speakers. A wall-size high resolution LED computer display flashed scenes from the Drug Runner video game that Goldman had been playing before their arrival. The scoreboard showed that he was winning the game. No surprise. The room glowed with soft, dim red light of the type used in meditation rooms—calming but obviously adequate to operate a computer by. Red, 50s swirling lava lamps graced each corner of the room. All in all, a cacophony of sound and light.

Wires were strewn and tangled haphazardly over the floor and connected to an array of high-speed computers and peripherals. A semicircular desk held three large, flat desk displays. Seemingly endless lines of white numbers on a black background streamed down the displays too fast for the untrained eye to follow them. The data was meaningless to Charlie and Thompson.

Thompson turned to Charlie. "How can anyone make sense out of that garbage?"

"That's what we're paying Goldman for."

"Here is what I found." Goldman laughed as he hit a few keys. The video game blacked out and another stream of numbers hit the wall display. "I cracked the Cartel network through Brooke's tie-in network," Goldman said. "They were foolish enough to provide Brooke with a direct link to their Cayman records. I found a "back door" an accounting program that gave me access to the system, and I was up and running. This was child's play. Any twelve-year-old hacker could do it. The military, now there's a tough nut to crack. They obviously didn't have the best security people. Should've hired me."

"Let's make this easy," Goldman said as he hit a few keys. An orderly Excel-like table of numbers hit the screen.

"Once I got in, the rest was pretty simple. Here's what you wanted—the records of the Cartel's planned shipments and overall inventories by country. The DEA and country authorities should be very interested. You can be big-time heroes. Or make a lot of side-money selling the data to the powers-that-be in a few countries. I've also located a major shipment due into Cayman on April 3rd. Looks like it might be worth a hundred million on the street, depending on the spot price of coke at the time. You have plenty of time to intercept the junk. It's coming in on the freighter "Monterey." Registered in Panama and a regular in Mexican-Caribbean trade."

"Fabulous work," Charlie said. "Now for the next items."

"What next items?" Goldman replied.

"An iPad and hard drive stolen from a big-time financier. We believe it may contain invaluable data tied into a murder, financial fraud, and the local drug trade. Should be interesting."

"Let's have a try. See how good they are. I Pads are usually pretty easy to crack. Some are foolish enough to only hide their data in a spreadsheet or word processing program with minimal security. The gadget doesn't have a lot of memory so it can't handle a lot of encryption."

Goldman carefully pried the iPad case open, exposing its guts, and attached two wires to a relatively large, multi pin square component in the center of an orderly green circuit board. He said that it was the central processor; the "chip." He fired up the iPad, connected it to a powerful computer, and a series of lines of code flashed on the big screen.

"Duck soup" he said as he keyed in a few lines of his own code. The computer took a few minutes to chew on the data and decode the program. A list of numbers and banks appeared: Switzerland, Vanuatu, Bermuda, The Cayman Islands, Liechtenstein, Singapore, Panama, and the Isle of Man.

"Phewooc," Charlie whistled. "What a gold mine. Half the major offshore banking countries in the world are there. I guess Brooke sure wanted to hedge his bets in case someone cracked one or two accounts."

"Those are the accounts we're looking for and the numbers needed to transfer funds to accounts that we set up. We'll take all the money, less your commission, of course."

"Fine. Give me a few minutes to prepare the data for you." Shortly, Goldman produced three memory sticks and said, "There are two red memory sticks with identical encrypted files of all of the data you saw here. The black memory stick contains the program that will break the encryption and reveal the files. Keep them safe and apart. With the set, you can pull the data up on an ordinary PC. Whatever you do, don't keep hard copy. It's easy to lose; easy to steal.

Goldman swiveled around in his chair to face Charlie and Harry.

"I expect to be paid as soon as you get into the accounts. No 30-day credit nonsense. Don't screw this up.

I'm doing it on spec. If I don't see the money, you'll hear from a Bulgarian "collection agency." They have a 100% record of recovering money from debtors—sometimes using painful techniques to "encourage" recalcitrants to pay up. Handing Charlie a slip of paper, he said, "Here's the account that you should transfer my money into."

"How do we know that you won't steal the money before we get to it?" Charlie said to Goldman.

"You don't. You'll have to trust me. Believe it or not, there's honor among hackers and their clients. But getting paid helps."

Goldman determined that the hard drive contained no useful data and took Charlie and Thompson to the airport.

"Next step for me is to set up the drug bust," Thompson said to Goldman, "What about you?"

"Transfer the funds to new accounts. Fast."

CHAPTER FIFTY-FIVE

Brenda linked her arm in Charlie's, looked him in the eye, and said, "Thank you again; I would never have found Gil's money without you. Ten billion dollars." She laughed. "I can spend that if I put my mind to it. It's a miracle of detection."

"Well, it's been interesting, to say the least," Charlie responded. "You likely won't thank me when you get my bill," he said, half seriously and with a chuckle. "But I think you can more than afford the toll."

They landed in Zurich via London and settled into a $3,000 per night suite, one of the lower priced extravagances at the Baur au lac Hotel. The hotel was in the heart of the old city and a five-minute walk to the city's fabled financial district and their destination. They were hardly there for the luxury, Indeed, they only intended to stay two nights before traveling by train to Lichtenstein. The most that they'd see of Zurich were banks and the view from their window of Lake Zurichsee and the distant Swiss Alps.

Charlie picked the Coutts Bank von Ernst AG, a centuries old, family-controlled operation for the transaction. The bank building was a formidable 19th century, three-story limestone structure on Stauffacherstrasse 1. The Von Ernst family founded it in the late 1700s, as one of the elite private banks in Switzerland. They served only the wealthiest clients and had never had a breach of security. Unlike a retail bank that offered loans, checking, and other ordinary services, the bank invested in safe securities, properties, bonds, and companies, for its own account and for its customers.

Two alert, armed, uniformed security men guarded the entrance. The lobby was a large mahogany paneled room with a busy crystal chandelier hanging from the ceiling. Hanging on one wall was a 1732 painting of the forbidding founder, sporting a white-powdered wig with his back hair gathered in a small, black silk bag. He had intelligent blue eyes and wore the business dress of the day—a red waistcoat trimmed with gold lace under a plain black coat with gold cloth buttons, and shirt with lace ruffles. He looked a bit like George Washington dressed for a dance. The furniture had the clean and spartan lines of the early 1800s Biedermeier School, arranged on a rich Persian rug. The receptionist was an all-business; a rather plain, gaunt-faced gray-haired woman, in a severe black dress, and pearl necklace. She wore just enough makeup to prevent her from looking like a cadaver. The woman caught their eyes immediately and, with a tight smile, ushered them to seats in front of her desk.

"May I ask, what is your business here?"

"We're here for an appointment with Herr Schwartz. I'm Mr. Braun and this is Ms. Baxter."

"Yes, he is expecting you. I'll ring him, and he will be down to pick you up momentarily. May I please see your passports and another form of photo identification as well? I'll have to inspect your briefcase and purse."

"Fine."

"May I offer you tea or coffee or a glass of wine?"

"No thanks," they said in unison.

Just as they completed their sign-in, Herr Schwartz (dressed in a black suit with a white shirt and a tasteful, modern, black and white print tie), ushered them up an elevator and to his office. Schwartz's office was modern—in contrast to the antique entry hall. There was a chrome and very dark mahogany desk, with a modern and famous Eaems, aluminum-framed, black leather desk chair. In front of the desk, arrayed around a Noguchi glass coffee table, were three le Corbusier armchairs in black leather and chrome. The rug was a plush dark gray and the walls were decorated with black and white photographs of famous scientists and inventors: Einstein, Fermi, Bohr, Edison, Tesla, and Jobs, among others. There was a chrome and glass eighteen-foot wide tank with tropical fish behind his desk. It contained miniature versions of fish found in Grand Cayman and other tropical waters: butterfly fish, rock dandies, blue tangs, fairy basletts, and soldier fish. All swam leisurely over a sand bottom with anemones, orange sponge, and sea grass. Charlie supposed it was to calm his guests and make them more amenable to parting with their money. Schwartz had a breathtaking view of the lake and its twenty-story fountain at the entrance to the small harbor. All in all, it symbolized Swiss efficiency, cold logic, and good taste.

Schwartz guided them to the armchairs and began to explain the procedure.

"First Madame," he said, "I'll need your passport and another photo ID and your signature on an account card. We'll then go to the ID room to complete the identification procedure, which is quite complex, but the most advanced and formidable in the business."

He led them into a austere room with an array of computers and equipment that looked like flatbed scanners, audio equipment, and a device like an ophthalmologist uses to examine your eyes.

"Here's what we're going to do. We'll take your picture and then get a scan of your retinas. We use it to get a print of your retinal pattern, which is unique to each person. Next you'll put your fingers and palms on that scanner. We not only get a picture of your finger and palm prints, but also the pattern of veins beneath both. Again, though a clever crook can duplicate fingerprints, they can't duplicate the unique venous patterns in the hand. Finally, we'll record your voice and produce a "voice print." When you call, the print will be compared with the telephone voice to insure that you are the caller."

Swinging a shapely leg and looking disgusted, Brenda said, "God almighty, is all of this crap really necessary?"

Charlie gave Brenda a cautionary look, hoping she wouldn't lose her legion temper. Schwartz threw a lingering glimpse at Brenda's leg, recovered his machine-like manner, and went on.

"Yes, I'm afraid that it is. Otherwise we can't guarantee that your account will be secure.

The retina and palm IDs will be used when you personally visit the bank or its London branch. You will access the account by phone most of the time. To do so, you'll have to identify yourself saying, 'Coutts Bank Brenda Baxter,' and give your account number. Once the voiceprint clears you, one of the three officers cleared to deal with your account will complete the transaction. One is available 24/7 as we operate in all time zones across the world. We like a human to talk with you and see if there are any problems or concerns and to insure that the transaction is what you really want. You'd be amazed at the number of people who misstate the amount of transfers or deposits. Is that understood?"

"Yes," Brenda said. "I'll be using the telephone most of the time. But how do I get account statements and balances and records of transfers?"

"They can be accessed by phone or encrypted computer files. We do not put out paper records for obvious reasons. We'll give you a small module to attach to your landline or fax to decode our encrypted messages. The device will allow you to use your phone for regular calls without interference. We'll also provide you with a cell phone with an encryption decoding program as well. It has extra security features built-in to insure that no one else can get into and use the program. So far, our devices and programs haven't proven unshakable. We employ a firm that does nothing but try to hack our security systems and correct any weaknesses."

Brenda completed the process with the machines and was given a slip of paper with her account number and passwords on it. She was warned to keep it private and make no copies. Better yet, memorize and destroy it. If she couldn't remember it, she would have to return to Switzerland to reopen the account. She was given a list of the three officers authorized to deal with her if there were any questions or any problems. "By the way," Schwartz continued, "Swiss law stipulates jail time and prohibitive fines for anyone divulging information about secret accounts. It also requires that we divulge the name and details of an account if a country, or the US federal government can show that the account is involved in fraud, or there's an indictment of the account holder for fraud. So keep your noses clean, or at least stay under the radar. Should you wish, establishing a residence in Brazil, which has no extradition treaty with the United States or Switzerland, might be prudent."

On the spot, Brenda transferred $2 billion from the Cayman account to her Coutt's account, and received her cell phone with a briefing on how to use it.. They were ushered out and had a leisurely lunch at Petermann's Kunststuben, one of the most elegant and expensive restaurants in the world. They took the train to Lichtenstein to open another account. The routine would be repeated in The Isle of Man, Vanuatu, Singapore, and Bermuda, before returning to Grand Cayman.

CHAPTER FIFTY-SIX

It was a late night for Thompson. Almost twelve o'clock when he left the office after cleaning up the absurd pile of paperwork that was on his desk. He called Amanda on his cell phone, knowing that she was up, knowing she was waiting.

"Sorry honey. I had to get the bloody paperwork out of the way. Is there anything to eat at home?"

"Cold conch stew, and maybe me. I'll heat both up for you. Which would you like first?"

"You know which. Give me ten."

Suddenly, he was dog-tired. He pocketed his phone, retrieved his keys, yawned, rubbed his eyes, walked out through his office door, and locked it. He entered the dimly lit room where his detectives worked. There were two rows of back-to-front desks, a typical arrangement where the men and women work face-to-face, in part to save space, in part to encourage cooperation between each partnership. There would be a cacophony of talking, joshing, laughter, and clacking of keyboards during the day. And now an eerie silence pervaded the room. It was as if the criminals had escaped from the detectives' files and were wafting, playing, and dancing around the room, flaunting their crimes, taunting Harry to catch them. Anxious to get home to Amanda, he hurried down the faux marble front staircase, swiped his security card to record his exit, hustled to his Honda, and climbed into the driver's seat.

Thompson senses a movement behind him. He glanced in the rearview mirror as a masked figure lunged toward him from the back seat, too fast for him to react. He was grabbed, arms pinned to his side by an extraordinarily powerful person. Thompson, cool and calculating, twisted, broke the man's grip, and jumped from the car in full flight. He hit the ground, bruised and bleeding from gravel scrapes on his face and shoulder. A second man bolted from behind a car, tackled him, and threw him to the ground, raising his hand to slug him in the head. Harry forcefully grabbed his crotch. The man screamed and reflexively loosened his grip. Harry struggled from beneath him, scrambled to his knees, rose and began to run. The first thug, who had a neck as thick as Thompson's thigh and arms like a lifetime weight lifter, punched him in the stomach and threw a brutal right to his jaw. Harry's head snapped hard to his left. He crumpled and lost consciousness. The man tied Thompson's hands and legs with duct tape, gagged him, and pulled a hood over his head just as Thompson groaned and began to come to. The gangster wrestled him into the back seat, climbed in beside him, pressed a gun into his ribs, and said, "Keep quiet and don't struggle. Otherwise we'll go and get your wife and both of you can go down together."

Thompson figured that there was nothing he could do at that point. He'd have to play along for the time being.

The bigger assailant said, "We're going to go to a nice, quiet, beautiful place to talk to you. Just talk. We don't like your messing around in the Cartel's business. Understand? Poncho, get moving."

As the tires squealed on the road, Harry nodded his head and fell silent. *These bastards are going to kill me. I know that. The Cartel never messes around. Sending a signal to anyone else who tries to bring them down. These guys are pros. But so am I.* They drove for a long time. *They have to be heading for the East End or North Shore. They're the only places that are more than a short drive from Georgetown.* The sound of the car tires on a paved road gave way to the crunch of rubber on a crushed coral drive. When they finally stopped, he heard the thundering sound of furious breakers. *A reef. It has to be the North Wall. No other surf on the island is that angry.* Thompson was yanked out of the car, grabbed under the arms, and dragged, heels down, toward the water. He was dripping sweat and struggling to breathe through his nose. He could feel harsh bumps as his feet rode over the gaps between planks. *A dock. Water. Not a good sign.* The sound of the waves increased and he was lifted onto a gently rocking floor. *A boat. Feels like a big one.*

The two men dragged a weakened Thompson into a chair on the back deck. His hands were handcuffed around the back of a chair and his legs duct-taped to the chair's base. His breathing was shallow and labored. Sweat drizzled down his face and over his body. His jaw throbbed. His mask was torn off, and a man he had never seen before stood staring down at him. The man who had black, venomous eyes drilled into a pockmarked and knife scarred face, pushed his nose onto Harry's. His breath was foul, smelling of cigarettes and whisky. *Not a local. This man has killed before. Many times.* His pulse raced. Beads of sweat ran into his eyes. He hurt.

Before he could size up the muscle-bound brute, a fist crashed into his cheeks, then his jaw. The world went blank for Thompson for a few seconds. He came to and tasted the metallic tang of blood running from his mouth. He sat still, breathing hard, looking around, checking out the situation. Through the corner of an eye, he saw Poncho climb up to the flying bridge twenty-five feet above the deck, invisible from below. He heard the boat's powerful engines start. They gurgled, then rumbled into a full-throated baritone as they accelerated out to sea. The man, called Roberto, ripped the tape off Thompson's mouth and kicked him on his side with a rib- breaking blow. Then, for good measure, he punched him in the stomach.

The breath knocked out of him, Thompson, sick to his stomach, dizzy and unfocused, pulled up his head and said, "You fucking maniacs. You won't get away with this. We'll track you down and feed you to the fish."

"Buddy," Roberto said in Spanish-accented English, "no fucking way. You're off to a bloody burial at sea. Mexico wants you dead. Sends a message to the other cops to lay off or they'll disappear too. Happy to kill 'em all. When we finish with you're off to a bloody burial at sea. Me and Poncho ain't pray'n for you either."

The man yanked Thompson's head up by his hair and started interrogating him. "What do you know about the Cartel's business on the island?"

"Nothing motherfucker."

"I'll ask you again; what do you know about our drug business?"

"You tell me."

Silence.

A hard uppercut snapped Thompson's head back. His mouth bled.

"Now, what do you know?"

"I know that you're all going to be in jail or dead real soon."

"We'll try again. What did the snitch tell you? Who did he finger?"

"He told us that you were a bunch of big bad pricks."

Roberto slammed his hands hard over the sides of Thompson's head, causing excruciating pain and bleeding from his ears. Thompson screamed. As the goon brought his face down again, staring into his eyes, Thompson head-butted him hard, sending him to the floor. His attacker didn't move. *Unconscious* he thought. Thompson tipped his chair forward falling on top of the man, immobilizing him. He wrestled the chair onto its side and maneuvered his tied hands into the thug's pants side pocket. Bingo. Luck the first time around. The handcuff keys. There was enough slack in the cuff chain for Thompson, struggling against his restraints, to open the cuffs. He untapped his ankles, painfully stood up, and kicked the man in the head twice to insure that he stayed unconscious. He smiled. Pain returned. He removed the man's 9mm Glock, took rope coiled on the deck, and hog-tied and gagged him as he plotted his next move.

They were entering, at full throttle, the channel through the North Wall reef, into the open ocean. The boat began to buck violently in the six-foot, white-capped waves. Thompson saw only one chance to save himself. He would go straight up the exposed ladder from the deck to the cabin roof. Then, he'd take another ladder from the roof to the bridge. He would slug the skipper from behind, knock him out, and take over the boat. Thompson hoped that any sounds of the recent mayhem were covered up by the engine noise and the water careening off the hull. There needed to be an element of surprise in his attack.

Adrenaline rush heightening, Thompson cautiously climbed up the slippery ladder, rung by rung. Halfway up, he was propelled sideways as the boat smacked and slewed in a trough. His slick street shoes slipped off the ladder. He grabbed the top rung and hung, knuckles white, swinging in the wind, the wet spray drenching him and clouding his vision. His arms ached and his fingers were slipping and losing their grip. His ribs screamed. He managed to catch the toe of one shoe on the edge of the ladder, push it onto a rung, and pull the other foot in beside it. His breath came in clusters of gasps. He paused for a moment. He hadn't been noticed. He strained to pull himself high enough so that his eyes were at the floor level of the flying bridge. He could see the skipper's feet firmly planted on the platform.

Thompson hoisted himself up the three remaining rungs and pulled the Glock from his back waistband. He jumped on the unstable deck, put a one-armed throat hold on the man, who tried to tear Thompson's arm away, but failed. Thompson shoved the gun under the man's jaw.

"Down the ladder or I'll shoot you."

The man wrenched away as the boat bucked violently through a huge wave. The gun fell onto the deck. The thug slipped on the spray-drenched deck, grabbed Thompson by the legs and yanked him over the deck's edge. They both plummeted down the ladder, bounced off of the cabin roof and landed in a squirming, flailing heap on the deck. Pilotless, the boat started moving in ever-widening circles. A few more orbits and they would be broken apart on the North Wall reef; battered and drowned.

The man pinned a shaken Thompson on the deck. He grabbed a two-pound lead diving weight and slammed Thompson on the side of his head. Thompson's bleeding head bounced to one side. He was stunned for a second and groaned. The man was off balance. Thompson, quickly alert, drew on his experience as a college wrestler and managed to break his assailant's hold, throw the man on his side, and get to his feet. Before Thompson could get his footing, the man staggered up, picked up a pile of rope, and threw it at Thompson, hoping to tangle him up so he could move in for the kill. It draped over Thompson's head and shoulders, but he shook it off and backed into the stern of the boat. As the enraged man ran toward him, Thompson picked up a pointed boat hook and jammed it into his assailant's stomach. The man screamed, the air whooshed from his lungs, and he doubled over, retching and holding his stomach. Thompson pushed him against the transom and hit him with a brutal uppercut and with such force that the thug flipped over into the sea—into an area known as Hammerhead Alley.

Thompson made sure that his other "guest" was secure. He quickly climbed up on the bridge. Just before the boat crashed onto the reef, he grabbed the wheel and wrenched the boat toward deep water. He called the harbor police and told them to expect an important "package" in about an hour. He piloted the boat back to Georgetown.

CHAPTER FIFTY-SEVEN

Zane's country safe house was invisible to the outside world, and most islanders thought it uninhabited. Only a few of his most trusted people knew about it. The house was an old, non-descript, ramshackle, wood-framed, one-story farmhouse with a collapsed cattle shed in back. The once-white paint on the siding was peeling away and showed the pockmarks of half a century of humid weather, ferocious storms, and summer scorch. Somehow, it had survived the periodic hurricanes that laced the island. The barbed wire enclosing a corral and grazing land was rusted, still intact, and a deterrent to curious wanderers.

The structure was located in the little-trafficked "boonies," some three miles from Georgetown, up the winding and lightly traveled East End Road. It was near a centuries-old path that was an ancient route from the south to the North End and used by Caribe Indians centuries before Europeans and slaves arrived around 1700. There was an uninviting, winding, half-mile, pot-holed, dirt driveway leading up to the house. The road offered many vantage points for sentinels and interception of unwanted guests. The house was situated on a large square of barren, cleared land, and no one could sneak up on the structure without being seen. It sported the same state-of-the-art surveillance devices used at the in-town safe house. The building was well shielded from the main road by low-lying, non-descript shrubs, small trees, and tall, native grass. Several magnificent flame trees and fragrant, over-grown frangipani dotted the plot. Zane had purchased the house and thirty acres of land decades ago as an investment for the future. Eventually he hoped that the newly growing suburbs of Cayman would seep onto his property after it had served his purpose and he had moved to another location as his profession dictated. He would be in on the ground floor of a building boom. Zane used the house as a depot for drugs to be sorted, re-packaged if necessary, and shipped to various customers. It was guarded around the clock. He felt very safe there.

Zane was at the house preparing for the arrival of the Monterey, a Panama-registered freighter carrying his latest shipment of drugs. The black Ford van used to transport drugs from the dock to the hideaway was gassed up, mechanically checked, and tires properly inflated. His BMW "chase" motorcycle was parked behind the van. The seven-man crew that would unload and transport the drugs, and the armed sentries guarding the house stood ready for a briefing.

"When our container is unloaded from the boat and on the dock, it will be located by Sam who will be there before the boat arrives. He knows the number of the Maersk container that the drugs are in. He'll radio its location. We'll cut a hole in the fence on the north side of the lot, which is dark and has no traffic in the middle of the night. You all have your individual assignments. Any questions?"

"What happens if we're seen? If the cops come?"

"Try to outrun them without gunfire. If they get too close, fire and try to get to one of the three "go-fast" boats tied up on the iron shore opposite this house. If you can't make it, give up. Try not to get yourselves killed.

"You've all done this before. We're going to be in place to get the drugs half an hour before the Monterey's estimated 2:00 AM docking.

"That's it. See you here at 1:00 AM. You're responsible for your own weapons, ammunition, and tools. Wear all black and blacken your faces."

CHAPTER FIFTY-EIGHT

Thompson's office was a barren anomaly in the sparkling, new, glass-encased police building, a testament to the island's wealth and emphasis on law and order. It was outfitted with an industrial, gray desk; black broken-back office chair held over from many past occupants; a phone; and a couple of rarely used file cabinets. His desk was piled with papers—unwritten reports, requests for information, bulletins, and the like. The only decoration, evidence of a human occupying the office, was a browning, scraggly ficus plant, begging for water and neglected by Thompson, who was not known for caring much about anything except his police work and now Amanda.

He hated paperwork and was constantly in trouble for not providing it to the bureaucracy, which he defined as an organization where a file for action was passed from hand to hand to hand and finally lost before anything was done. *The hell with it,* he thought.

He had two murders on his hands, Baxter and investment banker Whitney. But there were no murder weapon, no witnesses. Zilch. Brenda having been cleared, the only current suspects were Pat Sweeney and Savanna Lord who both hated the Baxter's guts. Herb Pierce, the man asked Gil for more money for their joint venture, was a no-go. His alibis checked out, and he went home to oversee the bankruptcy proceedings for Vista. The only connection between the two murders was that the weapon used in both was apparently a dive knife—a loose tie at best. There was a drug twist—Baxter was a heavy drug user, more than a casual sniff once in a while. Baxter apparently had unlimited supplies of just about every mind-bending substance on the planet. That meant he used a "heavy" connection, and not a penny-ante street vendor. Maybe Baxter didn't pay his bills, or a drug lord figured that he would expose his operation and have him killed. Thompson would have to follow up on this angle.

Baxter was also a gambler, which raised the possibility that he owed someone a lot of money and out of resolve or neglect didn't pay. The Chinese syndicates believed in quick "justice." He'd let the international authorities worry about the gambling slant.

Thompson's encrypted cell phone buzzed on his desk, as did Braun's who had returned to Cayman and was in his hotel room. It was a conference call from Goldman who said, "Charlie, Harry, you both on?"

"Yes, Yes."

"I have news for you," Goldman said. "I was surfing the Cartel's site and discovered that they're doing a huge business out of your backyard, or off your beach, whichever you prefer. Over half a billion dollars worth of coke has passed through you guys in the last couple of years— some for the local dudes and the remainder for the rest of the Caribbean and probably the US and beyond. I'm surprised that your drug guys aren't onto this Wal-Mart of goodies."

"Sam, we get the little guys, but can't find the king of the hill. I hope your info will get us to him," Thompson said.

"A Mexican container ship, the Monterey, left Vera Cruz headed for Grand Cayman two days ago. It's due in Cayman after midnight on Wednesday. It has about 100 kilos of coke stowed in container CCA 24965 from Tierramaraire SA. I don't have any more information. If I find any, I'll let you know."

Thompson became hyper-alert. His pulse and hope shot up. He sensed a big "kill."

"My god, we've wanted to ream a steam shovel up the ass of the cartel running the Cayman operation for a long time. This may be our chance. Any information about the names of their people here?"

"Not yet. They're referred to by code name, so I have to find the list linking the codes to real names. I'm hope there is one somewhere. I'll look. I did come across some useless information. I was able to break into the personal computer of one of the big guys. He thought that he was so smart to connect with the Internet though his allegedly unbustable network. Too bad. Appears that his code name is "el rey depredadou," which roughly means king of the assassins. He likes porn. Particularly the Ukrainian, Mexican, and American sites where you can video chat with a live woman who will do and say about anything that can be electronically transmitted. I'm sure that we'll soon have 3D holographic 'grope TV.' The big guy also loves video games. Plays them a lot. His favorite games read like manuals to mayhem: Saint's Row: The Third; Dead Space 3; Hit Man Resolution; God of War; and a real favorite, Call of Juarez, about cartel murders and wars in besieged Mexican cities."

"These imaginary slaughterers use a closet full of 'business equipment'—guns, automatic rifles, rockets, high explosives, throat-ripping knives, grenades, and garrotes. You name it. And great special effects—heads exploding like melons, guts spilling out on the ground, screams of torture, not to mention blasted buildings, bombed cars and bridges, and druggies and police going through magical gymnastics, vaporizing and reappearing. Armies' form and fight. Innocent citizens and kids are killed and neighborhoods destroyed. Oh yes. They have drones and fighter-bombers. And he plays the bad guy and almost always wins. By the way, their code name for the Cayman drug connection is 'Swimmer.' That's it. What else do you need now?"

"For now, nothing. We'll be in touch," Charlie said.

Harry added, "I have to hustle and get a raid set up."

"Good hunting," Goldman said.

Thompson hung up on Goldman, after asking Charlie to stay on the line and said, "Bingo. We have a little action at last.

CHAPTER FIFTY-NINE

Thompson called the harbormaster and found that the Monterey was to dock at 0130 the next day. There was no bad weather to delay them. It was to be offloaded immediately. He called Sam Sanders, the head of police Special Ops.

"Sam, I need your help. We have a hell of a drug bust coming up, and it's going to need a lot of firepower. We don't know where yet, but we'll bet it'll be a raid against a heavily defended safe house. They'll have cartel-type weapons—AK 47s, small arms, hand grenades, and RPGs. We have to trail the drugs from the dock, find out where they are off-loaded and move in. I'd guess we'll need ten men equipped for night action."

"OK. We'll give you an unmarked command car and three vans with the SWAT guys. They're looking for action anyway. Not a lot of demand on the island to keep them sharp. Have to send them to Miami all the time for brush-up training. I'll have plenty of 'uniforms' as well."

"What about help on the dock?"

"We'll station an officer disguised as a dockworker and another as a guard. They'll signal when they see the ship dock. They're seasoned men who've worked the waterfront and nailed a few bad guys before. There'll be a total of 18 guys for the operation. More than adequate."

"Thanks. I'll hook up with you and your men at 1140 in the police garage."

Thompson and Bridgewater, Thompson's sergeant assistant, secreted their unmarked car on the main road by the container yard. The three vans with the primed, heavily-armed SWAT teams parked off the road on side streets about a quarter mile from the dock's fences and gates. Two lookouts were stashed in bushes on two diagonal corners of the square container compound. Between the two of them, they could spot entrance and exit of vehicles from any direction. The "dockworker and guard" lurked in the dark shadows cast by stacked containers.

Thompson said to nobody, "Christ, it's taking forever," as he took a sip of his cold and acrid coffee out of boredom and the desire to stay sharp.

Bridgewater, stared out of the window, thinking about Jezebel, the woman that he met at "Elements" last night. He pleasurably mulled over his prospects for a heated tryst as soon as the operation was over.

Silence. Annoying silence. It was as hushed and dark as an empty coal mine. A night bird called. A hoarse hound bayed. The rattle of an aging, out-a-little-too-late, junk heap, weaving a bit, clattered by. *Someone ought to pick the damn guy up*, thought Thompson. In the rear view mirror, Thompson saw a light flicked on in a house behind them. *Early riser or bladder problems.* Silence.

Then came two blasts of a ship's horn and the rumbling sound of a boat reversing its engines hard. The radio squawked. Thompson and Bridgewater jerked alert and reached for the microphone at the same time, hands almost colliding. Thompson won. The whispering voice said, "They're docking. We'll hold tight until there's solid action on the docks. Copy?"

"Copy."

Thompson was primed for action. The vacuum of quiet was getting to him.

The engines of two dock cranes popped, caught, and grumbled to life. Their giant arms swung over the bow and stern of the Monterey's deck and began plucking off containers, carefully stacking them, back to front, on the dock staging area.

Thompson and Smyth waited and listened. Nothing. The radio squawked. The faux guard, Les, on the dock, whispered into his encrypted radio.

"Four people, dressed in black, are at the back of the lot and heading toward a couple of containers that were just off-loaded. They've stopped at one numbered CCA 24965. I tracked it from the crane. One has big hacksaw, and another, an acetylene torch. These are our guys. They're attacking the lock and lock bar on the door. I can't get closer without blowing my cover."

Thompson and Bridgewater heard the urgent rasping of a saw on metal over the radio.

"Don't move in closer," Thompson said. "I want you to find out how they're getting out of the place with the goods when the time comes."

"Roger."

The night became ominously quiet again. The metal rasping stopped, the night sounds went away, and the birds and animals seemingly waited with Thompson for something to happen. Thompson gnashed his teeth and sweated more than usual in the tropical heat. The air was dense, thick, making everyone's breathing labored. The radio beeped and crackled. Les was back on the radio. "From what I can see, they've cut the fence on the south side of the gate. Just opposite you. There's a black van and a motorcycle at the hole, and they're loading as fast as they can. The cargo looks like irons, blenders, air conditioners, and backyard grills. They're really moving."

Thompson replied. "Anyone armed?"

"A couple have automatic weapons slung over their shoulders. There are people in the car. I can't see how many, but I would assume that they're armed to the teeth. That would be a lot of coke to move without protection."

A few minutes (that felt like hours to Thompson), passed until Les piped in again.

"On your toes. They've almost finished loading and will be high-tailing it out of there fast. There's one guy on a motorcycle behind the van. I haven't a clue what he's there for unless he's a scout.

Thompson radioed the police and SWAT teams. "They're loading a van. Get ready and lock and load."

"Roger," came the reply.

"They're moving."

CHAPTER SIXTY

The van made tracks up South Sound Road toward Zane's country safe house. The police group, without lights, trailed the drug van at a respectable distance They stopped, still undetected, well short of the drug crew who started to unload their precious cargo. Other than the light from bright stars and the slimmest slice of a silver moon, there were no lights, inside or outside of the house. Night vision binoculars crisply showed the van being unloaded. It looked like there were six people--four unloading and two on guard. There didn't seem to be anyone else in or around the house—at least not helping with the cargo or visible around the house. The SWAT team, dressed in black, pulled night vision goggles down over their eyes, donned bullet proof Kevlar vests that would stop AK-47 rounds, and waited.

Their sergeant whispered, "Ready." There was a sharp series of clicks as the policemen chambered a round in their rifles. On the whispered signal "Go, go, go," they silently stepped out of their vans, crouched, and ran to surround and subdue the gang. They encircled the house, concealed, and unobserved, at a distance. A radio signal from the sergeant ordered them to go. As soon as they left the protection of the scrub brush and trees and entered open ground, the rapid crack of automatic weapon fire and orange muzzle flashes shattered the dead silent night. There was withering fire from behind the van and the front, side, and back windows. Apparently the drug crew had night vision glasses and laser sights too, because their fire was uncannily accurate.

One member of the SWAT team was hit in the throat and died instantly. His partner had both legs nearly severed at the knees and was bleeding to death. Some in front were knocked down and stunned by the force of multiple rounds hitting their vests. A police van was peppered with bullets; it rocked from the impact and looked like an oversize colander. It caught fire, exploded, and flipped end-over-end in an orange fireball. The patrolman inside the vehicle jumped out in time to escape injury. In position, a member of the SWAT team fired a small rocket containing a "flash-bang" through a house window. It exploded with an intense, disorienting, dazzling light and a head-splitting bang. He reloaded and followed with a second round.

Two men burst out of the front door with their hands over their heads. They were quickly thrown to the ground and handcuffed by two SWAT team members. Two shooters went to the front windows and fired back at the police. A fusillade of automatic weapon fire subdued and maybe killed them. Four men poured from the back of the house running toward the ocean where escape boats were stowed. Firing on the run, four policemen pursued them. One escapee dropped behind a tree and threw covering fire back at the police to give the others a chance to escape. One policeman went down screaming with wounds in both legs and bleeding profusely. The SWAT team took cover and fired back with no effect. The escapee left his cover and disappeared in the surrounding underbrush. Smoke lay low over the scene, and the house was furiously burning. The moans of the wounded could be heard over the whoosh and crackle of the fire.

Sargent Bridgewater radioed the Caymanian Coast Guard on their emergency channel.

"Coast Guard, come in. Emergency, emergency. This is Police Sargent Bridgewater. Do you read me? Over."

"Roger, we read you."

"We have three or four drug dealers heading on foot toward the Central Mangrove Wetlands. They likely have a very fast, armed escape boat hidden there. I would guess that they'll hit the water at the center of the bay shore. We think it likely that they'll head for Jamaica. Would you interdict and capture?"

"Roger."

A fast cutter was on its way in five minutes. The helicopter was launched in ten. Both were heavily armed. The Cartel's 1000 horsepower "go-fast" exited the dense mangroves and revved up to 110 mph in a calm sea.

CHAPTER SIXTY-ONE

Zane was supervising the unloading of the van's cargo when the firefight broke out. He jumped back on his motorcycle, an ultra-fast BMW 1200 S, and kicked it alive. He turned left on to a slender, barely passable footpath carved through the trees and brush. He sped through the surprised outlying SWAT team as the policemen fired into the cloud of dense yellow dust and gravel thrown up by the bike. Bullets whizzed, trees shattered, slugs spattered in the dust around Zane. Though the motorcycle was peppered with bullet holes, there was no significant damage. At the end of the path, Zane turned west on Seaview Road and accelerated to a blistering, barely stable, 110 miles per hour.

Out of the corner of his eye, Thompson had seen the motorcycle's headlight flood the road and the bike take off at high speed. *Trouble. SWAT doesn't need me at the scene at this point. Let's see who's so anxious to get out of here.*

Thompson went in pursuit in his specially modified, high-performance BMW 525i police car. His lights flashed and the raucous singsong of the siren split the once-peaceful night. Thompson matched the motorcycle's speed but could not gain on him. He could barely hold the car on the road in turns. *Christ, I feel like a horse and carriage chasing a Formula 1 racecar.* The road-hugging cycle turned north on Frank Sound Road.

Just before the road reached the North Sound, Zane took to open country and bounced wildly across a rough and furrowed cow pasture. His teeth chattered, his back and butt were hammered, his brain pounded inside his head. His headlight bounced up and down sporadically illuminating his way, making vision difficult. He barely missed a lone, sleeping cow standing in his way and veered onto a little known walking path toward the black, dense, mangrove swamps bordering the North Wall. This was a place where, even in daylight, kayak explorers got lost. Sliding to a stop, Zane dropped his bike by his "go-fasts—a sleek, black thirty-five foot banana boat with two 1000 horsepower carbureted Mercury custom quad cam racing engines. It could do 110 mph, 120 in a crunch, and cruise for 250 miles on a tank of gas. It could outrun any boat around and was fully fueled and ready to go.

The boat, its low-throated exhaust rhythmically gurgling, threaded slowly through the tangle-rooted mangroves, its way barely lit by a dim, shielded, bow light. Zane accelerated carefully, avoiding the sparse, spindly, leafless dead trees randomly dotting the open bay. Then, throttle wide-open, rooster tail flying, the boat entered the open ocean. Zane set the GPS-driven autopilot for a safe landing site on a hide-away on the western shore of Jamaica where he would be met by De and taken to safety. He breathed deeply. His tense stomach muscles relaxed, the throb in his neck went away and his pulse dropped to near normal. *I'm almost free. It's all over. Fucking millions lost. The boys will be in jail forever. I can never come back. Fuck.*

When the suspect had gone cross-country, Thompson screeched into a ninety-degree turn into the rutted pasture. He barely missed two fence posts and bounced wildly over ruts until he hit a ditch, and the car bottomed out and stalled. Harry knew the chase was over. He was certain that his quarry was headed for a boat, but couldn't get to the mangroves by car. He got out of the BMW and heard the motorcycle engine die. The boat engines started and moments later, roared. This was out of his hands.

Thompson radioed the US Coast Guard headquarters in Georgetown. He got permission to directly a drug interdiction cutter close to Grand Cayman. HQ gave orders to Captain Bain, commander of the cutter Monsoon, to take direction directly from Thompson.

Thompson was then patched through to Bain who was fifty miles off the north coast of Grand Cayman.

"Captain Bain, this is Inspector Thompson of the Caymanian Police. A major drug smuggler just left the north shore of Grand Cayman. We couldn't catch him on land. Can you put out a search and grab for us?"

"Roger, Inspector. HQ said to give you our fullest cooperation. What speed would you guess he's making?"

"His boat? Who knows? Try 120 mph. That seems par for the course for the hot boats."

"Where is he likely headed?"

"Probably the western shore of Jamaica. That's the closest island. Lots of isolated spots to hide in. A common destination for the drug smugglers."

"What are his likely coordinates now?"

"His starting coordinates were: 19.333°N and 81.267W."

"I'll plot a course that should intercept him. Once we get closer, and pick him up on radar, I'll launch our Dolphin attack helicopter to drag him in. It can make 175mph, so we'll be on top of him fast."

Bain continued "How many people?"

"I don't know."

"Armed?"

"Unquestionably. We guess that this guy may be the biggest drug lord in the Caribbean. It's a major coup if we can get him."

"I'm on it. Over and out."

CHAPTER SIXTY-TWO

The cutter turned southeast at flank speed. The radar operator, helicopter crews, and gunners, were called to their stations and told that they may shortly be on a night chase of an armed vessel. The mood on the cutter immediately became tense, no nonsense.

Minutes later the radar operator said, "Captain, I have a small vessel traveling southeast at high speed, bearing 140 degrees, and twenty-five miles out. Looks like he's doing about 100 miles per hour. Nothing else on the horizon."

Captain Bain maneuvered the cutter to an intercept course and launched the heavily armed Dolphin. The MH65C Dolphin helicopter dipped off the deck, returned to horizontal flight, rose to 1000 feet. The pilot acquired the target on radar and upped the bird's speed to 180 mph to head off the bogie.

Zane loosened his shirt, and the wind dried the sweat off of his face, but the furrows on his brow, his rapid pulse, and the knot in his stomach, remained. *On my way, but by no means there. And when we get there, by no means safe.* The craggy, lightly inhabited shore of western Jamaica was a good place to meet De at his shoreside hideout. But nothing was sure in this business.

After fifteen minutes, Zane's white-knuckle grip loosened on the wheel. His breathing calmed, and his gut relaxed as he listened to the steady roar of the engines. *Not gonna get caught at night. Fastest boat in the Caribbean. No drugs aboard. No profit, but out alive. Gonzales will want my head. Maybe not. Matter to fix after the shit dies down. Won't be the first time dat a district lord was busted by the fucking rozzers. I've gotta rebuild the business. Get any of the guys still free out of Cayman. Maybe go to Grenada. No competition. Government corrupt as hell. Too much heat in Jamaica. Have Fernando and Keith there already. Good guys.*

"Captain," the helicopter copilot said, "we've acquired the target. They're about twenty-five miles out. We'll be overhead in about fifteen minutes."

"Roger."

The distant whump whump of helicopter rotors was getting closer. Zane heard the threatening noise. He couldn't tell where the bird was coming from, but it couldn't be more than a few minutes away. He prepared for action. His only hope of escape was to down the helicopter, and that meant a rocket shot to the engines. Zane checked his fuel supply and instruments. Fuel was OK, but one engine was missing occasionally and running hot. He didn't have time to slow down to let the engine cool off or figure out what the problem was. He would have to take his chances. He laid his AK-47 and two extra clips on the seat next to him. He then dragged two compact shoulder fired surface-to-air missile out of their crate in the cabin, and onto the rear deck. It took 30 seconds to arm them. He was ready.

About a mile out, Captain Bain spotted the long, telltale bioluminescent wake of the target. Soon after, an oval-shaped spotlight beam from the helicopter swept over the boat like a dazzling white sun. Speakers blasted the required warning in English and Spanish: "Stop for Boarding. This is the US Coast Guard. Stop and you won't be hurt." Four Navy SEALS, from the toughest fighting unit in the world, donned their buoyancy compensators, tanks, signal lights, knives, masks, and fins, . They knew they would be doing a hostile capture. They couldn't wait. Inaction was their nemesis. The two side door gunners racked their machine guns. Two snipers were ready. Muscles taut. The chopper captain descended to five hundred feet above the target boat, putting his aircraft into action and into harm's way.

Zane gunned the engines to maximum rpm and cut his boat severely right. Its stern skidded on the water nearly swamping the vessel and capsizing it as it slammed, broadside, into an eight-foot wave. Water poured over the gunwale putting the deck awash. Turbulence from the helicopter's rotors threw stinging water into Zane's eyes nearly blinding him. He struggled and held onto the control module. As the boat crested another wave, he fell and crashed to the slippery deck. The heavy surface-to-air missile crate violently slid across the deck and pinned Zane to the back of the cabin. Bruised and near exhaustion, he struggled free of the container, reached the wheel, and circled his crippled craft to the rear of the enemy aircraft. He cut the engines, stopped the boat dead in its tracks, and grabbed the shoulder-aimed missile from its crate. He armed the projectile, aimed at the helicopter and fired. The rocket, trailing a corkscrew of smoke, hurtled toward the target just as the helicopter took evasive action, turning violently away from the boat. The heat-seeking rocket veered away from the target. It didn't have time to hone in on the target's hot engines. It missed what should have been an easy kill.

Zane locked his jaw, gunned the engines, and turned to position the boat for another shot. He never got it off. The telltale stuttering and splashes of machine gun fire stitched a long line, one hundred feet before the bow and stern of the boat—the last warning to stop before the chopper opened fire in earnest. Zane increased his speed to the maximum possible with his wounded boat. Adrenaline flowed. His heart raced. The spray blowing over the windshield into his eyes clouded his vision. It's over. *I'll give them a run for their money. I'm dead or in jail.* The helicopter maneuvered close to the boat. Zane could see the grim, staring faces of the men in the open door, their guns, their determined looks, their bodies tensed, waiting for action.

Fifty-millimeter machine gun bullets ripped off the fiberglass bow, submerging the bow, stopping the boat instantly, and almost flipping it stern over bow. Zane was thrown into the sea. Simultaneously, a sniper's incendiary round hit the engine, and the boat erupted in flame. The helicopter descended to wave-top level, almost drowning in its own spray. Hell bent for leather, the Navy SEALS splashed into the water. Zane struggled underwater and broke the surface, choking on seawater, gasping for breath, thrown up and down in the waves. Blood from a head wound clogged his vision. His right arm was useless and he could barely tread water.

Two SEALS grabbed Zane from behind, immobilizing him by pinning his arms together. Six-foot waves made every movement difficult, and potentially deadly to Zane who struggled in the water.

"You sons of bitches, let me go," Zane screamed as he dug his fingernails into his captor's face, drawing blood as he fought to get away.

"No fucking way," said a lieutenant who tightened his grip.

Two SEALS grabbed Zane by the hair, pushed his head underwater, and handcuffed him with plastic ties. *Small retribution for nearly wiping out the whole team*, the team leader thought. Zane coughed and sputtered when he was finally allowed to surface. He was fool enough to struggle again and was held under, this time much longer. He was on the verge of drowning. The SEALS didn't care whether he lived or died. He had tried to kill them.

The orange rescue vest, with a blinking strobe marking its place, descended from the chopper, swinging in a wide circle, and skipping off the tops of the breaking waves. On the third pass, a SEAL grabbed the device while three others held Zane, forced him into the seat-like inflated device, and buckled him in. Swinging, rotating, and jerking up and down in the wind, Zane was very slowly winched up to the helicopter. This would give the prisoner maximum discomfort: nausea, dizziness, disorientation, and ready for some intense questioning.

An angry sergeant said, "Why don't we cut him loose 'accidentally' and save ourselves a lot of work and the taxpayers a lot of money? Maybe a defective harness. It happens."

The captain replied, "That worked in Vietnam, but not in the drug war. We'd be court-martialed if we're caught. Besides, it's inhuman, and we don't play the game that way. Bring him in."

Two men grabbed Zane by the rescue rig, making sure to slam his head onto the doorframe. They roughly pulled his body onto the floor of the chopper. He was lifted out of the rescue vest and handcuffed to two steel rings on the helicopter bulkhead, his legs immobilized by plastic ties. He was seasick and barely conscious. Nobody gave a damn. He could wallow in his own vomit until they could hose him off back at the base.

The four SEALS were lifted, one at a time, back onto the helicopter, hyped, and none the worse for wear.

One said, "Not nearly as hard as training exercises."

CHAPTER SIXTY-THREE

Thompson, cruiser lights flashing, siren screaming, screeched to a stop in front of the drug house; he'd missed most of the action. The scene was clogged with ambulances, squad cars, and a throng of people in lime colored day-glow jackets marked "Police." The criminal investigation unit was there. He surveyed the scene. There were bodies of two drug smugglers sprawled in blood pools on the floor and two wounded policemen, one critical, on their way to the hospital. Four gunmen were on the loose, undoubtedly in a boat. The coast guard and harbor police would soon chase them down.

There were tens of millions of dollars worth of cocaine in the bullet-riddled van. Slugs during the firefight had chopped the drug bales, and little rivulets of white gold had poured onto the floor. Thompson tasted a small finger-smudge of the powder. Pure, uncut coke. A good haul for the drug lord, an even better one for the police.

Thompson entered the farmhouse through the splintered front door, which was tenuously hanging awry by one hinge. The walls were peppered with bullet holes. They looked like a sieve. Splintered wood and spent cartridges littered the floor. Guns lay where they were dropped. There were puddles of drying blood by two windows. The air smelled of gun smoke.

Firefight damage aside, Thompson could see that the house was decorated like any island farmer's house. A large screen TV, shattered by bullets, dominated the living room. There was a curiously intact green, plush couch and two bullet-sliced beige, vinyl-covered recliner chairs. Sports magazines and local and Jamaican newspapers were strewn on the floor from an upended coffee table. The worn and scarred floor, made of some non-descript soft wood, was littered with brass shell casings. A couple of cheap prints of Cayman's magnificent beaches and sunsets along with reggae posters hung askew on the walls. The beds were neatly made and there was a bath and tiny kitchen, both of which looked unused and were remarkably untouched.

On first pass, Thompson saw nothing unusual about the scene. There was no evidence of who was living in the house—no bills, photographs, letters, advertising flyers, address labels on magazines or significant trash. There were no drugs. A search of drawers yielded only the normal stuff of everyday life.

Later, forensics would rip out the walls and strip the furniture in search of drugs, guns, and clues. The floors would be ripped up. The property outside the structure would be searched, and the ground probed for drugs, guns and any other items that might help the case.. Maybe the fingerprinting and forensic experts would find something. Thompson was doubtful. Things just looked too orderly and carefully kept. The sign of a very cautious person who attends to detail.

A forensic technician and Sergeant Boylen, joined Thompson in his search of the kitchen. The cupboards contained the usual assortment of food—cereal, salsa, beans, canned fruit, flour, sugar, coffee, and rice. The refrigerator yielded beer, cheese, milk, frozen tacos and tortillas, and packaged dinners. Every box, every drawer, every shelf was emptied into trash bags. Nothing of interest.

Sergeant Boylen carefully felt around the inside of the cabinets for false panels that could conceal evidence. Two men helped him pull the refrigerator and stove out from the wall. He peered inside and in back of both and came up empty. Behind the wall-hung microwave however, almost hidden in a tangle of cords, was a small light switch.

Thompson flipped the switch on. There was a slight pause, and then a high-pitched whine started under the kitchen floor. The floorboards creaked, then separated slightly at one end and a man-size trapdoor slowly raised by hydraulic arms revealing treaded steel stairs. He couldn't find a light switch at the entrance to the room below. Thompson took out his flashlight and gun, and slowly, cautiously, moved down the unlit steps. His heartbeat fast, his breathing shallowed and his neck tensed.

He called out, "Police, come out with your hands up." No response.

He sensed motion, heard a slight scuffing sound, and swung around a corner, sweeping the room with his flashlight and gun, ready to fire. "Police, show yourself."

Again, a noise, this time a rapid thumping. Thompson squatted and faced the noise, his finger tightening on the trigger. The flashlight caught two yellow-green eyes staring at him from the floor in the distant corner. A scrawny, friendly, beige and white island dog rapped its tail on its pet bed as if greeting an old friend. Thompson sighed with relief. Otherwise the room was clear.

The inspector flipped on a light switch. The lights miraculously worked. He took a deep breath, relaxed his shoulders, and stared with amazement and admiration. He expected a sloppy, unprofessional, local drug operation. Instead he found a well-lit, high-tech command, control and distribution center for a major enterprise. It was literally a dry, impenetrable, air-conditioned concrete and steel box sunk into the coral substrate. A fortress.

Thompson cautiously moved between the rows of floor-to-ceiling, gray, steel, industrial storage shelves at one end of the room. A dozen or so bales of coke were stuffed into one shelf unit; the rest were empty, awaiting the large shipment that would never arrive. In the middle of the room was "the factory." The factory weighed and tested the incoming cocaine before storage to insure that they had received the correct quantity and purity. It was then repackaged into smaller containers: from street size vials and packets to kilo bricks for distribution in Grand Cayman and abroad. Under the tables were two crates of M-15 automatic rifles, a collection of 40-caliber Glocks, and ammunition.

At the other end of the room, colored lights were flashing and blinking on computer servers. Flat screen displays were lit with rows of streaming numbers. There were telephone headsets in front of the monitors. *Unbelievable. A high-tech business and communication center. How the hell did our phone and Internet monitoring boys miss this one?* Thompson had heard cartels had gone all out in their electronics, but this was beyond belief—right here in Grand Cayman. He'd hit the mother load. The evidence and leads will keep the Cayman Drug and Communication Sections, and the DEA busy for months as they trace the operation, hopefully, back to its origins.

"Sonofabitch," Thompson yelled, as he tripped over a dive bag and Pelican waterproof fiberglass photo case on the floor at the end of a drug shelf. He hit the concrete, cracking his jaw as he broke the fall with his hands. "Shit, Fuck. Fuck, fuck, fuck." His hands hurt; his jaw throbbed and a small stream of blood bubbled where his teeth had cut his lower lip. He angrily picked himself up and grabbed the bag. The bag and Pelican photo case were each marked with a single word: Zane. *Jesus fucking Christ. Zane's involved in this operation?* Thompson hurriedly, and in anticipation of solid evidence, unzipped and dumped out the dive bag. Strewn on the floor was the usual diver's gear—regulator, mask, fins, dive computer, wet suit, buoyancy vest, and regulator repair tools. Again, nothing of interest. Just ordinary diving gear.

Next, he used the screwdriver blade on his pocket-knife to pry open the locks on the Pelican case. Inside were a couple of Nikon camera bodies and assorted lenses nestled in eggshell foam—probably for Zane's cruise business. As an after-thought, he ripped out the thick lining glued to the photo case walls.

Behind the padding was a very, very sharp dive knife. Thompson picked out the knife with a handkerchief to preserve any fingerprints or blood that might be on it. He ran his finger along the razor sharp serrated cutting edge. Much sharper than any dive knife that he'd seen. No doubt specially sharpened. Thompson put the knife into an evidence bag to give to the CSU lieutenant.

He knew he had his man.

EPILOG

Harry, Charlie, and Amanda sat at a table at their usual table at Sunset House sipping pink gin—that quintessentially lethal English drink made with three shots of Tanqueray No.10 and a dash of angostura bitters, stirred, not shaken, and served in a stemmed cocktail glass. It was known for lubricating the mind, loosening the tongue, and arousing the libido, not that Harry and Amanda needed any help with the latter. They sat silent for a moment looking out toward the ocean, watching three slowly moving cruise ships slip by on a glassy sea and into a pink-blue, after-sunset sky.

"They're headed for Jamaica or Barbados to dump thousands of relaxers, explorers, and revelers onto some other island," Charlie said. "Maybe they're going back to the States—Miami or Ft. Lauderdale. Can you imagine the thousands of people onboard and fancy what each person, each unique individual is like—what they look like, their personalities and experiences, their ups and downs, problems and concerns, their successes and failures? There'll be the rich, the middle class out for their trip of the year, and those who can barely afford the journey and have scrimped for years to take a cruise. There'll be doctors, lawyers, business people, housewives, policemen, bridge clubs, gamblers, merchants, kids, pensioners and workmen. Most of them will be 'senior citizens.' A lot of people seeking the sun. Never cared to go on one myself. Don't like crowds, being herded."

Thompson interrupted. "I think that we should all congratulate ourselves. Look at what we've done in five months. Forensics found Zane's fingerprints and traces of Baxter's blood on the dive knife. The once mighty Zane will be tried for drug trafficking, first-degree murder, destruction of property, endangering the lives of others, and financial fraud. The toughest-on-crime judge in the Islands will preside. He'll get life without parole. In olden days, he would have been hung. We brought down Zane's drug ring in Cayman. And their Jamaica and Barbados operations will surely fall as a result of our efforts. That leaves other small dealers in the Caymans and bigger ones on other islands. But it's a start. And the Columbian cartel is now a small problem, but they are a potentially huge invader, like the Mexican's were."

"We owe cracking the case to Goldman and his brilliant hacking skills," Charlie said. He told me that he's too busy to take on any more projects for us. He's been hired by a consortium of the British, German, French, and Brazilian intelligence services to hack into NSA's system for monitoring e-mails and phone messages to and from their countries. Angela Merkel, that cold, calculating, vengeful, tubby German Prime Minister, was red with anger when she heard that her personal conversations with her husband and kids were captured. State secrets aside, maybe she does phone sex with hubby. Who knows?"

They all laughed, having trouble envisioning that powerful, stern, dowdy product of East Germany having sex at all.

Amanda piped in. "This is getting dull guys; can't we go on to more fun things like whether the Minister of Transport is taking bribes from Island Construction for the new Northern Bypass, or Lady Taylor being the lover of Sam Litchfield?"

"Forget it," Harry said. "I'd rather reminisce."

"Harry, the hottest topic in the whole deal is you and me. Remember the Hotel Saratoga in Havana?" she said with a mischievous, inviting, and I-can't-wait-to-get-out-of-here look in her eyes. "Did we ever get out of bed? And, of course you seduced me into getting married."

Harry blushed a bit, totally out of character for him, and anxious to have the subject changed.

Charlie pulled out a Habana Monte Cristo, bit off the end, and carefully lit it. "Best in the world," he said as a blue billow of eye-stinging, nose-assaulting, throat-rasping smoke blew over Amanda.

Amanda coughed, laughed, and said, "You prick, at least you could sit downwind. Smells like camel shit." With a faux sullen look, eyes squinting and staring at Charlie, she moved so that she was upwind of him in the typical, gentle, evening, offshore breeze blowing over the group.

Charlie continued, "Well, we got Brenda her money. We changed the ownership of the holding company to her name and are keeping the good investments and selling the rest. We got a retired former honcho out of the financial industry to oversee the ventures for a hefty eight-figure salary. There were actually some good companies in there. A couple of social networking sites—one where you can download pictures and transmit them instantly to your friends and a very popular Internet dating site. They owned a number of hotels and apartments in New York, London, Monaco, and half a dozen other cities. Brooke was smart and a good investor. He got into Apple, Google, Qualcom, and Expedia, early in the game. Of course, we paid taxes and fines owed and settled overdue accounts. Actually, some of the portfolio was a mess and had to be cleaned up. I eventually turned over about 20 billion dollars to Brenda—less Goldman's paltry fee. This puts her way up on the list of the Forbes's top billionaires.

"And guess what?" Charlie added. "She set up a 15 million dollar trust fund to cover the education of any children that you—Amanda and Harry—might have. The terms of the trust are quite liberal and carefully worded to allow you both to use the funds to enhance the kid's upbringing. And that includes houses, foreign travel, private schools, cultural events, and a lot more—anything to create a lifestyle to which the kids should become accustomed. And, of course, the criteria for spending are very liberal, and I'm administering the trust. My "fee" is pretty hefty too. Joke."

"Kids Harry? We definitely have to get going on this," Amanda said.

Harry retorted, "We've been working on it as hard as we can. Really, really hard."

Amanda laughed, and with a hopeful look in her eye, said, "Harry, we only need to pull the chemical plug. Does this mean kids are a go? I'm ready. And the family will need a few extra hands in the business by the time ours grow up."

Harry looked frightened and a bit pale, but hopeful.

Charlie interrupted. "I always wanted to be a close uncle. You know, the right to pollute the kid's minds and teach all sorts of oddball and off-the-wall things.

Now's as good a time as it gets. Maybe a lawyer in the family?"

"No way." Amanda intoned. "Based on this experience, I see lawyers as troublemakers, skirting the law, and putting themselves at risk as much as cops. A settled businessman or woman, maybe in the family business, would be just fine as long as they get an Ivy education."

"What happened to Brooke?" Amanda added.

Charlie looked very proud. "We cooperated with the police's fraud unit. Our investigation and the records that we found proved first-degree murder, securities fraud, and conspiracy to import drugs. He was arrested yesterday and will be locked up for life.

The group went silent for a while, contemplating the last vestiges of the orange and purple sunset and the rising moon and bright stars, and their own future.

"Well," Charlie said, breaking the silence, "back to boring estates and trusts. The law will never be the same for me. Any chance another case like this will come along?"

Harry said. "Probably. Keep the encrypted line."

ACKNOWLEDGEMENTS

My grateful appreciation to the many people who helped me complete this undertaking. They include:

My beautiful and intelligent wife, Kate Driesen, who edited every chapter as it came out of the printer, and the complete manuscript…and tolerated my mental absence during the writing of this book. Terry Greene and Sheldon Grebstein who critiqued the entire manuscript. The "No Name" writing group who reviewed chapters as they came along. Michael Grossman for his invaluable help on self-publishing. Betty Cotter, a fine teacher and author, who started me down the exciting road to fiction. Peter Milburn, of Dive Cayman, who began showing me the underwater delights of Grand Cayman forty-five years ago. And last, but not least, Charlie Kingsley, a lawyer, classmate and friend of sixty-five years who gave me the idea for the story.

I thank you all.

Made in the USA
Charleston, SC
14 August 2016